Hellfire from Paradise Ranch

Hellfire from Paradise Ranch

ON THE FRONT LINES OF DRONE
WARFARE

Joseba Zulaika

UNIVERSITY OF CALIFORNIA PRESS

University of California Press
Oakland, California

Cataloging-in-Publication Data is on file at the Library of Congress.

Names: Zulaika, Joseba, author.
Title: Hellfire from Paradise Ranch : on the front lines of drone warfare /
    Joseba Zulaika.
Description: Oakland, California : University of California Press, [2020] |
    Includes bibliographical references and index.
Identifiers: LCCN 2019023480 (print) | LCCN 2019023481 (ebook) |
    ISBN 9780520329744 (cloth) | ISBN 9780520974326 (epub)
Subjects: LCSH: Drone aircraft—Moral and ethical aspects—United
    States. | Terrorism—Prevention.
Classification: LCC UG1242.D7 Z85 2020 (print) | LCC UG1242.D7 (ebook) |
    DDC 358.4/24—dc23
LC record available at https://lccn.loc.gov/2019023480
LC ebook record available at https://lccn.loc.gov/2019023481

Manufactured in the United States of America

29 28 27 26 25 24 23 22 21 20
10 9 8 7 6 5 4 3 2 1

Prologue: Slaughterhouse-359

That was the number. He'd asked his bosses. Researched it. Three hundred and fifty-nine civilians he'd helped kill in 2009. That's what Cian Westmoreland, a former drone operator, was telling us in Las Vegas, at the end of March 2016, on a warm and radiant desert evening.

President Obama's numbers were different. He said that during his administration drone air strikes killed between 64 and 116 civilians. The same year Westmoreland was killing for his commander in chief, Obama was awarded the Nobel Peace Prize.

Whom to believe? And do the numbers really matter? And what inner imperative brought Westmoreland to stand before us at the Las Vegas Law School—head bowed, eyes fixed on an empty spot below the podium? A clean-cut figure in a black T-shirt, he cast the shadow of a broken man. Yes, he said, I killed those civilians. He had been twenty-two at the time. Now his own life, the real of who he was, was at stake. He said he was haunted by the memories, that he was in therapy. Slaughterhouse-359. He said it again, 359, raised his eyes, looked at us, added: "I'm here for those kids I helped kill." Then he lowered his head and became silent. The audience was startled, unable to find his inaccessible eyes. His confession was an act of utter defiance, a radically political act—the choice that saved him from insanity.

His testimony compelled me to write this book. Having published several books on terrorism and having lived three decades in Nevada, I couldn't avoid identifying with this vulnerable rebel. I was forced to hear the truth of his trauma. Westmoreland was the emblem of the American soldier when the soldier is the epitome of a nation's subjectivity.[1] He represented what it means to be American during these years of drone warfare—pilots hunting and shooting via satellite human targets thousands of miles away from Creech Air Force Base next to Las Vegas. You could sense his rage beneath the somberness.

Cian Westmoreland had been raised in the shadow of his family hero, General William Westmoreland, commander of US forces in Vietnam when Robert McNamara was secretary of defense, the same man who, during the World War II firebombing of Tokyo, had helped General Curtis LeMay incinerate one hundred thousand Japanese civilians in just one night. Such deaths had not traumatized McNamara and General Westmoreland, who remained proud of their military careers. Why couldn't Cian Westmoreland feel that way?

Ethics, you might say. But whose? At one time McNamara had argued it was unethical *not* to burn the fifty square miles of Japanese homes, thereby forcing American soldiers to battle and die on Tokyo's streets. Later, as an architect of the Vietnam War under presidents Kennedy and Johnson, McNamara conceded that US intervention in Vietnam had been "terribly wrong," a result of ignorance and bad judgment. He said that if he'd understood Vietnamese nationalism, and how wrong the domino theory was, millions of lives might have been saved. Still, asked if he ever felt guilty or traumatized by those millions of people he helped kill during World War II and the Vietnam War, he replied, "Never." Responsibility belonged to the president. Why couldn't Cian Westmoreland forget that number and feel the same?

His confession of murders was bad enough. But as bad, if not worse, was that his trauma, for almost everyone else, was *nonreal*. After all, according to President Obama, the mainstream media, and the general public, those whom drones kill are not innocent civilians but terrorists. Most politicians and military men subscribe to the ethical position, best illustrated by President Truman in Hiroshima, that sometimes killing innocent civilians is a necessary evil. So why couldn't Westmoreland feel that the killing was justified, that he'd done something honorable, instead of telling us he had become a war criminal?

Cian Westmoreland, emblematic American drone soldier, was our war criminal and our hero that spring evening in Las Vegas. We, his spell-bound audience, were Veterans for Peace members, Catholic radicals, Code Pink activists, writers, and filmmakers. We, eighty people in a country of 350 million who, polls suggest, overwhelmingly approve of drone warfare, had just driven the forty-six miles on Highway 95 back to Las Vegas from Creech Air Base, where we'd spent the day protesting killing people thousands of miles away by drone.[2]

A year after that first meeting with Westmoreland, during the Shut Down Creech protests in April the following year, he and Brandon Bryant were back in Las Vegas for the screening of *National Bird,* a documentary film featuring testimonies of former drone pilots.[3] Bryant was another former pilot turned whistle-blower who, upon his release from Creech Air Base, was awarded a scoreboard indicating he had helped kill 1,626 enemy combatants.[4] It wasn't some ideological objection that had caused his military leave; it was the trauma and his body's physical incapacity to keep killing serially in a casual manner.

Months later, in early October 2017, Code Pink organized another annual Week of Protest at Creech. This time, along with the drone victims, other killings were also on our minds—fifty-eight tourists killed and more than five hundred wounded in Las Vegas the weekend before by a gunman, Stephen Paddock, who, from his thirty-second-story room in the Mandalay Casino, rained bullets on people in the outdoor music festival below. One more mass shooting—there had been 521 reported (with four or more killed) during the previous 477 days.[5] News of the shooting focused on the unknown "motive" of the shooter; nothing was more disturbing to the public than the killer's normalcy. But for most Americans, killings from Creech do not present similar problems of incomprehension—the pilots are simply following orders. "Mass shooter and drone killer, both hunting people," read one protester's sign at Creech. However it's done, from Creech or hotel casino, it's killing *in* Las Vegas and *from* Las Vegas— America's emblematic city where novelist Hunter Thompson's two gonzo protagonists attempted their "savage journey to the heart of the American Dream."

Says protagonist Duke's attorney in Thompson's novel to a waitress in Las Vegas: "Let me explain it to you. . . . We're looking for the American Dream, and we were told it was somewhere in this area." This dialogue follows:

WAITRESS: Hey Lou, you know where the American Dream is?

ATT'Y (TO DUKE): She's asking the cook if he knows where the American Dream is.

WAITRESS: Five tacos, one taco burger. Do you know where the American Dream is? . . .

ATT'Y: All we were told was, go till you find the American Dream. Take this white Cadillac and go find the American Dream. It's somewhere in the Las Vegas area.[6]

Thompson's characters know that for a loser Las Vegas is the meanest town on earth but that for the would-be winner it's the city of desire that holds out the fantastic possibility of winning big—and that it's all bound up with war. "What do you *want?*" Duke harangues the desk clerk who has called him up in his room. "Where's the goddamn ice I ordered? Where's the booze? There's a war on, man! People are being killed!" "Oh . . . yes . . . yes . . . This terrible war. When will it end?" "Tell me . . . What do you *want?*"[7]

Las Vegas is the city of mirages, a portal to a time warp, where you can travel back to the Second World War, Cold War, Nuclear War, and Vietnam War, proceed through the present War on Terror and Drone War, and be propelled into future wars of fantastic technologies and apocalyptic terror. It is the place where a Great Military Barrack is married to a Great Whore. "Awww, mama . . . can this really . . . be the end?" Stephen Paddock might as well have been listening to Dylan's "Memphis Blues Again," ejaculating his bullets from the Mandalay Hotel-Casino. The man squeezing the trigger was also an emblem of the American Dream; he had become wealthy, enjoyed the gambler's life. Duke's friend Bruce with some surprise might have asked him: "You *found* the American Dream? . . . In *this* town?"[8] And Mr. Paddock might have answered with a Beatles song, "Yes, happiness *is* a warm gun."

The delirious youth culture of the 1960s and 1970s needed Bob Dylan, the Beatles, and Thompson's *Fear and Loathing in Las Vegas* to touch on what's hidden at the core of American dreaming. Today, if you want to take its measure, journey to Creech and witness Hellfire missiles launched from Paradise Ranch to distant countries in the larger Middle East, while drone pilots experience the hunter's thrills as well as, when things go wrong, revulsion and self-loathing.

And then consider the historic significance and contradictions of Obama's presidency, "whose power was bracketed by the same forces that bracketed the lives of black people everywhere"[9]—forces that became even more pronounced after Trump's election and his open complicity with the racist politics of white supremacy. In America, after two centuries of black slavery, Obama succeeded in channeling the rage of Malcolm X ("I don't see any American dream. I see an American nightmare") and the Christianity of Martin Luther King ("America is essentially . . . a dream yet unfulfilled") into a democratic victory of the progressive agenda, including his heroic passage of the Affordable Health Care Act and his promise to end the wars in Iraq and Afghanistan. Was it inevitable that Obama would end up sanctioning the crimes of the secretive drone warfare carried out by the US security state and redouble the drone attacks, institutionalizing the "kill lists," the signature strikes, and other violations of the basic rules of war? At the end of his administration Obama moderately circumscribed the CIA's role in drone strikes by executive order, limits that Trump quickly lifted. Obama, who inspired hope in me and my children, is the only president for whom I actively campaigned. It was painful to write this book. If even Obama, a man whose intelligence and decency I held in the highest esteem, was unable to rise above the illegal policies of a counterterror security state, where can we find the new type of politics he espoused as a candidate? Criticizing Presidents Bush or Trump is a given for any progressive position; in this post-Obama moment when things cannot get worse, the hard work, activist Dorothy Day's "harsh and dreadful love," is to face the bankruptcy of the Left regarding America's class warfare and military imperialism and, as Day and King did, demand new thinking and new action.[10]

As an ethnographer I am expected to interview people and listen to what they have to say. The US Air Force didn't allow me talk to drone pilots; a witness is the last thing a killer permits. So I could talk only to former pilots turned whistle-blowers, of which there are only a handful;

some of them I met in person, others I heard speak in films, or I read their interviews in the expanding literature and filmography on drones that is a growing ethnographic source. I was also able to talk with antidrone militants during protests at Creech Air Base where I couldn't reduce myself to be a detached anthropologist but felt required also, as part of the ethnography, to become myself a participant.

An ethnographic writer must make sense of a cultural complex through precise description and analysis. But mostly, as Clifford Geertz wrote, "Looking into dragons, not domesticating or abominating them, nor drowning them in vats of theory, is what anthropology has all been about."[11] When I finally met Bryant and Westmoreland, the two former drone operators with whom I'd been most eager to talk, I experienced a muteness in their presence I hadn't anticipated, for I realized I indeed was looking into dragons, and my wanting them to explain to me what drone killing is, the real of their experience, felt suddenly obscene—as if they could ever really tell me. At the core of this ethnographic essay is the silence imposed by the horror they were part of, leading to the confrontation between old and new ways of thinking and politics.

1 The Real

"Home of the Hunters"—the words inscribed atop Creech's entrance gate. This is not a metaphor. Drone pilots and operators are literally *hunters*. Drones are *hunter-killers*, named after animals: "predator," "hawk," "raven," "drone." Former pilots' memoirs refer to their killing of humans on the ground as hunting "rats," "pigeons," "chickens," "mice." The generic result is *bugsplat*. Killing another human being is the hardest act—unless it's translated into a fantasy of hunting, and then it's animals, not people, you are killing. At the sensory, conceptual, symbolic, and emotional levels, killing by drone turns into designated hunting, which doesn't have to be hard. Hunting and killing prey can even be sport, can be fun. Hunting is the Lacanian *real* of what drone pilots do.

Lieutenant Colonel Matt J. Martin's memoir, *Predator*, describes his years as a drone pilot at Creech. The idea of hunting echoes in almost every page of his narrative: "I was a patient, silent hunter;" "We were always hunting, day and night."[1] Pilots' main activity consisted of "watching from the sky like a bird of prey ready to strike."[2] Martin uses the biblical bestiary to explain his frame of mind: "I sometimes pondered how Adam might have gone back to the Garden of Eden and whacked the serpent."[3] Drone pilot Martin said of his victims: "Insurgents were like

7

having a house infested with rats; the more of them you killed, it seemed, the more they bred."[4] Drone pilots are told in training, "The bastards never know what hits them."[5] Like hunters for whom the trepidation of their first kill is forever imprinted in their memory, Martin talks of "my first kill" when "I drew in a deep breath, felt sweat stinging my eyes, tasted the bile of excitement in my mouth."[6] The military term for this hunting is *going kinetic*, and there is a "general eagerness in Nevada [at Creech] to 'go kinetic.'"[7] Killing can be exciting. It's just hunting.

Beginning with the general name *drone*, coined by two naval scientists in 1936 "after analyzing various names of insects and birds," the metaphoric links between drones and the bestiary are consistently preserved:[8] "Global Hawk," "Raven," "Wasp," "Dragon Runner," "Eagle Eye," "Vampire Bat," "SnakeBot," "Big Dog," "Centaur," "Polibot" (shifting from the form of a snake into a spider), "RoboLobster," "Polecat," "Peregrine UAV Killer" (after the peregrine falcon), "Marsupial" robots (one robot carried inside another). "Predator" was the name for the hero of them all until 2016. The latest generation of drones are mostly "Reapers." The Iraqis' name for drones is "vultures."[9]

Grégoire Chamayou's paradigm for drone warfare is *manhunting*. He argues that by eliminating all sense of reciprocity, by killing without any danger of the killer being killed as well, drone warfare "becomes absolutely unilateral. What could still claim to be combat is converted into a campaign of what is, quite simply, slaughter."[10] After 9/11 Bush declared that the new kind of warfare required "us to be on an international manhunt," while Rumsfeld asked, "How do we organize the Department of Defense for manhunts?"[11] Researchers called for a "national manhunting agency," "manhunting perfected and, most of all, made invisible."[12] Hunter-killer drones are instruments of such manhunting, "so asymmetrical that it is more like hunting than war"—to the point that many in the Pentagon feared that such "preemptive manhunting" could turn into another Phoenix Program of torture and murder.[13]

A RADIO EXCHANGE

The declassified radio transcripts below between the sensor, the pilot, the MC (mission coordinator), the joint terminal attack controller (call sign

"Jaguar 25," or Jag25), and the safety observer of a drone operation can be taken as a sample of drone hunting. They are reenacted in the film *National Bird,* which Brandon Bryant and Cian Westmoreland screened for us in Las Vegas. The drone operators have just noticed three trucks driving on an Afghan country road. Here are extracts of the exchanges:

SENSOR: Looks like people on the back of a pickup, one, two, three, at least five dudes so far. . . . That truck would make a beautiful target.

PILOT: Yeah.

MC. Screener said at least one child near SUV.

SENSOR: Bullshit. Where? I don't think they have kids out at this hour, I know they're shady but come on.

. . . .

MC: They are reviewing.

PILOT: Okay, review that shit. Why didn't he say possible child, why are they so quick to call fucking kids but not to call a fucking rifle.

SENSOR: I really doubt that "children" call, man. I really fucking hate that.

SENSOR: Picked up a third vehicle on their train.

MC: Guilty by association.

. . . .

SENSOR: They're praying. They are praying. Praying? I mean, seriously, that's what they do.

MC: They're going to do something nefarious.

. . . .

MC: Adolescent near the rear of the SUV.

SENSOR: Well, teenagers can fight.

MC: Pick up a weapon and you're a combatant. It's how that works.

PILOT: . . . Be advised, all passengers are finishing up praying, and rallying up near all three vehicles at this time.

SENSOR: Oh, sweet target. I'd try to go through the bed [people lying on a bed at the back of the truck], put it right center of the bed.

MC: Oh, that's perfect.

PILOT: . . . Our screeners are currently calling.

PILOT: Twenty-one MAMs [military-aged males], no females, and two possible children.

JAG25: Roger. When we say children are we talking teenagers or toddlers?

SENSOR: I would say about twelve, not toddlers. Something more towards adolescents or teens.

JAG25: We'll pass that along to the ground force commander. But like I said, twelve-thirteen years old with a weapon is just as dangerous.

SENSOR: Oh, we agree. Yeah.

MC: What's the master plan, fellas?

PILOT: I don't know. Hope we get to shoot the truck with all the dudes in it.

SENSOR: Yeah. . . . Sensor is in, the party begins!

PILOT: Yeah. All right, so the plan is, man, uh, we're going to watch this thing go down, the hells [Hellfire missiles] are going to take out as much as they can, and when they Winchester we can play cleanup.

SENSOR: Hey MC.

MC: Yes?

SENSOR: Remember, kill chain!

MC: Will do.

SENSOR: Roger. And

EXPLOSION

SENSOR: Oh . . . And there it goes!

PILOT: Our engagement.

SENSOR: Stand by.

. . . .

PILOT: They took the first [truck] and, uh, the last out. They're going to come back around.

SENSOR: Looks like they're surrendering. They're not running.

SAFETY OBSERVER: Dude, this is weird.

SENSOR: They hit it. [Explosion of the third truck]. You . . . These guys are just . . .

PILOT: Holy shit.

SENSOR: I don't know about this. This is weird.

PILOT: The lady is carrying a kid, huh? Maybe.

MC: No.

SENSOR: Huh, yeah.

MC: The baby, I think on the right. Yeah.

PILOT: Since the engagement we have not been able to PID [identify] any weapons.[14]

Twenty-three civilian members of a family, including two children, were killed in that attack, their scattered body parts collected and taken to their village amid sobbing and wailing. The film shows images of survivors in the hospital, their limbs amputated. Family members of the killed explain to the interviewers how they had stopped at a roadside rest area to pray. When they left they heard a plane they couldn't see. The mother of her dead boy says there were two black helicopters and a white drone. When their first vehicle was hit, everyone panicked and the men told the women and children to get out of the truck so that the attackers could see they were civilians. But the bombing continued. One woman raised her child above her head to show they were not fighters. One man asks: How can't these allegedly precision weapons distinguish women and children from combatants?

Hunting involves looking for a "beautiful target." A truck filled with people, "military-aged males" is perfect for a strike. "They were always trying to kill people," explains Heather, a former drone pilot, in the film. "All these officers, it looks good on their résumé if they kill more people." But there are children. Toddlers or adolescents? "Oh, sweet target!" Praying? Call the kill chain. "The party begins!" The Creech pilot hits the first, then a second truck. A woman is showing her child to heaven. A third missile hits the third truck. No weapons. "This is weird."

Some of these massacres were later claimed to be human errors. General Stanley McChrystal apologized to the country after the previously mentioned massacre. But massacres are built into the US policy of manhunting. Human rights researchers have documented scores of abuses that appear to be illegal actions, amounting to war crimes, such as *double-tap* strikes (against first responders) and strikes deliberately targeting funerals and weddings—dozens of them have been documented by the Bureau of Investigative Journalism and the Stanford and New York University law schools.[15] A hunter doesn't respect funerals, weddings, or prayers.

THE KILL LIST

There is live video screening of drone attacks, directly transmitted from Creech to US officials in Washington. But that's not enough. The White House wanted real action. So a *kill list* was established. Obama was playing the leading role, the Hunter in Chief. The White House staff for national security, exempt from review by Congress, would play a substantial role in the hunting expeditions for killing suspected terrorists. According to a *New York Times* report detailing how the killings were decided in Washington, every Tuesday more than one hundred members of the national security apparatus, "a grim debating society" headed by the president, would gather by videoconference to discuss targets and recommend to the president who should be next to die—every strike in Yemen, Somalia, and Libya and the riskier ones in Pakistan.[16]

Candidates for the kill list were hotly debated. There were issues that required clarification, such as "What's a Qaeda facilitator?" "If I open a gate and you drive through it, am I a facilitator?" someone wondered. If men are loading a truck with fertilizers, how do you know if they are making bombs or just farming? Obama's chief of staff, William Daley, observed: "The president accepts as a fact that a certain amount of screw-ups are going to happen."[17] People close to Obama were impressed by his "striking self-confidence." As national security adviser Thomas Donilon put it, "He's a president who is quite comfortable with the use of force on behalf of the

United States." Cameron P. Munter, ambassador to Pakistan, was even more blunt: Obama "didn't realize his main job was to kill people."[18]

That killing was part of the ordinary business of the day at the White House can be glimpsed from the following interaction between Obama and his close national security advisor and speechwriter Ben Rhodes. At the end of the first term, when Obama asked Rhodes what he wanted to be engaged with during the second term, Rhodes complained that the administration lacked political ambition and had not taken on issues like normalizing relations with Cuba but mostly that "I'm tired of just being the guy who defends drones." Obama understood instantly: "So, more Cuba, less killing. Look, I feel you." The president offered Rhodes the opportunity to take the lead on some projects of interest to him but insisted, "I'd like you to stay where you are. . . . You're not just an advisor, you're a friend."[19] They were friends and partners at the White House not only while they collaborated on writing Obama's great speeches for Prague and Cairo and Oslo, but also while they went hunting terrorists in the Middle East and Africa. Not only Creech but also the White House had turned into the "Home of the Hunters."

Obama "insisted on approving every new name on an expanding 'kill list,' poring over terrorist suspects' biographies on what one official calls the macabre 'baseball cards' of an unconventional war."[20] During the first six months of 2011 there were 145 drone strikes against Gaddafi's regime alone, even while the Obama administration denied there was a war against Libya.[21] What did Obama know from the baseball card profiles of the potential terrorists? According to one report, of the approximately 3,000 people killed by drones up to June of 2011, the CIA knew the names of only 125, and it considered only 35 of them as "high value targets."[22] But why should a hunter know the names of the wild prey he is going to kill? Only pets and tamed animals have names.

Did these killings really diminish the terrorism problem posed by al-Qaeda and affiliates? David Kilcullen, a "counterterrorist guru," close associate of General David Petraeus in the "surge" to end the war in Iraq, and someone who knew the situation well, didn't think so. He told Congress in April 2009, "Since 2006, we've killed 14 senior Al-Qaeda leaders using drone strikes; in the same period, we've killed 700 Pakistani civilians in the same area. The drone strikes are highly unpopular. They are deeply aggravating to the population. And they've given rise to a feeling of anger that coalesces the population around the extremists and leads to spikes of extremism. . . . The current path that we are on is leading us to loss of Pakistani government control over its own population."[23] The ratio of fifty civilians killed for each militant was, for Kilcullen, "immoral," and led to a self-generating process of further violence, a view reiterated in other internal CIA documents.[24]

The London-based Bureau of Investigative Journalism is the most cited database regarding victims of drone warfare. As of June 2018, the Bureau estimated that between 7,854 and 10,918 people had been killed by American drones in Pakistan, Afghanistan, Yemen, and Somalia; of these, between 751 and 1,555, following the BIJ's own definitions, were "civilians,"[25] and among these, 262 to 335 were children.[26] Some Western estimates put the number of combatants among the dead at 85 percent. A very different calculation was given by the Pakistani daily *Dawn*: it estimated that of the 708 people killed by drones in 2009 alone, only five were known militants. The other major English-speaking daily in Pakistan, the *News*, estimated that of the 701 people killed by drones between January 2006 and April 2007, only 14 were known militants.[27] Why the wide disparity between these numbers and the accepted Western estimates? A major explanation has to do with the notion of "signature strike"—in which the meaning of "combatant" is decided on the basis of a pattern of life, geographical location, or guilt by association.

There are, however, other well-informed Western sources that concur with Kilcullen's 50-to-1 estimate. Peter Bergen and Megan Braun report that since 2004 some forty-nine militant leaders have been killed in drone strikes, constituting "2% of all drone-related fatalities."[28] The 2012 report *Living under Drones,* produced by the Stanford's International Human Rights and Conflict Resolution Clinic and the NYU School of Law's Global Justice Clinic, similarly found, for Pakistan specifically, that "the number of 'high-level' targets killed as a percentage of total casualties is extremely low—estimated at just 2%."[29] Bergen and Jennifer Rowland reviewed the drone campaign in Pakistan between 2004 and December 31, 2013, and affirmed that the fifty-eight militant leaders whose death were confirmed by at least two credible news sources "account for only 2 percent of all drone-related fatalities in Pakistan."[30]

Signature strikes are based on patterns of behavior observed on the ground from a drone ten thousand feet in the sky. William Arkin's "Data

Machine"—the vast system of data collection for national security pur-
poses that is leading to increasingly automated surveillance and warfare—
would define a signature as "a distinctive basic characteristic or set of
characteristics that consistently re-occurs and uniquely identifies a piece
of equipment, activity, individual, or event."[31] Signature strikes target
"groups of men who bear certain signatures, or defining characteristics
associated with terrorist activity, but whose identities aren't known."[32]
What those "defining characteristics" are has never been made explicit
to the public. By 2012 the CIA had clearance to treat armed men traveling
by truck in Pakistan, a country where gun ownership is common, as
individuals whose "pattern of life" warranted a lethal strike, with the dead
being counted as "militants."[33] An extension of such cavalier acceptance of
group killing is the frequency with which drone attacks on militants are
carried out at night. A study by an academic group and the BIJ found
that "houses are twice as likely to be attacked at night compared with the
afternoon ... when families were likely to be at home and gathered
together."[34]

President Obama's main counterterrorism chief, John Brennan, claimed
in August 2011 that not a single noncombatant had been killed in a year of
strikes. This derives from accepting a simple premise: "Military-age males
in a strike zone [are] combatants ... unless there is explicit intelligence
posthumously proving them innocent."[35] That is, you *are* a terrorist if you
are in a zone where there are terrorists, because "in fact, simply *being a
male capable of taking up arms* in a territory deemed 'hostile' sufficed in
the minds of the drone program administrators to dispatch the suspect and
label the homicide an 'act of war.'"[36] (This logic still does not take into
account the estimated three hundred children killed by drones). As a CIA
officer told Jane Mayer of the *New Yorker*, "No tall man with a beard is safe
anywhere in Southwest Asia."[37] Other officials candidly admitted that they
"were killing a large number of terrorist suspects, even when the C.I.A.
analysts were not certain beforehand of their presence."[38] In short, signature strikes ordinarily imply that the identity of the people killed is
unknown. In 2012 President Obama approved TADS, "terrorist attack dis-
ruption strikes," in Yemen—strikes on unknown people who are deemed to
be linked to terrorism. Frequently the NSA approves drone attacks by looking at the activity of a SIM card, not the actual content of the phone call;

this led one former drone operator to "believe that the drone program amounts to little more than death by unreliable metadata."[39]

Laurie Calhoun writes: "Preemptive war and summary execution of suspects are two sides of the same tyrannical coin." Such executions are protected by the secrecy of the perpetrators and the procedures used to target, death sentences issued by a president-appointed committee of bureaucrats with no provision for appeal or surrender. Calhoun points out that "military dictators have always executed their suspected enemies without trial," and she wonders how the Predator drone program's "*institutional* homicide differs from the outrageous mass murders perpetrated by the tyrants of the past."[40]

Terrorists are people stripped of names, citizenship, national identity. They have no rights, no personal defense, no due process. They represent nothing, allegedly belong to no group, family, or country. We make of them the embodiment of *bare life* in the manner described by authors such as Michel Foucault or Giorgio Agamben. In the Greek distinction between *zoe* (living beings in their natural state that include people and animals) and *bios* (human individuals in society), terrorists belong to *zoe*, to bare life, the equivalent of what, in Roman law, was the figure of *homo sacer*, someone "who may be killed and yet not sacrificed."[41] The reduction of people into animal-like bare life is not marginal to the politics of the war of terror; it constitutes it. Hence the centrality of the hunter's ethos. "Double taps" are an extreme instance of the reduction of terrorists to bare life to be killed with no due process and with no ordinary rites of burial. *Homo sacer* or "sacred man," in its double aspect of abjection and sacrality, is a figure close to the anthropological notion of taboo: someone who produces at once awe and horror.[42]

The politics of the drone provides a startling example of how politics is turned into *biopolitics*, a transformation produced by modernity, according to Foucault—that is, central to the mechanisms of state power are the calculations about natural or bare life itself, "a kind of bestialization of man achieved through the most sophisticated political techniques."[43] For Agamben, such a biopolitics of bare life "signals a radical transformation of the political-philosophical categories of classical thought."[44] Achille Mbembé has added the notion of *necropolitics*, that is, a politics in which "the ultimate expression of sovereignty resides . . . in the power and the capacity to dictate who may live and who must die."[45] In the current world, terrorism provides evidence for such views. A political axiom in the current War on Terror is that it is the sovereign state's right to place the attribute "terrorist" on someone, who then becomes an individual outside human law (so that he can be killed without homicide being committed) or divine law (so that his death is not a valid sacrifice to any community and disrespect toward his religious burial is not a sacrilege). A major criticism by Dick Cheney and other Republicans against the new Obama administration was that, for a while, it appeared as if they were going to treat the terrorists as "criminals"—that is, allowing them a right to due judicial process and punishment, an intolerable concession in the post- 9/11 mind-set that defines the terrorists as bare life just to be hunted and exterminated.

A HUNTER'S WORLD

I once spent several autumns running after wild boars with a group of twenty to thirty Basque hunters before I wrote an ethnographic essay on their mind-set and emotional life. What impressed me were the ways this type of hunting reduces the universe into an elementary semiotics of tracks, barks, and smells, as well as its specific use of the senses, its symbolism, and what I called its "erotics."[46] A hunter is a man possessed by desire who needs a kill. If, for Chamayou and for Hugh Gusterson, hunting is the true paradigm of the drone pilot, a theory of hunting is perhaps the best cultural and subjective analogue to a theory of the drone.

The hunter's initial premise is that the human senses—hearing, sight, smell, touch—must be reduced to the level of animal communication. The wild beast in flight is concrete only in the tracks and scent it leaves behind—traces that are transmitted through invisible air, that the dog perceives and translates into barking. The hunter, upon hearing the barking, has to interpret the authenticity, intensity, modality, and direction of the signals and guess the location of the animal before approaching the spot where it might be hiding. The sensorial and cognitive gaps between human and wild animal are such that one wonders how the hunter can trust his own guesses. Yet a successful catch shows that the hunter comes to know a lot about his object of desire. But what kind of "knowledge" is this, based on tracks, blind smell, wordless barking?

To understand the hunter's reduced sensorial field, one should differenti-
ate between the primary-level senses of smell and touch (which lack a defi-
nite semantic space) and the secondary-level senses of hearing and sight
(whose words, images, and colors form semantic hierarchies, relationships,
and incompatibilities). Smell and touch dominate the hunt, and hearing is
also vital but not at the level of speech. As for sight, the hunter uses it in a
sort of process of elimination—normally the hunter imagines the image of
the fugitive prey but doesn't see it except as a momentary "apparition" pre-
ceding an immediate kill. You can watch a domestic animal endlessly, but a
wild animal is elusive, travels under cover of night. As in the children's game
Hide and Seek, "seeing" is "killing" and wins the game. The visual paradox
of the hunter consists in transforming the erratic image of the fantasized
wild animal into the still life of an inert animal. Only then can he touch it.

One could say that the hunter's claims to "knowledge" rely on *olfactory*
information, based primarily on the dog's sniffing and the guesswork that
guides the hunter. Instinctual, intuitive knowledge is related to the sense
of smell, as when you "smell" danger. The hunter never "knows" for certain
the moves of his prey; he can only guess what it will do. In the absence of
fixed knowledge, a shaman-like "divination" of the prey's behavior is the
only type of knowledge left to him. The ordinary notion of "truth" doesn't
apply to guesswork or fantasy—we are already in the domain of symbolism. No hypothesis can falsify the result when we are guessing or divining.
The only certitude is the kill.

In hunting you establish imaginary boundaries, fences, strategic barriers to control and trap the beast—close a passage, surround an area, point
to the center of a field. The hunter's success requires a strategy of enclo-
sures, and "freedom" consists in not being subjected to them. The erratic
animal will pass through these imaginary circles imposed by the hunter's
"rites of passage." One theory of symbolism argues that when conceptual or
encyclopedic knowledge fails, symbolic knowledge kicks in.[47] This same
theory applies to the hunter, whose substantive lacunae in sensory and
conceptual knowledge must be replaced with conjectures and intuitions.

In his memoir, *Predator,* in which he continuously says he thought of his
victims as wild animals and of himself as a hunter, drone pilot Martin
engaged with the enemy opponent not as a human to interact with at the
level of the human senses—face to face, speaking, listening—but as a *target.*

For hours a drone operator pursues a hidden, invisible enemy; suddenly the enemy appears and sets in motion a hot chase, the goal being the elimination of the target with the joystick—it's called a "targeted killing." Since the pilot is far removed from any personal interaction, the face of the fugitive is invisible, and in the absence of any witness the pilot kills the target as the hunter who sees only an object of a lower *species*. The pilot does not see an individualized target down below but a *group* for a "signature strike." Collateral damage is assumed as intrinsic to war—the killing of up to thirty bystanders for each combatant is taken as a rule in drone warfare, according to a former analyst.[48] Victims of drones are mostly generic individuals, deprived of their individuality and banded into a biopolitical group identity, as wild animals are seen on the basis of habitat and species. Categorical shifting from individual to group, from member to species, is decisive for the diffusion of responsibility regarding the actual killing.

Consistent with the paradigm of the hunt, the only knowledge the drone pilot is allowed about the terrorist is at the animal level—tracks that require policing, momentary sightings, guesswork and information on his whereabouts, fictions of his beastly nature. The hunter cannot engage with the prey at the human sensory level except as a moving target for elimination, cannot know about the motives, ideas, or values of the terrorist except in terms of guesses and fantasy. Ignorance of the terrorist's subjectivity is a condition for hunting him. You would be contaminated by being in the presence of such an untouchable, by talking to or shaking his hand. By definition you can never touch a wild beast, nor should you touch a tabooed terrorist—except by killing him.

A hunter who begins to perceive the subjectivity of his prey in privacy is already committing a category mistake. The pilot/hunter's primary axiom must be simple: I am the hunter, my enemy is an animal target—not an individual citizen. There is no rule for privacy in animal life; neither there should be for those under drone surveillance, for their privacy has been turned into a public domain, into Predator porn, observed from above potentially by countless people. The peeping drone with its "eye in the sky" should recognize no privacy, say, for a lovemaking couple below—which makes their sexual behavior akin to the nonprivate sex of animals.[49] The risk for pilots comes from feeling that they actually are intruding into the private lives of the people they hunt, when instead of the terrorist wild beast they begin to see a fully domesticated house animal. The two types of killings, of wild or tame animals, are categorically different for a hunter. The drone pilot, watching the prey for days and weeks, can end up feeling he is using a hunter's strategy against a domestic pet.

DON'T CAPTURE, KILL

US senator Saxby Chambliss succinctly summed up the basic change in terrorism policy under the Obama administration: "to take out high-value targets, versus capturing high-value targets."[50] The Bush administration's policy had been, for the most part, to keep suspected terrorists at Guantánamo and torture them. The Obama administration chose to assassinate them instead. The Trump administration followed Obama's lead. Capture is messy and could lead to domestication. Hunters prefer to kill.

There are countless cases to document the Obama administration policy of "Don't capture, kill." Bilal el-Berjawi, stripped of his British citizenship before he was killed by a US drone, had been "under surveillance for several years as he traveled back and forth between the UK and East Africa yet [British and American intelligence] did not capture him. Instead the United States hunted him down and killed him in Somalia."[51] The authors of the Pentagon's Intelligence, Surveillance, and Reconnaissance Task Force study "admit frankly that capturing terrorists is a rare occurrence."[52] It is true that a capture could become a source of information. But the Guantánamo prisoners showed that their prosecution presents messy problems; the Obama and Trump administrations preferred to avoid these.

As a *New York Times* journalist put it, "The bottom line is clear: killing is more convenient than capture for both the United States and the foreign countries where the strikes occur."[53] Killing is also cheaper than keeping the target in jail indefinitely. As a result, there were "virtually no captures by American agencies."[54] Senator Lindsey Graham admitted in 2013: "We lack, as a nation, a place to put terrorists if we catch them. I can tell you that the operators are in a bad spot out there. They know that if they capture a guy, it creates a nightmare. And it's just easier to kill 'em."[55] Vice President Cheney had a point when he criticized the Obama administration "for being so weak that it has given up on trying to capture and interrogate the bad guys and instead just kills them."[56] Targeted killing from a distance was "clean" and easy, "the antithesis of the dirty, intimate work of interrogation."[57] As John Rizzo, a career CIA lawyer who had approved the CIA's infamous detention-and-interrogation program, put it, "Once the interrogation was gone, all that was left was the killing."[58] The *Guardian* reported that US special forces routinely killed suspects, even civilians, without attempting capture.[59] In some cases there was not enough evidence to hold an Afghan suspected in custody, but there was enough of a narrative to assassinate him.[60] This was the reality of the counterterrorist policy under Obama, which continues under Trump: don't bother with capture, just kill the suspected terrorists. It's hunting.

During the first year of Obama's presidency, the CIA was after Saleh Ali Saleh Nabhan, a member of al-Qaeda's East African branch. Killing him would be a major victory, but capturing him would provide an intelligence windfall. In a meeting chaired by Admiral Michael Mullen, Obama was given the options of killing Nabhan with missiles, with a helicopter-borne assault, or doing a "snatch and grab" operation, the last tactically the most attractive but also the riskiest option. And there was a problem: "Where would Nabhan be taken if the military succeeded in capturing him? Nine months into its own war on al-Qaeda, the Obama administration had no detention policy for terrorists captured outside established war zones like Afghanistan or Iraq."[61] As one of the people involved in the mission explained it, "We didn't capture him because it would have been hard to find a place to put him."[62] Guantánamo and Bagram prisons were out of the question. So was bringing him to the US or turning to an anarchic Somalia. As General James Cartwright, vice-chairman of the Joint Chiefs, summed it up, the military is required to take surrendering enemies into custody, but "We do not have a plausible strategy."[63]

Klaidman sums it up in *Kill or Capture:* "The inability to detain terror suspects was creating perverse incentives that favored killing or releasing suspected terrorists over capturing them."[64] While testifying to the Senate Armed Services Committee, Admiral William McRaven recognized that a capture outside Afghanistan "is always a difficult issue for us."[65] The Obama administration's often-repeated mantra to reassure the public was the lie that killing was the last option when capture was not possible. The actual policy was just the opposite: don't capture, kill. Yes, we can.

The acceptance of the rationale for assassination and not capture hinges on the insistence that the enemy is not only a combatant but something else—a terrorist. A year into his presidency, in a tense meeting with top counterterrorism and political advisers gathered in the Situation Room, Obama read aloud US district judge William Young's sentencing of Richard Reid, the so-called Shoe Bomber:

> This is the sentence that is provided for by our statutes, it is a fair and just sentence. . . . You are not an enemy combatant. You are a terrorist. You are not a soldier in any war. You are a terrorist. To give you that reference, to call you a soldier gives you far too much stature. . . .
> . . . You are a terrorist. And we do not negotiate with terrorists. We do not treat with terrorists. We do not sign documents with terrorists. We hunt them down one by one.[66]

This mantra of "you are a terrorist" is the cornerstone of a mind-set that categorically separates *them* from *us*—the premise that justifies "hunting" them.

The license to kill terrorists and the new normal for Predator drone assassinations was not accepted as a matter of course initially by everyone in counterterrorism. To understand how a "new normal" for drone assassinations was established as counterterrorist policy, one change sums it up with precision: replace the rule of law—the work of police, judges, jailers— with the law of hunting. Interviewed by the 9/11 Commission soon after the attacks, then head of the CIA, George Tenet, was asked "whether he, as Director of the Central Intelligence, should operate an armed Predator." He replied to the members of the commission, "This is new ground," and he raised key issues, asking: "What is the chain of command? Who takes the shot? Are America's leaders comfortable with the CIA doing this, going outside of normal military command and control?"[67] The assistant director, Charles Allen, said that he or the Agency's number-three man, A. B. "Buzzy" Krongard, "would be happy to pull the trigger." But "Tenet was appalled." He added that no CIA personnel had such authority to use drones to summarily assassinate people, even terrorists. Considering the repercussions of getting into the business of assassinations, then CIA's deputy director John McLaughlin commented: "You can't underestimate the cultural change that comes with gaining lethal authority. When people say to me, 'It's not a big deal,' I say to them, 'Have you ever killed anyone?'

It is a big deal. You start thinking about things differently."[68] You start thinking like the assassin Mafia guy you watched in a Coppola film. Or you start thinking like a hunter.

In sum, the CIA bosses knew exactly what the changes for fighting the War on Terror required: assassination outside the boundaries of law. Before this new war, Janet Reno, the attorney general and top law enforcement official from 1993 until 2001, "didn't support tacit presidential approval authorizing Afghan proxies to kill bin Laden"; she labeled it "illegal."[69] Also when then top FBI counterterrorism official had been presented with a scheme to kidnap bin Laden and make him disappear, he objected, saying, "I'm a lawman, not a killer."[70] The new normal of the post-9/11 state of exception replaced assassination with "targeted killing." The CIA's deputy director for operations, Jose Rodriguez, found a convenient solution to any difficulty presented by such killing: "He decided to outsource the killing program to Blackwater employees."[71]

Assassinations had long been the CIA's modus operandi. One need only think of the modern political history of Iran, Guatemala, Indonesia, Chile, and more. To help in training for the business of killing, the Agency organized "a study in assassination" guide.[72] The manual included an explicit warning: "Assassination can seldom be employed with a clear conscience. Persons who are morally squeamish should not attempt it."[73] By executive order President Ford banned the policy of assassination in 1976, a ban later reaffirmed by presidents Carter and Reagan. But by 1983 the CIA was back to its former practice of supporting Nicaraguan Contras. Reagan sanctioned state-sponsored assassination in his 1986 attack against Gaddafi.

The normalized yet extraordinary results of this policy of "Don't capture, kill" can be seen in a proposal made in March 2009 by Chairman of the Joint Chiefs of Staff Admiral Mullen to destroy the entire Somali training camp (one hundred people? two hundred people?) in order to kill the one target they were after. Obama went around the table asking every member of the national security team what each one thought. The so-called "principals" of the national security group had no objections. Finally, General Cartwright said: "If there is a person in the camp who is a clear threat to the United States we should go after him. But carpet-bombing a country is a really bad precedent."[74] Obama agreed with him and the strike was canceled, an early timidity that would appear amateurish in light of his later decisions. In March of 2016 a drone strike attacked a training camp in Somalia and killed 150 Shabab militants without a single peep from the Obama administration or any notice from the general public. And so it goes.

The policy of "Mow them all down" that had looked so bad earlier was now acceptable. Its legality was based on a post-9/11 declaration, fifteen years earlier, that allowed violent action against the perpetrators of that massacre. Al Shabab was founded in 2006 and was attacked under the claim that it was associated with AQAP (al-Qaeda in the Arabian Peninsula), which was forged in Yemen in 2009. Al Shabab had armed itself with M16s and AK-47s that could be found for a hundred dollars in the Mogadishu weapons bazaar, weapons and ammunition that the Obama administration had shipped to Somalia's embattled government, forty tons of them, on sale in the market.[75] First create the terrorists, then hunt them.

In March of 2019 there was news that "US airstrikes kill hundreds in Somalia."[76] In 2018 the air strikes had killed 326 suspected Shabab, but in 2019, the news stated, during January and February alone US Africa Command reported killing 225 people in twenty-four strikes. This was happening while President Trump was scaling back operations against similar Islamist insurgencies elsewhere. Trying to make sense of the escalation of the air strikes, "a range of current and former officials said no seismic strategic shift explains the increased airstrikes and higher body count." The US ambassador to Somalia from 2016 to 2017, Stephen Schwartz, said: "It could be there is some well-thought-out strategy behind all of this, but I really doubt it." One way to explain the attacks is that in the new type of drone warfare "a new cultural sensibility emerges in which killing the enemy of the state is an extension of play."[77] The hunters are having fun.

HUNTING WILD NATIVE AMERICANS

Antidrone protests at Creech take place on land plundered from the Shoshone. Once you are there, you can't avoid becoming aware of America's history of genocide against its native people. You realize how close in space and time are the hunting of wild terrorists from Creech and the hunting of "wild" Indians whose lands are now occupied by the Creech

Air Force Base and the Nevada Test Site (NTS), part of the much larger Nellis Air Force Range with its 5,470 square miles, the size of Connecticut. The historical causes, meanings, and consequences of the expropriation of these lands can be argued; beyond dispute is that the white man institutionalized not long ago a form of *manhunting* for natives—a chapter in American history captured, among others, by Benjamin Madley's recent book *An American Genocide*.[78]

Before contact with Europeans, five million or more native Americans inhabited what is now the continental United States; by 1900 fewer than 250,000 remained. Indian "removal" was a precondition for the opening of American lands to modern capitalist society and "played a foundational role in facilitating the conquest and colonization of millions of square miles, the real estate and natural resources on which the country was built."[79] The ideological justification for the genocide was, as Secretary of War Lewis Cass declared in 1830, that natives were "a barbarous people . . . [who] cannot live in contact with a civilized community."[80] In the words of historian Hubert Howe Bancroft, what happened to the native Indians in the American West "was one of the last human hunts of civilization, and the basest and most brutal of them all."[81]

The term *human hunt* as applied to this historical period obviously must be understood in its most literal sense—a hunt actively sanctioned by the US government from the 1840s to the 1870s, when California's native Indian population plunged from 150,000 to 30,000; by 1880, a census would record only 16,277.[82] Madley concludes that between 1846 and 1873, "at least 9,492 to 16,094 California Indians, and probably more," were hunted and killed. While the natives also responded with violence, they killed fewer than 1,500 non-Indians.[83]

Madley typifies the violence as "genocide" after a detailed analysis of the "sustained political will—at both state and federal levels—to create the laws, policies, and well-funded killing machine that carried it out and ensured its continuation over several decades."[84] Such "Indian-hunting operations," as they were called, were condoned by the army, the press, the state's supreme court, and the US Senate. The killings were justified as "self-defense," and "war provided the context and the smokescreen for intentional mass murder."[85] The myth of inevitable extinction displaced the notions of fate, nature, or Providence as the agents of extermination;

in 1851, California governor Peter Burnett prophesied that "a war of extermination will continue to be waged between the races, until the Indian
race becomes extinct" and pushed state legislators "to institutionalize the
state-sponsored hunting and killing" of Indians.[86]

Between 1846 and 1873, approximately 80 percent of all California
Indians died; there were more than 370 massacres, many of which left no
survivors, or little children only.[87] As an alternative to mining, legislators
offered $5 to $15 a day, paid by Congress, to hundreds of militiamen signing on to Indian-hunting expeditions that were broadly supported by voters.[88] As the *Sacramento Transcript* had it, "Savages . . . infest a great part
of the richest mines."[89] Plunder and high wages were incentives for killing.
There was also "great excitement amongst the men" for the hunting
itself.[90] In 1851 California supported six well-publicized Indian-hunting
ranger militia expeditions that killed at least 143 Indians.[91] In Shasta City
Indian killing was institutionalized when authorities offered "five dollars
for every Indian head brought to them."[92] In April 1852, a man disappeared and whites organized a killing squad at Weaverville against the
Wintu village, massacring almost every villager and returning from the
hunt in gory triumph with "one hundred and forty-nine scalps hanging to
their girdles," which provoked "you can well imagine the wild excitement
and joy at the extermination of the tribe. Indian scalps were nailed to
many door posts in that town for quite a while."[93] Seventy-five to eighty-
eight percent of the Modoc tribe were killed, including several chiefs who
were hanged before their heads were cut off and shipped to the Army
Medical Museum in Washington, D.C.[94] As for the standpoint of the US
Congress, it never called for the extermination of Indians, "but it emphatically approved genocide ex post facto by paying California for the killings
carried out by its militia."[95] It was the traditional logic of the imperial
powers, which saw the colonies' original inhabitants as "savages," with no
regular armies of their own and thus no distinction between combatants
and noncombatants, or between "enemy" and "criminal," and no possibility of concluding peace with them: "That colonies might be ruled over in
absolute lawlessness stems from the racial denial of any common bond
between the conqueror and the native."[96]

The categorizing of Indians as *barbarians* justified the burning of
villages and massacres—which prefigured the burning of Vietnamese vil-

lages in the 1960s and 1970s, much as the portrayal of Negroes as savages justified their slavery or lynching. In Baldwin's words, "No black person can afford to forget that the history of this country is genocidal, from where the buffalo once roamed to where our ancestors were slaughtered (from New Orleans to New York, from Birmingham to Boston) and to the Caribbean to Hiroshima and Nagasaki to Saigon."[97] The classification of Negroes and Indians as barbarians until over a century ago again prefigures, in the same American West that includes Creech, the classification of terrorists as barbarians, with the cultural premises and murderous results similar then and now. In an era that boasts the most sophisticated robotic systems, animal categories define drones and their victims in a war conceived as a fight between civilization and barbarism. It's just hunting.

KILLING AND SEX: THE MARTIAL CITY OF PROSTITUTES

Killing and sex are linked in the hunter's experience and in the soldier's battlefront experience.[98] Both traditional forms of masculinity, war and hunting produce pleasure. Military psychologists talk about the experience confirmed by many soldiers that "squeezing the trigger—releasing a hail of bullets—gives enormous pleasure and satisfaction. These are the pleasures of combat . . . of the primal aggression, the release, and the orgasmic discharge."[99] As a Vietnam veteran put it, "A gun is power. To some people carrying a gun was like having a permanent hard-on. It was a pure sexual trip every time you got to pull the trigger."[100]

Hunters told me about the erotic displacement from sex to the killing of the wild prey. They compared the pleasure of hitting and catching the beast with sexual climax—"Both things are the same," one told me. Killing in war also becomes sexualized; as a veteran put it to psychiatrist Theodore Nadelson, "Christ, I got off on it, killing . . . I thought, more than once, back then 'I'd rather fight than screw.'" Another veteran said: "I had been firing, in an ambush [of Vietcong]. I saw them fall; when I put it a new clip, I saw I had a hard-on." A former Marine confessed: "The first time I killed, I puked and I messed myself, I swear. . . . The fifth man I killed . . . I got off on it, I got hard. . . . Now if that is normal, what kind of animals are we?"[101]

For the hunter it's not enough to shoot the flying bird: you must retrieve it and touch it—the feel of it in your hand is part of what constitutes successful hunting. When you catch and kill a wild boar and skin it with your bare bloodied hands, all your senses are immersed in the steaming body of the beast. An added dimension of this eroticism is the hunters' professed paradoxical *love* for the animals they hunt. Some torturer guards in Abu Ghraib and Guantánamo also found displaced pleasure by engaging sexually with the inmates in a degrading manner.[102]

When I was a student in Franco's Spain, in 1975 I was required to do "military service," a period of military training that I took to be a kind of initiation into the rituals of manhood in primitive societies.[103] The readiness to blindly follow military commands and to kill when ordered requires a harsh transformation of the self—the initiate must be subjected to paradoxical Catch-22s until he becomes resigned and ready to comply with whatever is ordered. As future soldiers, we were subject to the symbolic castration of having to surrender our lives and sexualities to the cause of the Mother Country, while at the same time, separated from families and peers, we were given great sexual license to visit nearby brothels. These two positions are antithetical on the surface only, for they are simultaneous in military culture—the asexuality of the military surrender of one's own life to the country, compensated with the promiscuity of buying sex or raping as part of the battle.

A similar complementarity obtains between Nellis Air Force Base in Nevada's southern desert and the city of Las Vegas—Nellis and its doppelganger Strip. The image of Las Vegas as a uniquely successful gaming and tourism city replete with escort services can't conceal its other dimension essential to the town's history—Las Vegas as a *martial metropolis*.[104] Historians have shown that Las Vegas conforms to this model and that "war, not wagering, triggered the city's first period of dramatic growth."[105] The history of Las Vegas's economic development shows that the city of sex and excess grew in parallel with the nation's busiest air force base and the continent's foremost nuclear test site.

With the Cold War and proliferation of nuclear weapons, the robustness of Las Vegas's war economy was ensured for decades to come. Even if it was known as a resort city, Las Vegas had transformed into a martial city. But how was the initial decision to build a military airfield there achieved?

Legend has it a chicken sandwich was responsible. As a famished brigadier general H.W. Harms landed in Las Vegas in October 1940 and went to a nearby café for a chicken sandwich, he happened to meet a prominent local businessman, R.B. Griffith, who urged him to consider the possibility of a base near Las Vegas. The general agreed. Days later Griffith wrote to the military portraying Las Vegas as the perfect location for the army airfield, promising the lease of the land for $1 a year, and boasting of the city's good schools, churches, newspapers, and opportunities for recreation—except that "Griffith predictably failed to mention the town's notorious reputation for providing somewhat less wholesome forms of entertainment."[106] What the town had to offer the military included apparently the benefits of that notorious reputation as well. There was in fact a famed Texas brothel called the Chicken Ranch—opened in 1917 to serve the army men fighting in World War I and named so because during the Depression you could pay with chicken in lieu of cash.[107] General John L. DeWitt was concerned over the potential for distraction that all-night taverns and casinos might present to the servicemen in Las Vegas. Casino and bar owners agreed to a voluntary program to limit hours of operation, a decision that didn't last long. Patriotism required a tip of the hat to virtue and sacrifice before the dirty business of sex and killing could be engaged in.

Beginning with the construction of the Boulder Dam (completed in 1935), "Las Vegas benefited from a sudden outpouring of federal reclamation, relief, and, after 1939, defense programs."[108] Until then the Helldorado (a play on words from "El Dorado") Rodeo and Parade, begun in the 1930s, had been the town's most successful promotion.[109] Franklin Roosevelt's New Deal pledged millions more. Just eight miles northeast of the city, Nellis was created in anticipation of World War II, with the establishment in January 1941 of the Las Vegas Army Air Corps Gunnery School, and "by June, the school was graduating four thousand students every five or six weeks."[110] By 1943 the gunnery school had become home to over eighteen thousand trainees; by 1945 it was the largest in the nation.[111] The influx of soldiers, war workers, and government money was decisive in the early stages of development. Las Vegas resort facilities provided "the release of pent-up hysteria which characterized both military and civilian personnel."[112]

World War II and its aftermath "really transformed the sleepy little desert town," in the words of historian Gerald Nash, and "accomplished a reshaping of the region's economy that would have taken more than forty years in peacetime."[113] Western states benefited the most from the wartime boom, with California doubling its per capita income and tripling its manufacturing output from 1940 to 1945. Las Vegas underwent a similar transformation to become a full-fledged martial metropolis. "During the war, the gunnery school brought multi-million dollar payrolls and much needed infrastructural improvements to the Las Vegas Valley."[114] Nellis Air Base had 12,955 personnel by 1945. Part of the war effort was the production of magnesium, and in 1942 the world's largest magnesium plant was opened in Las Vegas; it produced up to 120 tons per day and employed over 13,000 workers—their payroll five times greater than the total of all other industrial wages in Nevada. By the end of the war Las Vegas had become "a new desert getaway for people eager to have fun and celebrate the permissive morality that became popular during the war."[115] Las Vegas benefited directly from "the great expansion of the 1920s that brought two million midwesterners and their automobiles to Los Angeles County."[116] As Mike Davis put it, the Las Vegas "miracle" demonstrates "Edward Abbey's worst nightmares about the emergence of an apocalyptic urbanism in the Southwest," while confirming that Las Vegas "in essence, is a hyperbolic Los Angeles—the Land of Sunshine on fast-forward."

Because Las Vegas up through the 1960s was the "most segregated city in the nation,"[117] many of its black workers could not find housing and were forced to live on the Westside in tent villages, trailer parks, and even cars. From the early 1940s "the growing number of white tourists expected a Jim Crow town,"[118] and blacks, who numbered over ten thousand by the late 1950s, became unwelcome at any of the resorts on Freemont Street or the Strip—even while headliners filling showrooms were black performers such as Nat King Cole, Sammy Davis Jr., or Lena Horne, who had to spend the night in Westside rooming houses. There is a story that in 1953, when the black entertainer Dorothy Dandridge dipped her foot in the pool of the Hotel Last Frontier, the pool became so racially "contaminated" that the hotel drained it in an act of purification.

In 1950 the Korean War gave new relevance to Nellis, the training ground for nearly every airman who flew in Korea. On a section of the Nellis Bombing Range, in December 1950 President Truman created the 1,350-square-mile NTS; there, sixty-five miles north of Las Vegas, between

1951 and 1992, close to a thousand nuclear weapons explosions were carried out. Truman had declared Las Vegas a "critical defense area" in 1952. "As the 1950s began, it was obvious that tourism and defense spending would be the two industries that would drive the growth of Las Vegas."[119] Defense continued to grow, along with the city—"Nellis Air Force Base was second only to tourism as the largest sector of Las Vegas economy."[120] To the gaming resorts and escort services there was now the advertised bonus of "atomic tourism," which had people flocking to Las Vegas to watch nuclear mushrooms while toasting with "atomic cocktails."[121] In 1990 the economic influence of the test site was estimated at $1 billion. Contrary to what some feared, the end of the Cold War and the moratorium on nuclear testing did not dry up the funds that the NTS contributed to the local economy. The economy diversified into various defense-related projects: "Hazardous materials handling, counterterrorism exercises, seismic testing, and sub-critical nuclear testing are a few of the site's current operations."[122] By then, though still economically relevant, the military had been overshadowed by the tourism economy of megaresorts and casinos. This was the period in which the Mob ruled Las Vegas.[123]

As for the systemic linkage between the military and prostitution, it has been studied mostly by feminist scholars. Cynthia Enloe wrote: "Military bases and prostitution have been assumed to 'go together.' But it has taken calculated policies to sustain that fit." These include "policies to shape men's sexuality, to ensure battle readiness, to regulate businesses, to structure women's economic opportunities, to influence military wives, to socialize women soldiers, and to design systems of policing, entertainment, and public health. It is striking that these policies have been so successfully made invisible around most bases."[124] In Las Vegas, some of the best-known brothels are close to Nellis. Without the compliant sexuality of prostitutes, "Would many American men be able to sustain their own identities, their visions of themselves as manly enough to act as soldiers?"[125] In the web of social and political relationships between the military and civilian cultures, sexuality is pivotal. The implication is that militarized masculinity is historically built around prostitutes. As in hunting and war, at Creech too, for the pilots who kill with drones during the day and can resort to escort services in Las Vegas at night, sexual relations take on a meaning of their own.

THE TRANSFORMATION OF A HUNTER

How do you change a teenager into a hunter-killer? The transformation is, at once, so minimal it is almost imperceptible and so real it changes everything. Drone pilot Martin identified himself with a hawk—"I wondered if a mouse might not feel like that just before a *hawk* dropped out of the sky to snatch it up with piercing talons."[126] His profession makes him feel comparable to a falconer with centuries-old skill at catching prey by training a hawk. "Global Hawk" is the name of one of the drones; with high-resolution radars and long-range sensors, it provides surveillance over as much as forty thousand square miles a day. Both the falconer and the drone pilot long to have a hawk's vision, to feel solitary and invulnerable while looking down on the world from on high.[127]

In his confrontation with the wild "dirty pig," the hunter undergoes a dramatic subjective transformation. The wild animal's nature is symbolically dirty, almost to the point of being taboo, and it produces in the hunter an enormous sense of danger—even if it's essentially imaginary danger. The creation of taboo around the terrorists also goes to the heart of counterterrorism, which has long advocated complete absence of contact with them so that there can be no risk of empathy.[128] Whether the hunter is confronted with a boar or a quail, in his fantasy it appears to be a life-or-death situation. Wildness becomes a defining component in his subjectivity, and killing the animal implies for the hunter conquering the beast outside as well as the beast inside. Emotion takes hold of the hunter at that final moment of "cleansing," as I learned from my work with the Basque hunters. By overcoming his animal/human antinomies and by putting an end to his desire and fantasy, the hunter is *moved* into a trance-like state. By internalizing the behavior of the animal in order to correctly guess its erratic moves, the hunter is able to leave behind a cultural persona and combine it with animal metaphors predicated on himself while undergoing a sort of ritualized transformation.[129]

For the pilots at Creech turned hunters like Martin, the transformation into hawks echoes the intense identification between falconer and hawk described by Helen Macdonald in her *H Is for Hawk*. By identifying with the trained hunting animal, you perform a "moral magic trick": you are "allowed to experience all your vital, sincere desires, even your most bloodthirsty ones, in total innocence. *You could be true to yourself.*[130] At the same time you are not responsible for the killing, for it is the hawk, the drone you have been commanded to pilot, not you, who in a kind of "de-realization" is doing the killing in a strange unrecognizable world. Still, the falconer/pilot, despite this exhilarating freedom, knows deep down that "he is an executioner . . . and he should be wearing a mask."[131]

Macdonald hoods her hawk when she returns home from the kill. She thinks of Abu Ghraib, the photographs of the hooded tortured prisoners tied and bound to perches of steel, and the use of hooding, eliminating sight to calm the bird or the man to be executed. She says the word *hood* feels like a hot stone in her mouth;[132] the word in Arabic is *burqa*, the head-and-body covering worn by Muslim women and banned by European countries. One of the constant features recounted by Guantánamo prisoners when describing their tortures is being hooded. Executioners and the military have a tradition of blindfolding or hooding prisoners who are to be executed.

When Macdonald first went hawk-hunting with her parents as a child, she was a spectator only. Years later when the father she adored unexpectedly died, she dealt with her rage from that loss by turning herself into a falconer killer. She admitted that "I forgot I was human at all."[133] Macdonald realized that she was no longer the same person: "I was astounded by the radical change in subjectivity it had instilled: how the world dissolved to nothing, yet was so real and tangible it almost hurt."[134] She feels the savage energy of the hawk whose instinctive desire is to wait, watch, target, and *"kill kill kill."*[135] She recognized, *"I am not Helen any more. I am the hawk woman."*[136] So Martin felt as a hawk at Creech. And so the pilots Westmoreland and Bryant must have felt: I am not Cian any more, I am not Brandon any more, I am the drone/hawk man.

"OUR PRESIDENT HAS BECOME AN ASSASSIN"

Before his inauguration as president, Obama had been preoccupied and withdrawn because of a false alarm that Somali terrorists were planning to attack during the event. Three days later, on January 23, 2009, CIA director Michael V. Hayden briefed Obama on news that the CIA was launching the Obama presidency's first strike. It was an inaugural moment in the CIA's relationship with Obama. Hayden "went into granular levels of detail, describing the 'geometry' of the operation, the intelligence it was based on, and the risk of collateral damage." Obama "began to grow impatient,"[137] then authorized the two drone strikes.

By maneuvering a joystick and a keypad, a pilot from Creech Air Force Base, seven thousand miles from Pakistan's Waziristan province, launched the Hellfire missile held beneath the wing of the Predator. The missile hit the compound of Malik Gukistan Khan, a tribal elder and member of a progovernment peace committee who was entertaining visitors at the moment of the strike. It failed to hit its intended high-value targets. The drone operators, who had been observing the compound for hours through the drone's infrared camera, had to know that there were many people in the compound. The strike killed Mr. Khan, members of his family, and their visitors on the spot. Seventy-two hours into Obama's presidency, and the attack killed some twenty-three people, possibly as many as twenty of them civilians, in an action he authorized.[138] "He's been blooded, just like you would a hunting dog," a former White House official said, capturing the significance of the moment for Obama.[139] Immediately after his inauguration, the CIA had been eager to involve the new president in a drone strike. When Brennan informed the president about the botching of the attack, "Obama was disturbed."[140] But by then Obama's blood baptism was a permanent mark.

Obama was disturbed, and yet, during his first National Security Council meeting days later, he authorized "a CIA plan to further expand strikes on Pakistan."[141] *We Kill Because We Can* is the title of Laurie Calhoun's book on drone warfare. There would be no US compensation for the slaughtered Khan family. Hunters don't recompense their victims.

But the issue was still whether Obama had what it took to be Manhunter in Chief. Obama was most bothered by a column David Brooks had written in the *New York Times*.[142] The moderate Brooks had spoken to military experts "who follow the war for a living" and who were worried not about Obama's policy choices but about something else: "Their concerns are about Obama the man." Brooks concluded that "the most important meeting" for Obama "isn't with the Joint Chiefs and cabinet secretaries. It's the one with the mirror." There was no mystery in what this meant for Obama: "Why is this whole thing framed around whether I have any balls?"[143] he asked. Did he have the balls? The American public was about to find out.

Constitutional due process requires that the government, after arresting and informing a person of the charges against him, must provide a fair trial. The position of the US administrations is that neither criminal law nor international law protects the targets of the War on Terror; they exist in a legal "black hole."[144] The authorization of use of force after 9/11 has been invoked to justify targeted killings. By the end of his first year in office, a drone bombing led Obama's counterterrorism team to build "the infrastructure for a formalized US assassination program" as the centerpiece of national security; it was criticized by many, including Desmond Tutu, as "illegal, immoral, and unwise."[145] Ben Emmerson, the United Nations special rapporteur, in January 2013 noted that the US use of drones for targeted killings in foreign countries against a stateless enemy, without geographical or temporal limits, "is heavily disputed by most States, and by the majority of international lawyers outside the United States of America."[146]

Regarding the US policy on assassinations, the words of Martin Indyk, ambassador to Israel, are often quoted: "The United States government is very clearly on the record as against targeted assassinations. . . . They are extrajudicial killings, and we do not support that."[147] That was before 9/11. Now the US has hundreds of drones (Predators, Reapers, Global Hawks) with the aim of assassinating terrorists. As a former high-ranking US intelligence official put it, "We are the only country on Earth who thinks that we're in a global war with Al Qaeda and that we have the right to take the fight to the enemy outside of internationally agreed theaters of conflict."[148] Such a claim was shared by the previous UN rapporteur, Philip Alston, who said that the "exception" of terrorism "creates the expansion of the relevant category to include any enemies of the State, social misfits, political opponents, or others."[149] This opens a self-serving opportunity to challenge the entire international human rights system, so that "assertions by Obama administration officials, as well as by scholars, that these operations comply with international standards are undermined by the total absence of any forms of credible transparency or verifiable accountability."[150] According to Alston, "Outside the context of armed conflict, the use of drones for targeted killing is almost never likely to be legal."[151] He described the drone program as "a vaguely defined license to kill."[152]

The basic reality is that we live in a state of exception by which actions that ordinarily are illegal and immoral are tolerable because of the claim that the fight against the Terrorist demands them. Abu Ghraib and Guantánamo provided indelible images of torture. Yet one of the CIA officers who oversaw torture and later took part in destroying the videotaped evidence, Gina Haspel, is currently the head of the CIA under President Trump. Many cases of extrajudicial "rendition" or "torture by proxy" have been documented, including disappeared people formerly in US custody—"At least a dozen people once held by the CIA remain nowhere to be found."[153] And so it goes.

Whose "law" is the one invoked by the Bush and Obama and Trump administrations to authorize drone warfare? It is not a law published in any US Code or enacted in any concrete manner by Congress; there is no regulation issued by any federal agency, and no legality has been adjudicated by a federal court. The administration officials insist that the drone strikes are lawful, "but the 'law' they invoked was their own. It was written by executive branch lawyers behind closed doors, withheld from the public and even from Congress, and shielded from judicial review," concludes Jameel Jaffer, former deputy legal director of the ACLU who, for almost a decade, litigated some of the most significant post-9/11 cases of US counterterrorism policy.[154] The Office of Legal Counsel is supposed to play the role of the government's "conscience." Yet under Bush the office signed off on the NSA's warrantless wiretapping program and held that al-Qaeda prisoners are not entitled to the Geneva Conventions, that prisoners have no right to habeas corpus, and that the president can lawfully permit the use of torture.

Under Obama the OLC continued to approve the drone assassination program, even against American citizens. For decades the US government had characterized targeted killings as "assassination." After 9/11 the government could kill suspects, including American citizens, without having to justify its action in court. "If this is law, it is law without limits—law without constraint," wrote Jaffer.[155] Journalist Jeremy Scahill summed it up: "Drones are a tool, not a policy. The policy is assassination."[156] The corollary and centerpiece of Obama's assassination program was that "he, and he alone, has the power to target people, including American citizens, anywhere they are found in the world and order them executed on his unilateral command."[157] We kill because we can.

Bush carried out some fifty drone strikes in Pakistan. Overall Obama authorized roughly five hundred drone strikes (this does not include the drone strikes carried out in Iraq, Afghanistan, Syria, Yemen, Somalia, and

Libya).[158] In 2009, Cian Westmoreland concluded he had helped kill 359 civilians; in 2010 alone 128 strikes were carried out in the tribal areas of Pakistan, killing more than 700 people. The every-Tuesday meetings to review the "kill list" belonged to Obama, the president who institutionalized the program. Human rights researchers used to documenting the worst abuses could hardly believe the Obama administration had authorized and normalized these illegal actions. The question whether the US was violating Pakistan's sovereignty and legality depended on Pakistani consent. According to the Stanford and NYU law schools, "Repeated public statements by Pakistani officials, which intensified in 2012—declaring that US strikes are illegal, counter-productive, and violate the country's sovereignty—clearly cast doubt on whether Pakistan consents to ongoing operations," and "The legality of so-called 'signature strikes' is highly suspect."[159] In a less restrained mode, many agree with Phyllis Bennis's conclusion: "The reality is that the US assassinations are the actions of a rogue state."[160]

Soon Obama would oversee new tactics such as "the deliberate targeting of first-responders and funeral-goers in Pakistan, which would eventually lead to a UN team investigating his administration for possible war crimes."[161] At least fifteen cases of "double-tap" strikes against first responders helping the injured have been documented, and more than eighteen instances of funerals targeted by the CIA's drones have been identified by Stanford and NYU law schools.[162] Jo Becker and Scott Shane's report detailed how Obama ordered killing the leader of the Pakistani Taliban, Baitullah Mehsud, when "he was not an imminent threat to the United States,"[163] even though he knew Mehsud to be in the company of his wife and other family members. Obama boasted of having "taken" him in his weekly radio address. So did Rahm Emanuel, who recognized the attack as politically advantageous.[164] Some in Washington considered it a "goodwill kill" for Pakistani officials.[165] Mehsud's killing had required sixteen missile strikes during fourteen months, and between 207 and 321 additional people killed as collateral.[166] "I voted for him," a colleague confided to me about Obama, "and he made me complicit in his crimes."

According to Edward Snowden, in September 2010, forty-four targets were slated for death or capture in Afghanistan's Kunar Province. The targets were ranked in significance from 1 (the most) to 4 (the least). Only one of the forty-four targets rose to the priority of 1; more than 80 percent were priority 3. Still, regardless of their significance or insignificance, "The United States ultimately devoted the same resources to picking off locally affiliated militants as it did to the campaign against the group responsible for 9/11."[167] After thousands of killings, some in the US special operations began to question the value of their targets in Afghanistan; a former SEAL officer in June 2015 told the *New York Times*, "By 2010, guys were going after street thugs. The most highly trained force in the world, chasing after street thugs."[168]

The first drone strike in Yemen, on December 17, 2009, killed, in addition to the intended target, two neighboring families and left a trail of cluster bombs that later killed many more people; videos of victim children's body parts flooded YouTube. During the same period, as witnessed by author Chris Woods, some 350,000 civilians were ordered to leave their lands and, under pressure from the Obama administration the Pakistani army entered the province of South Waziristan and "simply flattened" entire areas.[169] As civilians fled to North Waziristan, the Americans insisted the army follow and "clean" the territory of terrorists; the army's unwillingness to do so resulted in the undoing of relationships between Washington and Islamabad.

Joby Warrick, the *Washington Post* correspondent, described one double-tapping attack on the funeral mourners of a midlevel Taliban commander as deliberate; the expectation was that Mehsud and a few lieutenants would come to the burial. The funeral attracted hundreds of mourners. The US drone operators followed the policy of double-tapping and fired a missile against the civilian gathering, killing eighty-three people, including ten children and four tribal elders. Woods carried an investigation for the London Sunday *Times* and "was able to confirm ten incidents in which first responders had been deliberately targeted."[170] As Christof Heyns, the UN special rapporteur, stated, "If civilian 'rescuers' are indeed being intentionally targeted, there is no doubt about the law: those strikes are a war crime."[171] Woods's findings were corroborated by the findings of Amnesty International and the law schools of Stanford and New York University.[172] Of the seventy-four people killed in such follow-up strikes, only twenty-six were confirmed as Taliban—but then Obama didn't consider the Taliban a terrorist group.[173] As Calhoun pointed out, it has always been the prerogative of tyrants to execute suspected enemies without trial.[174]

"At first, some intelligence experts were uneasy about drone attacks," observes Jane Mayer; but years later, "There is no longer any doubt that targeted killing has become official policy. . . . Now . . . nobody in the government calls it assassination."[175] They are all convinced hunters now. And so is the American public. Fully 77 percent of liberal Democrats agree with the use of drones, and 67 percent of moderate or conservative Democrats approve of Guantánamo Bay.[176] This is the shame of America. And the policy has ominous potential repercussions. The president now has the power to kill Americans outside the battlefield and without judicial process. Further, although the number of killings by Obama's drone warfare pales compared with Bush's conventional warfare, "the expansive Predator drone program is far more insidious, given the potential for adoption by governments all over the world, in emulation of the USA executive."[177]

"Our president has become an assassin," said the writer Nicholson Baker in an interview with the *New York Times*. "This sickens me and makes me want to stop writing altogether."[178] These are the hardest words for a writer to say. Cornel West, who campaigned for Obama, said, "Barack Obama is a war criminal . . . because his drones have killed 233 innocent children."[179] Confronted in his harsh indictment by Bill Maher, West added: "It is out of deep love, brother."

DUAL SOVEREIGN POWER

"Who makes these decisions? Where do they make them, and where's my opportunity to intervene?," asked President Obama when he was first introduced to "signature strikes" and realized that killing women and children was part of the concept.[180] Initially, Obama had problems grasping the concept, and it's not difficult to guess why. There is a clear category for killing groups of people on the basis of their appearance, the place where they live, or the company they are in—"multiple murder." But Obama was being told now that signature strikes were legal, moral, a clean form of warfare, the ultimate and most efficient measure in counterterrorism's tool kit. The CIA director Hayden defended it forcefully as a simple case of math—you kill more presumed terrorists by targeting groups than by targeting individuals. Obama's initial reaction was one of resistance: "That's not good enough for me."[181] As a black man himself, he was well aware of the platitude that the arbitrary killing of civilians on the basis of their looks or patterns of life is, here and everywhere, just murder. But he was now being told that this was a different reality in a different period: technically, militarily, morally, politically, and in every other way you can rationalize, this type of killing was now conceptualized as "signature strike," no longer as "murder" or "assassination." Obama had difficulty understanding, but mostly accepting, the change of meaning. Who decides when murder ceases to be murder? That was historically the exceptional prerogative of the sovereign. Obama was now the sovereign. By the end of the meeting Obama "relented on both signature strikes and delegation authority" and authorized them.[182] We kill because we can.

In 2012 Obama signed into law the provision of indefinite detention of US citizens, something he had previously deemed a "legal black hole." And then he added that he did not altogether agree with the law: "I have signed this bill despite having serious reservations with certain provisions."[183] In this and other cases, what had been a red line for Senator Obama was now required by the security state. Obama the constitutional scholar knew that the exception he was signing was an aberration. His close adviser and speechwriter Rhodes wrote that Obama's "views did not necessarily reflect those of the US Government."[184] It raises the question, by whose authority is an order being imposed that creates, for the sake of expediency, an "Alternative United States of America" accountable to no one?[185]

In his book *An American Utopia*, Fredric Jameson recently reintroduced the old Leninist idea of "dual power"—referring to the coexistence in Russia in 1917 of an official provisional government and the informal, unofficial government of a network of workers' councils.[186] In various historical instances of dual power that Jameson cites—organizations such as Hamas, enclaves such as Chiapas, some mass uprisings, and local communes during the French Revolution—"the networks to which people turn for practical help and leadership on a daily basis in effect . . . become an alternate government" that exists alongside the official government without directly challenging it—in Foucauldian terms, exhibiting an opposition or a tension between governmentality and sovereignty. Perhaps the most striking cases of *dual sovereignties* are the ones studied by anthropologists in societies where there is an opposition and complementarity between the jural/administrative power of chiefs on the one hand and the secretive, mystical authority of priests and sorcerers on the other. Current counterterrorist policies suggest another case of the takeover of ordinary government processes by the security state in what amounts to a modality of dual power.

Many cultures are governed by the premise that "men are subject to the power of unseen forces and personages."[187] One way of coping with these mystical forces is to embody them in the person of the ruler—the so-called "divine king" studied by generations of anthropologists. In some cultures this exceptional individual was at once "a priest and a murderer,"[188] (for when the old king weakened, he was challenged to a duel and killed by the contender, who then became the new king/priest). "Dual sovereignty" consisted in the "complementarity between the practical government exercised by the settlement chiefs and the ritual unification provided by the sacerdotal office of the king."[189]

Terrorists share the duality of being "priests" (martyrs) for their followers and "murderers" for the rest.[190] But that same fundamental duality is also embodied by counterterrorist officers who express "their distaste . . . for the prospect of being turned into mere assassins" but who, thanks to the Data Machine, turned into something else: "a new class of warrior . . . not quite military, not quite CIA, and certainly not lawmen . . . x-men."[191] Their hallmark is that "they cross the lines . . . They are soldiers, policemen, and covert operators all rolled into one. No border holds them back, and similarly, no conventional law applies. . . . They are armed with technologies that are only tangentially arms."[192]

Drone pilots turned hunters live out this duality. In his memoir, Martin tries to convey to the reader how drone pilots are *ordinary* guys—anything but murderers. His relationship to his wife is an anchor of normalcy. In his Prologue he mentions his Predator with Hellfire missiles raining "death from above . . . fire with the sound of skies ripping apart on doomsday. Like Armageddon or something," then says, "I remembered that Trish had asked me to pick up a gallon of milk on the way home."[193] But any sense of normalcy is constantly challenged by the actual predicament he is in. He is acutely aware that he sometimes lives in an "alternate world and persona" or in a "parallel universe."[194]

One world is the control station from which he flies a drone in Iraq or Afghanistan; the other his home in Las Vegas. He enters his control station with a "cup of coffee in hand and fresh from out of a warm bed with my wife."[195] His care for her as she faces a life-threatening cancer, a preoccupation hand in hand with his worries about killing innocent bystanders, humanizes him. After the devastating incident when they kill two children, he calls his wife, although he cannot share with her his "revulsion and self-loathing because of what we have done." He calls her because he "just wanted to hear [her] voice."[196] She feels something is wrong, but when he asks about her doctor's appointment, it's she who exclaims, "I'm frightened," and he is the one who must listen and care. She tells him, "What you're doing is saving lives." He replies, "This is why I love you."[197] She makes him something other than a killer, which allows him to go on killing.

The nexus between open political processes and covert actions required in the War on Terror parallels a similar dual sovereignty in democracy—an arrangement in which legal authority is complemented by a power that finds its legitimacy in the elusive principle of *national security*. If overt politics is based on the rule of law, covert politics is grounded on secret information not to be shared with the public. As Dana Priest and Arkin put it, "The government Barack Obama was about to inherit had really become two governments: the one its citizens were familiar with, operated more or less in the open; the other a parallel top secret government whose parts had mushroomed in less than a decade into a gigantic sprawling universe of its own, visible to only a carefully vetted cadre—and its entirety, as Pentagon intelligence chief James Clapper admitted, visible only to God."[198] The two alternate worlds are territorially and architecturally marked in Washington.[199]

As Obama took office it soon became obvious that he would keep intact most of the previous Bush-Chaney administration's counterterrorism policies. He banned torture, but his CIA chief admitted that they would continue the implementation of "extraordinary rendition"—or torture by proxy carried out for the US in other countries.[200] He promised greater transparency, but his Justice Department reasserted the state secrets privilege; his administration brought more leak-related prosecutions than all previous administrations combined. He ordered Guantánamo closed, but his cabinet members testified that the prison was lawful and he backed off under political pressure. He closed the CIA's black-site prisons, but CIA drone strikes multiplied.[201]

The interaction between the ambassador and the CIA station chief in countries where the US is engaged in war presents a relevant structural point of conflict between the two sets of rules—the official versus the secret. Such was the case in Pakistan when Ambassador Munter demanded he be notified and have veto power on drone strikes and was rebuffed by the CIA chief.[202] When the turf war between the two powers reached Obama's top advisers and Munter, participating in the meeting via video link, began making his case, Defense Secretary Leon Panetta cut him off midsentence, "telling him that the CIA had the authority to do what it wanted in Pakistan. It didn't need to get the ambassador's approval for anything." Secretary of State Clinton defended Munter. "No, Hillary," Panetta said, "it's you who are flat wrong."[203] Stunned silence followed. Obama had the final word. Panetta had swung through the revolving door of the two alternative powers. He "had publicly accused the CIA of breaking American law by committing acts of torture," but after he became head of the CIA he was "forcefully arguing that the details of those acts be kept secret from the public."[204] Obama rewarded Panetta by granting him every one of his requests: "The CIA gets what it wants."[205] No wonder that some people in Washington were "comparing Obama to Michael Corleone as the CIA was conducting more assassinations than at any point in its history."[206] Another CIA source told Andrew Cockburn, "You know, our president has his brutal side."[207]

The policy of "Don't capture, kill" provided striking cases of the two sets of rules. Woods was told by an officer that there might be situations in which there was "not enough evidence to hold the man [an Afghan suspected insurgent] in custody" but that there were "suitable grounds to assassinate him."[208] The rules for capturing and jailing are aspects of ordinary political and judicial processes, but these need not apply when one can apply the rule of covert war, where killing is outside law and morality—a simpler, more expeditious act. CIA director Hayden said about the killing of Anwar al-Awlaki: "We needed a court order to eavesdrop on him but we didn't need a court order to kill him. Isn't that something?"[209] Human rights apply to normal citizens, killing with impunity to "terrorists." Citizens can be searched and arrested; terrorists must be hunted and killed. Similarly, Judge John Bates asked: "How is it that judicial approval is required when the United States decides to target a US citizen overseas for electronic surveillance . . . but judicial scrutiny is prohibited . . . when the United States decides to target a US citizen overseas for death? How does that all make sense?"[210] The two sets of rules explain it: killing terrorists doesn't break any law; eavesdropping on civilians without warrant is a breach of law.

The first day in office Obama signed an executive order requiring Guantánamo to be closed within a year. But soon, despite support for doing so by the administration heavyweights, the lofty appeals for regaining the "moral high ground" proved rhetorical promises only. From early on, his abrasive chief of staff Emanuel was concerned about "whether Obama was really going to risk a second term to protect the constitutional rights of a bunch of terrorists held in Guantánamo."[211] White House counsel Greg Craig, knowing "that Obama could dismantle the legal architecture of the Bush-Cheney war on terror with a stroke of the pen," pushed for a clean break with Bush's legacy.[212] But days after his inauguration, on February 9, a case brought by five terrorism suspects tortured under the CIA's extraordinary-rendition program would make sure that the Bush-Cheney agenda of secrecy continued—the Obama administration advanced the very same "state secrets" argument to dismiss the case. "This is not change," Anthony Romero, head of the ACLU, was quoted on the front page of the *New York Times*. "This is definitely more of the same. Candidate Obama ran on a platform that would reform the abuse of state secrets, but President Obama's Justice Department has disappointingly reneged on that important civil liberties issue."[213] A year later the ACLU would be running a campaign with a picture of Obama morphing into Bush—it was "the Bush-Obama doctrine" on terrorism.

While advisers fought bitterly among themselves and, at times, nobody seemed to be in charge of policy, it was unclear what Obama himself believed. Eric Holder soon realized that his efforts to close Guantánamo would come to nothing—"It was not a compromise. It was a capitulation."[214] Congress was blamed for preventing the president from fulfilling his pledge, "but that's not the whole story," as Connie Bruck showed in a long *New Yorker* essay.[215] Craig, who made enemies in the White House and was reprimanded for his commitment to freeing Uighurs from Guantánamo and ultimately stripped of all authority on terrorism policy, was stunned that the White House folded without resistance in "a demonstration that we did not really have the political will to deal with Guantánamo."[216] Everybody knew that the unfortunate Chinese Uighurs had been brought to Guantánamo by mistake, yet there was no will to free even them.

Indefinite preventive detention had been one of the red lines Obama had drawn against Bush's War on Terror. In 2006 he stated how truly exceptional it would be ("We would be hard pressed to find a conservative or liberal in American today, whether Republican or Democrat, academic or layman") not to "subscribe to the basic set of individual liberties identified by the Founders and enshrined in our Constitution and our common law." He listed some of those undisputable and unexceptionable liberties, including "the right not to be detained by the state without due process; the right to a fair and speedy trial."[217] As one of the obvious negative consequences of trampling these axiomatic legal principles, Obama added: "When we detain suspects indefinitely without trial, we weaken our ability to pressure for human rights and the rule of law in despotic regimes."[218] But on May 20, 2009, in a meeting with civil libertarians and human right activists, the issue was contentious. The president asked whether they saw any alternative to preventive detention for terror suspects. The head of Human Rights Watch, Kenneth Roth, warned Obama about the precedent it would set and how it might lead to legitimizing Vladimir Putin's "assassination campaign."[219] On December 31, 2011, Obama signed into law indefinite detention without charge or trial and without temporal or geographic limitations. Signing into law something you don't believe in recalls Peter Sloterdijk's formula of cynical reason: "They know very well what they are doing, but still, they are doing it."[220] The ideological illusion "is not on the side of knowledge, it is already on the side of reality, of what people are doing." Terrorism provides a context to show that ideology fundamentally is not an illusion masking the reality of things; it's rather "an (unconscious) fantasy structuring our social reality itself."[221] In Eric Holder's words, it was a season of "capitulation."

Thus the Obama era continued Guantánamo, indefinite detention, and extrajudicial killings by drones—all officially sanctioned and normalized by the very president who had been elected because he opposed them, and broadly accepted by the general public, including the Left. It was all part of the post-9/11 state of exception, meaning that lawbreaking approved by the highest officials would go unpunished, a situation in which "it is impossible to distinguish transgression of the law from the execution of the law, such that what violates a rule and what conforms to it coincide without any remainder."[222]

Such a state of exception claims its own justification in the war against Evil. But for those of us who identified with Obama and what his candidacy stood for, Evil takes a far more sinister mode than moral sermonizing that an external Evil "does exist in the world." Our predicament has much more to do with Alain Badiou's ethics by which the problem of Evil "arises as the . . . *effect of the Good itself.* That is to say: it is only because there are truths, and only to the extent that there are subjects of these truths, that there is Evil." Many of Obama's supporters believed we were agents of transformation, but we ended up with a definition by which "Evil is the process of a simulacrum of truth. And in its essence . . . it is terror directed at everyone," the final result being that we have fallen under "the figure of Evil . . . through an encounter with the Good."[223] The affirmations and subsequent perversions of the truths that candidate Obama embodied, later turned into simulacra broadly accepted by the Left, became a most insidious Evil that remains with us during the Trump era.

In the dual-power scheme, the president is at the summit and straddles both sets of rules. But there might be cases in which the question arises whether the president is, in fact, informed as to what is going on in the secret world—for "While conventional military forces fought in the light, another war went on in the dark."[224] Intrinsically linked to its dubious legality, secrecy is at the heart of this parallel universe. Even the statistics on civilian deaths become a state secret; each time a news source mentions them, they are denied as enemy propaganda. One reason for denial is obvious: since for much of the world the drone program is a policy of assassination, the US might be acting as a rogue state.[225] When challenged by lawsuits in court, the CIA has argued that it cannot confirm or deny even the existence of the drone campaign. The government's control of information has found little resistance in the courts.

Arkin's study of drone warfare concentrates on the ever-present and decisive influence of the "Data Machine." He considers that its growing capacity "facilitated (and maybe even demanded) the creation of two sets of rules—two sets that have profound consequences. One is open and the other is in the shadows, one subject to scrutiny by the news media and public opinion and even normal laws, the other doing the dirty work that is often too difficult for humankind." It is not *the* CIA that primarily operates the Black Box, Arkin writes, but a counterterrorist elite *within* the CIA. In this world, "The result is incredible secrecy and an alliance with people more powerful than those in delegated positions of power."[226]

Arkin finds in such secrecy the genesis of much warrantless surveillance and many other lawless practices that are unaccounted for, including the drone program. It went further than mere overreliance on technology; it implied "an automaticity that suggested that public servants and even the president had no choice in the matter, that indeed our entire system of national security was in its way becoming autonomous and unmanned."[227] The Data Machine kept growing, like a building without an architect, by adding new black boxes and capabilities and hydra-headed developments. By 2007 the disagreement over the drone program and the Data Machine's central control had reached a climax; people began complaining "that no one was in charge, that no one in the Pentagon was exercising control over competing programs."[228] It reached a point by which "the ultimate scourge" of the Data Machine policies and technologies was "that no one really knows the totality of the system."[229] The Data Machine turned into a killing machine, unmanned, self-contained, with functions that used to belong to combat forces made faceless. The NSA called its technology for finding targets by geolocating their cell phones "Little Boy," the name for the Hiroshima bomb—except that in Hiroshima the killers were real aviators who dropped bombs that left an infernal mushroom cloud as evidence of the murder. With the Data Machine the killing was silent and invisible. This went beyond the priest/murderer ambivalence. The duality here consisted in politicians speaking of national security and moral dilemmas ("Evil does exist in the world") while the Machine did the dirty work.

And how did the lawyers deal with the legal and ethical problems posed by defending security state policies such as "Don't capture, kill"? Not everyone is easily turned into a hunter of terrorists. Harold Koh was a Yale professor, a liberal idealist and former critic of Bush's torture program, who became top lawyer for the State Department under Obama. Many expected that, with Koh at the State Department, the US approach to international human rights law would drastically change. But it didn't. In the end, the Obama White House "accepted nearly all of the counterterrorism policies of the second Bush term. . . . They chose not to change key policies, such as reliance on . . . drones to target and kill terrorism suspects, with an enthusiasm that surprised even insiders that had worked in the Bush administration."[230] When he took his position, Koh thought of drone strikes as "extrajudicial killings,"[231] but then he came to support those who wanted to expand the covert program. Trying to stop a targeted killing, he confided, "would be like pulling a lever to stop a massive freight train barreling down the tracks."[232]

Koh had a unique role in ensuring that the drone assassination program and targeted killings conformed to law. Forgetting what he had thought previously, now he simply accepted the killings' legality. While studying government hit lists, he found himself wondering, "How did I go from being a law professor to someone involved in killing?"[233] His counterpart attorney at the Pentagon was Jeh C. Johnson. These two top lawyers at the State and Pentagon developed a competitive relationship and were soon on a collision course. Behind their squabbling over, say, whether Belkacem Bensayah's activities amounted to "substantial support" for al-Qaeda (Johnson) or little more than an insignificant monetary donation to al-Qaeda (Koh), the real issue was whom to detain indefinitely and whom to target for killing.

In December 2009, the hawkish Johnson was at his Pentagon office when an aide brought him a set of baseball cards with information regarding three potential targets; he had forty-five minutes to prepare for a meeting that would decide their fate. Soon on a secure conference call he was asked, "Well, what's it going to be? Yes or no, can we take the shots?"[234] The verdict was yes for two of the targets and no for the third, as this suspect was likely to be surrounded by children and women. It was easier to say yes than no under military pressure; Johnson thought of Koh's metaphor—the runaway train. Later he learned from human rights groups that the drone attack he had authorized killed dozens of civilians. "If I were Catholic, I'd have to go to confession," he confided.[235]

But something must have happened to Johnson, for a few weeks later, as another operation was being planned against members of the Shabab, to the surprise of his Pentagon colleagues he was no longer willing to approve the killings. Johnson's abdication of his role had a direct impact on his adversary lawyer, provoking a reversal of roles by which Koh now became the defender of the covert assassination program and offered to deliver a speech on the subject. Behind his back the White House began calling him "Killer Koh"; the military and the CIA loved the Nixon-goes-to-China idea of the liberal Koh now being the public face of drone assassination. In the meantime, the military put pressure on Johnson to reverse course, which he did by the end of the year.

The ordinary descriptor for officials involved in an assassination program is obvious enough: assassins. Yet nothing is further from how counterterrorists portray themselves, which conforms more to Edmund Leach's insight that the counterterrorist officials are engaged in a priest-like fight that is "a religiously sanctioned moral duty."[236] Brennan, Obama's chief counterterrorist "guide" steering him to targeted killings, was described as "a person of genuine moral rectitude . . . a priest with extremely strong moral values."[237] Brennan had studied with Franciscan nuns, gone to a seminary to become a priest (while dreaming of becoming the first American pope), studied in a Catholic university, read Saint Augustine.[238] Such invocations of priest-like qualities in people involved in assassination evoke the figure of the inquisitor, immersed in moral values so high that the actual torture and killing of victims was justified as a method to produce truth and justice (if the victim's soul was not in sin, his or her torture and death were minor events compared with the reward of going to heaven forever). In the case of Brennan and Obama, the reward is not heaven but national security. Brennan was in fact deputy director of the CIA from 2001 to 2003 when the agency put in practice the extraordinary-rendition and torture programs.[239]

Obama's involvement in the assassination program is likewise preceded by reports that he is a "student of writings on war by Augustine and Thomas."[240] Gandhi, King, and Niebuhr are among his heroes. The priest's power, unlike the politician's, rests on the charisma and secrecy of his high calling, subject to nothing but his conscience. "Under Obama, the justification for holding such unaccountable power was the good character of the president and his staff."[241] Obama is the president who would "order the targeted killing of an American citizen, in a country with which the United States was not at war, in secret and without the benefit of a trial."[242] In short, the entire drone assassination program, including the extraordinary presidential power to order the execution of an American citizen without due process, rests on the priestly charisma of the "personal legitimacy of the president."[243] One could say that a critical aspect of such legitimacy, as Evans-Pritchard said of the king's role among the Shilluk, is "not so much governmental as sacerdotal."[244] The sovereign, once again, is at once priest and assassin.

As if to exorcise the unsavory consequences of the priest/assassin matrix, close to the end of his second term, on July 1, 2016, Obama signed an executive order committing future administrations to strict measures regarding civilian casualties and the annual release of basic statistics on counterterrorism strikes, the very things his own didn't follow.[245] The expressions "the protection of civilians" and "minimizing civilian casualties" are repeated fifteen times in the order—as if future rhetorical lawfulness might erase past manhunting. President Trump would take full advantage of the much-expanded counterterrorism apparatus and powers bequeathed by Obama. On January 29, 2017, during the first week of his presidency, news surfaced of twenty-five civilians killed by drones in Yemen. Trump "oversaw five times as many lethal strikes during his first seven months in office as Obama did during his last six months, analysts believe."[246] Not only did Trump not deliver the annual report (he signed an executive order against the reporting requirement), but during his first year the number of drone strikes doubled in Somalia and tripled in Yemen.[247] Under Trump, the White House continues to thrive as "Home of the Hunters."

2 Fantasy and the Art of Drone Assassination

As much as the brutality of the hunt, what alarms Cian Westmoreland and Brandon Bryant most is the normalcy of the ideological *fantasy* by which the general public accepts drone warfare. That was the hardest thing to explain to their Las Vegas audience: "The thing that scares me most about [drone] war is not the brutality," observed Westmoreland, "[but] the civility of it—the fact that everybody can go about their business without any understanding that you are destroying lives."[1] Diffusion of accountability for the killings allows the illusion that nobody is responsible for them.

"I fed the system, that's all I did," Westmoreland explained, "and you think about how benign that sounds, being a technician . . . [until] you realize that it is you that is the vital link there." Westmorland had built a data-relay station as a technician responsible for the communications infrastructure of the drone program. "It is important to understand, not excuse the behavior of what is happening [at Creech]," he added, insisting on the daily normalcy of the pilots' killing predicament.

The Holocaust was the result of ordinary people, not monsters, argued Hannah Arendt, a "banality of evil"— people simply follow orders, as the Westmorelands and the Bryants and the McNamaras did. Eichmann was boringly *normal*. Arendt emphasized the responsibility of the onlookers regarding the mass crimes. She underlined that *"in general the degree of responsibility increases as we draw further away from the man who uses the fatal instrument with his own hands."*[2] Arendt's conclusion was familiar to Westmoreland and Bryant: "This new type of criminal . . . commits his crimes under circumstances that make it well-nigh impossible for him to know or to feel that he is doing wrong."[3] The normalcy that matters most to Westmoreland and Bryant is not that drone pilots kill but that the US public justifies it all for the sake of an alleged national security—the normalcy of the ideological fantasy that allows and condones the killing.

THE REAL AND THE FANTASY

A valid theory of fantasy is one in which fantasy is not equal to the *not-real*, rather *"constitutes a dimension of the real."*[4] This view of fantasy is very unlike the representational realism of the media, in which "representation becomes a moment of the reproduction and consolidation of the real."[5] A positivist view of the real stabilizes itself by the fantasmatic exclusion of all absence as unreal. Terrorism is that disavowed exclusion, included in the system as exception, that solidifies and gives ground to the politically real. Thus the exceptional phantom "assumes the status of the real, that is, when the two become compellingly conflated,"[6] and fantasy emerges masked as the real. As Laura Nader remarks, counterterrorism in many of its forms "appears as fantasy requiring terror in the name of ending terror, when in reality the elimination of terror is the apotheosis of terror."[7]

Drone pilot Matt Martin's memoir illustrates the struggle between fantasy and the real. His narrative describes a volunteer who goes hunting "poor bastards" and "rats" to save American lives, "like God hurling thunderbolts from afar."[8] Martin and his comrades couldn't wait for the twelve-week class for pilot certification to end, so they could get to "the real thing."[9] Once this real thing begins, Martin feels his chest tighten and his "breathing shallowed" when he is asked to sparkle the target with infrared laser. He is "electrified, adrenalized" that his team "shot the technical college full of holes, destroying large portions of it and killing only God knew how many people." It would take time for the reality of what he had done to sink in, "for 'real' to become *real.*"[10]

Martin's sensations are so orgasmic that he is "almost ashamed to admit to [his wife] the thrill I felt the moment I prepared to squeeze the trigger."[11] While holding to the thought that his wife will offer absolution for his killings, Martin admits that at times he feels squeamish about his thrills, even scolds himself for feeling thrilled, but in the end he returns to his ideological slogan that "Predator allowed us to be less brutal."[12]

While confronting "the real," Martin's fantasy makes him see himself in the position of an all-seeing God; in another moment he fantasizes he is General George Patton proclaiming, "Screw them ragheaded sonsofbitches. Blow that mosque back to the tenth century, then go in there and piss on the corpses."[13] The Israeli prime minister Manachem Begin once stated that destroying Yasser Arafat's headquarters in Beirut was like sending the Israeli army to Berlin to destroy Hitler, to which Amos Oz replied, "Hitler is already dead, my dear Prime Minister. . . . You reveal to the public eye a strange urge to resuscitate Hitler in order to kill him every day in the guise of terrorists."[14] Drone pilots are caught in a similar fantasy—killing alleged terrorists on the ground is like killing *the* Hitler-like Terrorist.

Bryant and Westmoreland struggled to answer the question: What is real and what is fantasy in drone warfare? Betrayed by trauma, they found no refuge in the public's presumption of their ignorance and condemned themselves for complicity in murder. For Westmoreland and Bryant, unlike their Commander-in-Chief in his Nobel Peace Prize acceptance speech, Evil was not metaphysical or externally embodied in Hitler-like monsters; it was what *they*, as drone operators, had done.

A historical precedent to the interplay between killing and fantasy is the case discussed earlier of the hunting of native Americans. But an even earlier encounter is between the Europeans and the Native Americans, and it is instructive to revisit the kind of debates it generated. When Columbus first described the native people of the Caribbean in his 1492 *Diario del primer viaje,* he recognized them as handsome, gentle, "normal" people. The urge for conquest, however, requires invention, and soon rumors spread that the natives were subhuman, dog-headed *cannibals* (the word derives from the Spanish for Caribs) who couldn't have a human soul—an act of fantasy and naming that was critical for Europeans to justify enslaving or killing them.

Much as there were "barbarians" during the Greek and Roman periods, in the Middle Ages the figure of the Wild Man was opposed to "civilized" people on the basis of *law*. The heir to the Wild Man is "the terrorist," as anthropologist Edmund Leach pointed out; he noted that the "'other' comes to be categorized as a wild animal, [and] then every imaginable form of terroristic activity is not only attributed to the other side but becomes permissible for oneself."[15] Such an archetypal figure of a wholly anomalous individual works in the way myth worked in ancient cultures, Hayden White observed, "that is, as a projection of repressed desires and anxieties . . . [a world] in which fictions (such as wildness, barbarism, savagery) are treated, not as *conceptual instruments* . . . or as *symbols* . . . but as *signs* designating the existence of things or entities whose attributes bear just those qualities that the imagination, for whatever reasons, insists they must bear."[16] If in the past dog-headed humans were instances of such remythification, currently the figure of the Terrorist gives ground to a reality the menace of which is felt to be greater than the one posed by the superpower Soviet Union during the Cold War. The task of a critical approach to terrorism is to see how the real of such a war is necessarily imbued in fantasy.

James Baldwin, the grandson of a slave, argued in a debate with William Buckley that "leaving aside all the physical facts . . . [the] rape or murder . . . [and] the bloody catalogue of oppression which we are, in one way, too familiar with already, what [the system] does to the subjugated— is *to destroy his sense of reality*."[17] What concerned Baldwin was that his own country's "system of reality" required the fantasy of Hollywood stories "designed to reassure us that no crime was committed. We've made a legend out of a massacre [against the Native Americans]."[18] Baldwin was saying that the ultimate horror, beyond even the oppressions that can be catalogued, is losing the sense of what oppression actually is, what crime is—losing the very reality of cultural and moral order. For Westmoreland and Bryant also, a catastrophe added to their killings was the fear of losing their very "sense of reality" and the fear that the public might view their trauma simply as private lunacy.

Baldwin's assessment was that Americans "deluded themselves for so long that they really don't think I'm human. . . . And this means that they have become in themselves moral monsters."[19] Whether dealing with the Negro or the Terrorist, Westmoreland and Bryant couldn't agree more with Baldwin that "this problem, which they [Americans] invented in order to safeguard their purity, has made of them criminals and monsters, and it is destroying them."[20] At the root of the problem of the white man's hatred "is terror, a bottomless and nameless terror, which focuses on this dread figure, an entity which lives only in his mind."[21] The condition behind the malaise, for Baldwin, is that "people in general cannot bear very much reality. . . . They prefer fantasy to a truthful re-creation of their experience."[22]

The dialectics between fantasy and the real is the terrain on which Westmoreland and Bryant crashed; their victims revealed to them the truth of Baldwin's words: "You cannot lynch me . . . without becoming something monstrous yourselves."[23] Baldwin knew the function that he served for white society when he said: "I'm a man. But if you think I'm a nigger, it means you need him."[24] "Why does the US *need* the Terrorist?" the drone pilots were asking us in Las Vegas, the place of sanctioned fantasy. It is said that "what happens in Vegas stays in Vegas," but Westmoreland and Bryant were subverting the structure of Vegas's fantasy by making sure that what happened in Las Vegas/Creech would not stay in Las Vegas/Creech.

LAS VEGAS LOVE

Since at least the time of the *Iliad* and its epic war fought for Helen of Troy, "women have always been a part of the plunder of warfare."[25] The sexualized fantasy relationship between the soldier and his weapon has long been recognized. For the Creech pilot it is the drone that embodies all the phallic qualities of the gun. But while the traditional soldier carried with him into war sublimated fantasies about women staying at home, for whom he was willing to sacrifice his life, the Creech drone pilot lives in Las Vegas and returns daily to his partner at home or to the city's night life.

The history of Las Vegas is a combination of the military-industrial complex and capitalist consumerism. By the end of the twentieth century Las Vegas was the fastest-growing city in the US. "From 1970 to 2000, the population soared from 270,000 to more than 1.3 million."[26] The Strip became a world tourist destination, with forty million visitors a year. The city's character is best revealed through literary figures such as the Great

Gatsby and his "colossal fantasies." There is no better place than Las Vegas to consider the structure of capitalist desire and assess how it succeeds or fails to deliver the satisfactions it promises. "Capitalism's adherence to the fantasy of success at the expense of the necessity of failure is essential to its functioning."[27] In the casino things are symbolic; the reality of money, turned into gambler's chips, evaporates into nothing but a means to keep score. Money turned to chips turned to faith—all grounded on the fantasy of the casino's instant wealth.

The labyrinthine casinos illustrate how, while we believe we may win, the failure to realize our desire becomes a form of satisfaction as we perpetuate the losing—thus proving the psychoanalytical insight that *failure* is foundational to the ways the subject finds enjoyment. This seeming contradiction led Freud to formulate the notion of "death drive" as determinant of any subject. His concluding remark in *Beyond the Pleasure Principle,* "The pleasure principle seems actually to serve the death instincts," applies to the subject's psychic structure,[28] but it also serves to describe the relationship between the Las Vegas casinos and the Nevada Test Site (NTS) military complex to the north of the city. In Norman Brown's words, "Freud was right in positing a death instinct, and the development of weapons of destruction makes our present dilemma plain: we either come to terms with our unconscious instincts and drives—with life and with death—or else we surely die."[29]

If Las Vegas is a city ruled by the "pleasure principle," what happens to love there? The word typically translates into dating or escort services and is one more commodity you can pay for. Essentially, the traumatic aspect of love is exchanged for transitory romance. As a Las Vegas prostitute, Jami Rodman, put it, "For men, sex is almost never about love. It's about fantasy and busting a nut," and the difference between a good escort and a bad escort "is how well we act on the illusion and the fantasy."[30] In Las Vegas, where sex is sold as "an expensive fantasy experience," the opportunities for the fantasy of love are infinite.[31] Thousands of trafficked prostitutes, streetwalkers, brothel women, working girls freelancing from casinos, and agency call girls are at the client's disposal. "Sex is the world's longest-running con," writes Rodman about her Las Vegas experience. "A hard dick, a wet vagina, and the high of an orgasm can make a man and woman believe anything. It makes us believe we're in love. Or we want to believe we are. Sometimes we do fall in love. For escorts and clients, it's inevitable."[32]

The first rule of the game is "Don't get attached."[33] Rodman wrote that the fantasy life begins with "crossing over" and acquiring a different name and identity for one's prostitute persona—in her case, she was Haley Heston. With such a new identity the job is easier because "it's not really us making the decisions. Somehow, as Haley, everything seemed less real. *If Haley doesn't work out, I can always go back to Jami. I can always go back to my real life one day, and forget Haley existed,* I told myself."[34] Rodman's perception that "it's not really us making the decisions" is also at the core of drone pilots' experience—we are simply following orders.

Rodman realizes she is making "dirty money" but at the same time "living the American dream."[35] A dating service sells love as both novel and predictable, as if it were a commodity, to eliminate the traumatic core and risk of the love encounter. The hunters' distinction between domesticated and wild sex echoes here. Wild sex is "free" from any institutional attachment, a hunter's "see it/kill it" never to be repeated. The *killing* a client does with an escort is presumed to be "free," "wild," and always "new." And yet the reality might be cast as the opposite, for what is truly *wild* is the violent onslaught of love, the trauma of losing one's identity in the unexpected encounter, whereas "romance . . . domesticates the trauma of love."[36] Romance replaces the lost object with the attainment of the object of desire. "The transformation of love into romance is an attempt to keep love in the field of desire and fantasy. . . . As long as we desire without loving, we remain on safe ground."[37] Drone pilots can reduce their traumatic experience of war to *zero deaths* among their ranks at Creech and, through dating services, reduce their experience of love to *zero risk.*

Down the Strip past Paradise is the Las Vegas Trump Tower, with its gold-infused windows and gigantic gold-plated letters TRUMP at its top rising above the other buildings—a sixty-four-story luxury hotel, condominium, and timeshare with twelve hundred rooms, Las Vegas's tallest building. Here Gatsby and what F. Scott Fitzgerald called the "colossal vitality of his illusion" have been reactivated by Trump's presidency.[38] Trump's method is quite simple: "The final key to the way I promote is bravado. I play to people's fantasies."[39] *Gatsby* is the story "of a national 'shipwreck' that's looming on the outer edge of the 1920s."[40] Gatsby appears a captive of Fate, not its master. He embodies the promise of America. The novel is not primarily about sex or an illicit affair but "above all. . . . about the titanic power of dreams."[41] Fitzgerald tried to explain to a friend that "the whole burden of this novel—[is] the loss of those illusions that give such color to the world that you don't care whether things are true or false as long as they partake of the magical glory."[42] Such is also the power of dreams at the nexus of Las Vegas and the NTS/Creech AFB, neon lights and drone technologies, which "renders the American Dream irresistible and heartbreaking and buoyant, all at once."[43] Here, in Nevada's bombed and radioactive desert and fantasy paradise, Gatsby's conclusion obtains: " We beat on, boats against the current, borne back ceaselessly into the past."[44]

Trump's promise of greatness and happiness can be matched only with Tony Hsieh's Happiness City in downtown Las Vegas. Hsieh sold his online shoe retailer, Zappos, to Amazon for a billion dollars, bought sixty acres of derelict real estate, vacant lots, and grimy motels a few miles north of the Strip, and started Delivering Happiness, a consultancy business. He presented his Downtown Project as a plan to revitalize and transform downtown Las Vegas into an entrepreneurial paradise of happiness and innovation and got hundreds of would-be entrepreneurs to join him. "The idea was that it would be not just a collection of businesses but a constructed utopian community, founded on the principle that work and life should not be considered separate."[45] It was going to be "one big party" where the word *don't* was banned.[46]

Americans work more hours than in any other industrialized world; half of them eat alone; only one out of three socializes with a neighbor; 40 percent of people over age fifty live without a companion.[47] And yet enjoyment and happiness are a sort of *duty* in American capitalism, one that if unfulfilled adds to people's anxiety as if it were a moral blemish. Such society needs a happiness industry, and Las Vegas, with 96 percent of its Strip located in the unincorporated town of Paradise, and with its military branch of Area 51 also called Paradise Ranch and Dreamland, is happiness's iconic place.[48] Poverty, injustice, migration, wars . . . they exist, but what the happiness industry advertises is that what matters most is the mind's positive attitude and perspective. Still, "Can the Pursuit of Happiness Kill You?" ran the title of the tech publication *Re/code,* giving statistics that showed that the "Downtown Project's suicide rate [was] at around five times the Las Vegas rate."[49] (Las Vegas's suicide rate is already an average city's double).[50] It'd be hard to find another place where the battle between the American Dream and its deadly real is as visible as here: Hsieh's laboratory for a "global movement of happiness" is next to hundreds of street homeless and just a few miles from the military complex where for over half a century nuclear explosions were regularly tested and where now the "Home of the Hunters" is located in Indian Springs across from Creech AFB.[51]

INDIAN SPRINGS: UFOS AND DRONES

Indian Springs is a small town of about a thousand inhabitants, forty-five miles north of Las Vegas on Highway 95. Native Americans settled there for the water. During the early days of the twentieth century Indian Springs was a railroad station between Tonopah and Las Vegas and, following the attack on Pearl Harbor, a training camp for the Army Air Force. After World War II, the Indian Springs Air Force was reactivated for aircraft research and the development of new weapons systems, including nuclear arms testing. Nearby is the Nevada Test and Training Range, inside which is the highly classified secretive place known as Area 51. Since January 27, 1951, when an air force bomber dropped the first atomic bomb on US soil inside the NTS, 105 nuclear bombs aboveground and 828 underground have been detonated there. In 1946 the US had two nuclear bombs, in 1955 a stockpile of 2,280. Indian Springs was the closest town to the stockpile.

But Indian Springs would also be known for something quite different from the latest military technologies—extreme fantasy associated with UFOs. By the 1990s a new generation of UAVs [unmanned aerial vehicles] was being developed in Area 51. Unmanned craft, without windows, cockpits, or need to protect a pilot, took on "otherworldly" forms, including the shapes of flying saucers. Indeed, the drone industry evolved in close association with science fiction. "How many UAVs, flying secretly, had been taken for UFOs?," wondered writer Phil Patton. His book on Area 51 contends that with the most recent UAV Predator at the El Mirage site, "the government may be manipulating, even generating, UFO reports to conceal secret programs."[52] He writes: "For years, UAV inhabited a world of their own, a shadow of a shadow," and wondered, "How long had they been flying out of Dreamland?"[53] Commanded by Colonel Steven L. Hampton, the first official squadron of UAVs, soon to be deployed to the Bosnia war, took shape at Indian Springs, the same town where the UFO lore has it that Bob Lazar was debriefed by extraterrestrials.[54] In short, the initial secret drones operated from Area 51 were at once UAVs and UFOs, surveillance tools and props for fantasy.

In the first week of July of 1947, something that has remained clouded in mystery helped spawn the phenomenon of UFOs: two flying discs with no wings and no tail, nothing like a conventional aircraft, hovering sporadically then continuing to fly, were observed and tracked by US Signal Corps engineers. One of them crashed near a ranch in Roswell, New Mexico. Was it a Russian drone Stalin sent to scare Americans? As crazy as it appears, after interviews with scientists and engineers who worked in Area 51 and tens of thousands of pages of newly declassified materials, that's the conclusion of investigative journalist Annie Jacobsen in a Pulitzer Prize finalist book on Area 51.[55]

An earlier event aired on Halloween Eve in 1938, the CBS radio broadcast of H. G. Wells's *The War of the Worlds* showed the dangers of mass hysteria over the fantasy of extraterrestrial life. Even though the broadcast stated at the outset that the Orson Welles's performance was science fiction, many listeners believed that Martians transported in "a huge cylinder" were actually attacking Earth. When thousands of people began calling the radio station, the police sent a reassuring teletype noting that the broadcast was "an imaginary affair." But the hysteria was beyond control, with many people believing the end of the world had come. More than twelve thousand news stories discussed the apocalyptic broadcast in the following month as the nation was suffering the fears associated with Hitler's troops invading Czechoslovakia. Roswell, Area 51, H. G. Wells, Orson Welles—it all had proven to the security state in most graphic terms one indisputable truth: the national danger posed by the force of fantasy on a mass scale.

Everything about Area 51 was *black*—that is, secret from Congress and the American public. Its secrets included the latest military systems such as the U-2 planes, whose presence in the Nevada, California, and Utah skies, at twice the altitude of commercial airplanes, turned into UFO sightings. The same month as the Roswell incident more than 850 UFO sightings were reported. The CIA created a program to record these sightings with the goal of persuading the public that there was nothing unusual in the phenomenon. But with the arms race in full swing, little did the CIA know how impotent their efforts would be once the image of the UFO had taken hold of the collective imagination. The file on unidentified flying objects remains to this day one of the most top secrets of the CIA and the Air Force.

The press learned that the air force had been keeping a file on UFOs, even while publicly denying it. The air force announced it was ending its UFO research but then launched another even more secret UFO project.[56] The public was not to know about the government's obsession with flying saucers. But on April 7, 1952, *Life* magazine published a sixteen-page article on UFOs, which began with the revelation that "the Air Force is now ready to concede that many saucer and fireball sightings still defy explanation."[57] The CIA and air force's cover-up showed the public something was being concealed. The collective hysteria that their own secrecy had generated was out of control. It would grow worse in time. Jacobsen surmises that the Cold War conspiracy theories around Area 51, "the ones peopled by aliens, piloted by UFOs, set in underground cities and on movie sets of the moon . . . all stand to aid and assist the Atomic Energy Commission in keeping the public away from secret truths."[58] Jacobsen notes that over six hundred million pages remain classified and that we know next to nothing about what went on in Area 51.

There is a direct correlation between secrecy and conspiracy theories. While Area 51's existence was officially denied and while new weapon systems were being developed and tested there, it became the site of intense fantasy. As proof of the aestheticization of war, Area 51 has been the setting for more than sixty movies, TV shows, and video games.[59] *Star Wars* was the blockbuster that began the genre. During the Cold War, Area 51 conflated the development of weapons systems with the fantasy supplement of extraterrestrial sightings and conspiracy theories. "Military science fiction" is science fiction's most popular theme. "Each year, approximately five major science fiction movies linked to war are released."[60] The link between war, fantasy, and science fiction is what requires aesthetics—

a space where drones are not a horror of the nuclear age but an alternative real of robotic wonder and human evolution.

Drones are not limited to military use, but they were originally and still are mostly military driven. Those who work in the industry admit the influence of science fiction on war technologies.[61] Not surprisingly, "a striking amount of government officials . . . read science fiction."[62] Harry Truman is known to have loved it. Ronald Reagan liked Jules Verne. *Star Trek,* the NBC series that generated five other TV shows, ten movies, and an entire library of over four thousand books, is one example of science fiction's influence on new technologies. Robotics turns into reality what science fiction presents as a magic fantasy of invulnerability.[63] Flying the remote-controlled unmanned drones is frequently compared to playing a *video game.* Military researchers are in fact modeling the robot controllers "after the PlayStation because that's what these 18-, 19-year-old Marines have been playing with pretty much all of their lives."[64] Turning war into a continuation of the kids' video games further confuses the virtual and the real, "play" and "war."

"Dreamland [is] the critical core of the bomb," wrote Patton.[65] This is a world grounded in secrecy and in "mystery engendering fantasy."[66] Within two months of the crash at Roswell, 90 percent of Americans had read or heard about UFOs. For psychoanalyst Carl Jung, flying saucers were "spontaneous fantasy images, dreams, and the products of active imagination."[67] But crucial for our study is that flying saucers "marched along in neat parallel to McCarthyism and the Red Scare."[68] Fantasy is a two-sided coin with images of the paradisiacal world on one side and images of fear and terror on the other.

The CIA officer Richard Bissell was all for new technologies but "was most interested in the psychology of CIA operations, the manipulation of public opinion, the creation of illusory forces rather than the use of actual weapons."[69] He knew that the Cold War would mostly have to be fought at the level of the imagination and that a sophisticated system such as the U-2 plane was as much a psychological weapon as a reconnaissance tool.

Just as there is a direct link between Roswell and Area 51, there is also a link between Dreamland and Las Vegas—and between Las Vegas and Hollywood. Not only is Area 51's Dreamland close to Las Vegas, "the city that never sleeps," but it is at the city's very core—its own *American dream,* fed by the two-faced fantasies of extraterrestrial life and apocalyptic doom, erotic frenzy and suicidal fate. As for Hollywood, during the romantic period in the history of Las Vegas, Howard Hughes set aviation records and created an alliance between Hollywood and aerospace—that is, "Vegas was L.A. distillate, a step further into fantasy than even Hollywood would go."[70]

The president most closely connected to the Hollywood of Las Vegas and Area 51 was Ronald Reagan, former actor of "Morning Again in America," and proponent of "Star Wars" (Strategic Defense Initiative), a science fiction strategy engineered in Area 51.[71] Reagan delivered his "Star Wars" speech on March 23, 1983, soon after "black" budgets for weapons increased from $892 million in 1981 to $8.6 billion in 1987. Area 51 was the natural test site for high-tech antimissile weapons, energy beams, UAVs, lasers, and other technologies. "Reagan believed in *Wunderwaffe*, wonder weapons," wrote Patton. "This belief was deeply rooted in his Hollywood past.... The Star Wars-era ray guns were anticipated in Reagan's Brass Bancroft films of the thirties and forties, which introduced similar themes." Reagan's idealistic laser beams "were defensive, just as the Lone Ranger uses his silver bullets not to kill people but to knock the guns out of the hands of the bad guys. It was a dream of peace without bloodshed."[72]

It was the two-sided coin of fantasy: a Hollywood dream of worldwide peace on the one side and Star Wars weapons against the "Evil Empire" on the other. In a startling moment at the Reykjavik summit of 1986, Reagan proposed getting rid of nuclear missiles. But there was one problem—he wanted to continue his Star Wars experiments for the deployment of strategic defenses. When Gorbachev set the condition that SDI research be reduced to the laboratory, the talks broke down. For the peace initiative to be real, not just one side but both sides of the fantasy had to be dismantled. Reagan's administration went back to developing the ten-warhead MX ICBMs based in 4,600 silos hidden across Nevada and Utah.

There are cultural and imaginary continuities between the Cold War and the War on Terror, as studied by Joseph Masco—the recognition that the "'new' counterterror state in 2001 was actually a repetition, modeled in language and tone on the launch of the national security state in 1947."[73] From the beginning, the security state knew the power of fantasy, not only as a peril to be exploited by the enemy by provoking mass hysteria à la Orson Welles, but also as a fear-generating asset for controlling a docile citizenry. If "after the bombings of Hiroshima and Nagasaki [the Cold War] was fought incessantly at the level of imagination," so it is in the current War on Terror.[74] As the atomic bomb tested in the Nevada desert became "the national fetish" during the Cold War, the weaponized drone in the same place projects a similarly fetishistic object—the new robotic unmanned weapon turned into the *image* of technological superiority in a world in which the empire's actual military record is abysmal.[75]

Area 51/Paradise Ranch shows that "the true conspiracy of Power resides in the very notion of conspiracy."[76] The myth of a secret, all-powerful parallel power, the organization within the organization, has been a hallmark of totalitarian regimes. When terrorism replaced communism, a prominent aspect of public fantasies became the conspiratorial notion that, given the hidden and catastrophic power of the terrorists, we must have our own ultra-secret agency and its own clandestine sources of information to legitimate actions that might exceed the rule of law. The conspiracy epicenter is no longer populated by MX ICBMs and extraterrestrial aliens; they have been replaced by drones and terrorist aliens.

The CIA and the air force came together in the winter of 2000 to work on a drone project at Area 51. Their goal was to arm a reconnaissance Predator with Hellfire missiles. The first successful tests took place on February 21, 2001. The transition from the Cold War to the War on Terror is a shift from *deterrence* to *preemption* and entails a change in the imaginary from the symbolic fiction of world hegemony based on nuclear power (fantasy as stabilizing dream) to the spectral reality of world disorder under the ubiquitous menace of terrorism (fantasy as unconquerable chaos). In deterrence the security state is engaged in securing defense systems never to be used—the threat is based largely on ritual display. In preemption, one must endlessly predict future acts of war. The apocalyptic power ascribed to terrorism, which then requires the state of exception, is best explained by its access to such a counterterror framework of fantasy.

FANTASY AND THE PASSION FOR IGNORANCE

In the early 1950s in Las Vegas, the nuclear tests with their mushrooms rising to the sky were entertainment for tourists and celebrated as a harbinger of a new period of humanity. The mushroom cloud became a national symbol, taking hold of popular culture with signs of "Atomic Café" and "Atomic Motel" along cross-country highways. *Our Friend the Atom,* a book for children, was published by Disney. In Las Vegas, the Flamingo Hotel designed a popular request, the "atomic hairdo." In Strip bars and at breakfast parties after the predawn tests, the "atomic cocktail" became a sensation—equal parts vodka, brandy, and champagne, with a dash of sherry. People were swinging to the tune of "Atomic Bomb Bounce," and a Miss Atomic Bomb contest was sponsored by the Sands Hotel.[77]

The fatal effects of atomic radiation were immediately evident with flocks of dying sheep and other effects on people. But the government's assurances that the tests presented no health risks were quickly accepted by the American public. The evidence supporting the health risks of radiation couldn't be more compelling, yet the will for ignorance won the day. The reality was that, according to 1997 estimates by the National Cancer Institute, "bomb tests conducted in Nevada during the 1950s may cause 10,000 to 75,000 extra thyroid cancers,"[78] and "there were few, if any, Americans in the contingent forty-eight states at the time . . . [who] were not exposed to some level of fallout."[79] If Hiroshima and Nagasaki were not considered sufficient evidence that atomic radiation kills, how could science prove it? In fantasy one can argue that *they* are after all Japanese, and who can be sure that *we* Americans will also die of atomic radiation? When "downwinders" got cancer and died, courts ruled in favor of the Atomic Energy Commission and against the victims.[80] Hollywood came to the aid of atomic warfare with realistic quasi-documentaries or science fiction doomsday scenarios. Atomic bombs were bad only in the hands of evil communists. It would take more than three decades before Judge Bruce Jenkins awarded a total of nearly $2.5 million to ten plaintiffs.[81]

In the tradition of ignoring the effects of radiation fallout, drone killings also belong to the category of "unknown knowns"—things that we know while pretending we don't, or "things that we don't know that we know—which is precisely the Freudian unconscious."[82] Information on counterterrorist practices, such as those revealed by Westmoreland or Bryant, is discarded as "disavowed beliefs, suppositions and obscene practices we pretend not to know about, even though they form the background of our public values."[83] If one believes them, the dissonance with what one reads or hears in the daily news becomes unbearable.

At the root of the pervasive recourse to fantasy in terrorism discourse is the existence of a systemic *passion* for ignorance—in the psychoanalytic sense of ignorance as an active refusal to know. Critical studies of terrorism discourse have long pointed out a crisis of knowledge in terrorism studies characterized by "the perversion of temporality, the logic of taboo, non-hypothetical knowledge, secret information, the passion for 'expert' ignorance, mystical causation and dual sovereignty."[84] In Richard Jackson's characterization, the crisis is "the condition where *lack of knowledge* is the main thing we *know* about the terrorist threat."[85] A sign of this crisis has been the difficulties of defining not only the term itself but the interpretive frameworks of events covered by the concept of terrorism.

Counterterrorism, as strategy, is founded on the tabooing of the Terrorist subject as someone who must not be seen or heard; even making any attempt at "understanding" his or her alleged political or moral claims is suspected of being a "justification" of terrorist acts. Counterterrorism has created a new industry of thousands of government organizations and private companies, with more than 250,000 private contractors working on top-secret programs and over 850,000 Americans with top-secret clearances.[86] Their mission is to study subjects with whom they are forbidden to meet, talk, or engage in person-to-person interaction. In sum, ignorance of the Terrorist subject is the inaugural condition of the counterterrorist episteme. A critical analysis of counterterrorism would start with identifying the blind spots in our knowledge of terrorism and recognizing the role of fantasy as central to this fabricated culture of taboo.

It is frequently observed that the National Security Agency is drowning in intelligence. It "now ingests 1.7 billion pieces of intercepted communications every twenty-four hours."[87] After 9/11, government agencies published some fifty thousand intelligence reports. However, the usefulness of the reports depends on the quality of the analysis. Dana Priest and William Arkin's conclusion is that "Top Secret America . . . [has] grown so big and so unwieldy and no one, still, [is] actually in charge."[88] This explains, for example, the fact that British intelligence knew that Umar Farouk Abdulmutallab, the Nigerian known as the "Underwear Bomber," was connected to Anwar al-Awlaki (the young man's father had contacted CIA officers at the US embassy in Abuja, Nigeria, to alert them to the danger posed by his son's "extremely religious views"), yet Abdulmutallab's name was not added to the No Fly List, nor was his US visa revoked.[89]

Forty percent of the US military budget is secret.[90] So are the budgets of intelligence agencies. The number of newly classified documents "has tripled to over 23 million,"[91] with the secret-keeping price tag of $10 billion a year. The intelligence community recognizes that the crisis in counterterrorist knowledge relates to the nature and context of the intelligence gathered.

David Kilcullen's internal criticism of counterterrorism goes to the core when he dares to question a *belief-based* intelligence: "Why did most countries (including those who opposed the Iraq war) believe in 2002 that Saddam Hussein had WMDs? Because they were intercepting the regime's communications, and many senior Iraqi regime members believed Iraq had them."[92] Kilcullen is referring to the fact that, after the removal of Hussein, there was declassified information, based on the FBI's interviews, that Hussein had, in fact, been *bluffing* about his own possession of weapons of mass destruction to keep regional enemies such as Iran in check. In short, the US went to war with Iraq, in good part, because counterterrorism was unable to sort out the misinformation Hussein himself had planted. The problem is fundamentally epistemological: how to sort out an actual threat from a feigned one, the real from the fantasy. It is the kind of problem an ethnographer faces in an alien culture or a detective in solving a crime.

I have argued elsewhere that the catastrophic intelligence failures leading to 9/11 are in good part direct consequences of such unwillingness to engage with the terrorists' political subjectivity.[93] The future hijackers had left a long track of evidence of their presence in the US. Nineteen months before 9/11, the CIA knew that two of the plotters, Nawaf al Hazmi and Khalid al Mihdhar, had flown from Kuala Lumpur to Los Angeles after a meeting with bin Laden. Hazmi and Mihdhar, who were in frequent contact with the other plotters, didn't even change their names to open their bank accounts, obtain driver's licenses, or attend flight training schools. Hazmi's name was in San Diego's phone book. A report made public on August 21, 2017, stated that fifty to sixty CIA officers knew of the presence of Hazmi and Mihdhar in the US.[94] Then in July 2001 there was the

"Phoenix Memo" sent to the FBI headquarters by one of their agents alerting them to the possibility that jihadists sent by bin Laden were training in Arizona; one of them, Zacarias Moussaoui, was even arrested by the Minneapolis office of the FBI. In the search for the failures leading to the attacks, *The 9/11 Commission Report* identified as the initial one a failure of "imagination."[95] But hijacking planes to crash against emblematic buildings had already been imagined, and "a Congressional inquiry into intelligence activities before Sept. 11 found twelve reports over a seven-year period suggesting that terrorists might use airplanes as weapons."[96] By the summer of 2001 the drumbeat of threats was such that "the system was blinking red," in the words of the CIA director George Tenet, but there was no way apparently to uncover a plot that was being hatched in plain sight. Why such inexplicable blindness? The information was in the system, so why did the system refuse to recognize it and act on it?

It's not enough to claim the obvious failure of communication between the agencies. Something else has to be taken into account, and that's counterterrorism's basic ignorance of the culture, thinking, and political subjectivities of the terrorists. It was the will of the plotters, the capacity for decision of humiliated people, including their willingness for suicidal action, that was ignored. The prevailing counterterrorist attitude was one of disdain for the tabooed terrorists as ignorant fanatics, cowards with no backbone and no moral compass, easily vulnerable to informants and manipulated in the courts, as proven in the aftermath of first attacks against the Twin Towers. The counterterrorist system was unable to read the abundant evidence out in the open because they did not link it to the despised enemy's desires, motivations, and potential for madness. Such contempt for the terrorists' subjectivity is a crucial dimension of "the passion for ignorance" that is grounded in counterterrorist impasses as an ideology and a mind-set. The evidence is there, but, as in the case of the proverbially "dumb policeman" in detective stories, the counterterrorist can read it only in the most literal terms while being easily fooled by the criminal—when what is needed is the approach of a detective who can read the desire and the inner workings of the suspect's mind.[97]

The systemic ignorance about the terrorists is also responsible for counterterrorism's inability to detect the element of bluff in the terrorist agenda. The end result of such ignorance is that, as Kilcullen said of bin

Laden, "we have turned a mouse into an elephant," and that the War on Terror has "largely played into the hands of this AQ [al-Qaeda] exhaustion strategy." He called for "a radical rethinking of some key Western policies, strategies, and attitudes."[98] Indeed, one needs a lot of fantasy to create an enemy Terrorist in Iraq, where there was none, to justify an annual spending "in excess of $400 million *per day.*"[99]

Nor are Kilcullen's proposals radical or controversial; rather, "Much of the best strategic work by the State Department, defense departments of contributing powers, and NATO planners conforms exactly to these prescriptions."[100] Kilcullen saw the decision to invade Iraq as "an extremely serious strategic error" and warned against it, but so did "almost every other counterinsurgency professional."[101] How was it that the military establishment *knew* that the consequences of a war in Iraq would be disastrous, officers were aware that the hubris of American military efficacy was breathtaking, and yet the US went to war? Similarly counterterrorism *knows* that drones produce further terrorism by killing civilians (as we will argue in chapter 3), and knows that with "every one of these dead noncombatants [there is] an alienated family, a new desire for revenge, and more recruits for a militant movement that has grown exponentially even as drone strikes have increased."[102] Yet this is currently the central counterterrorist policy. Rumsfeld's philosophizing about things we know and don't know pretends to be engaged in a war "against the unknown," when in reality counterterrorism is primarily driven, as Lisa Stampnitzky argues, by a "politics of anti-knowledge."[103]

Most significant, ignorance is mandatory for justifying "signature strikes" that kill people simply on the basis of cultural life patterns. As shown by Pakistani anthropologist and former politician Akbar Ahmed, who lives in Washington, D.C., the truth is that knowledge of local cultural patterns is to be avoided at all costs. The American lack of understanding of Muslim societies and the "mixture of ignorance, arrogance, and prejudice" of American foreign policy Ahmed finds simply "puzzling."[104] He quotes Peter Bergen, the terrorism expert who "exploded the myth of al-Qaeda as a global force" and said the American public is not ready to be told that the risk of al-Qaeda "may have been overblown all along."[105] While wondering at the consequences of such policies in trillions of dollars and hundreds of thousands of lives, Ahmed concludes, "Americans had information about everything, yet they understood nothing."[106] But this is what is to be expected as the result of a passionate ignorance turned into the fundamental dimension of counterterrorism's ideological fantasy—in the precise sense that "'ideological' is a social reality whose very existence implies the non-knowledge of its participants as to its essence."[107]

"WHAT DO YOU WANT?" FANTASY AS EVIDENCE

In his February 5, 2003, debriefing at the United Nations Security Council, standing before a tapestry reproduction of Picasso's *Guernica* covered with a blue curtain, Colin Powell began: "My colleagues, every statement I make today is backed up by sources, solid sources. These are not assertions. What we're giving you are facts and conclusions based on solid intelligence."[108] At the outset Powell established his axiomatic nexus; he had come, he said, "to share . . . what the United States knows about Iraq's weapons of mass destruction as well as Iraq's involvement in terrorism." He enlisted a plethora of facts for what was, he emphatically insisted, irrefutable evidence from a variety of sources. Hussein's possession of WMDs was definitive and indisputable, he said. But, he continued, this was not the worst. "Our concern is not just about these illicit weapons. . . . It's the way [they] can be connected to terrorists and terrorist organizations that have no compunction about using such devices against innocent people around the world." He concluded that "leaving Saddam Hussein in possession of weapons of mass destruction for a few more months or years is not an option. Not in a post-September 11th world." Powell's deployment of this counterterror state's "secrecy/threat matrix" was an impressive performance and commanded world attention[109]—except there were no weapons of mass destruction in Iraq. His long list of "facts," and the media's collusion, amounted to no evidence whatsoever.

Drone warfare also needs evidence to justify killings, most of which consists of information about group association, not individual guilt. Sociologists and anthropologists have long studied the crucial role of the Durkheimian "collective representations": ideas, beliefs, values, fears, and emotions elaborated and held collectively by a society. Historians also speak "of the realm of imaginary representations, a realm that also has a history, fed not by 'facts' alone but also by 'interpretations.'"[110] As with Powell's "evidence," we should ask to what extent the Cold War and the War on Terror are also situated at the nexus of history and fiction.[111]

Terry Castle, discussing the intense interest aroused by the ghost story *An Adventure* (1911), observes: "The prime symptom of *Adventure*-mania [is] a passion for invoking 'evidence.'"[112] It is one thing to explain how someone might see a ghost, but when *two* see the same delusion Castle is led to investigate the nature of collective hallucinations, invoking Freud's lament that we possess "no explanation of the nature of suggestion" and ideological transference.[113] The "passion for invoking evidence" when there is none is characteristic not only of ghost stories but of Powell's and others' claims of terrorism based on secret evidence and requires that we consider the modern notion of fantasy not as mere dream but as that which gives consistency to what we call reality.

Che vuoi? What do you want? What is bothering you? In psychoanalytic theory, "fantasy is an *answer* to this '*Che vuoi?*', an attempt to fill out the void of the question with an answer. In the case of anti-Semitism, the answer to 'What does the Jew want?' is a fantasy of 'Jewish conspiracy': a mysterious power of Jews to manipulate events, to pull the strings behind the scenes."[114] In the case of suspect Muslim migrants in a rich European country, the answer to "What do Muslims want?" might be, as in Switzerland, a referendum against their building a minaret because of a fear that it will lead to a terrorist plot. In Žižek's words, "The crucial point that must be made on a theoretical level is that fantasy functions as a construction. . . . By giving us a definitive answer to the question 'What does the Other want?', it enables us to evade the unbearable deadlock in which the Other wants something from us."[115] This is the case in situations of torture when the victim, in an effort to escape unbearable pain, is ready to say anything, including the construction of a fantasy narrative, begging the torturer, "What do you want to hear?"

When his torturers asked Mohamedou Ould Slahi whether the confessions they extracted from him after months of torture were true, he answered: "I don't care as long as you are pleased. So if you want to buy, I am selling."[116] Slahi is but one example of the hundreds of people taken to Guantánamo with no record of wrongdoing who provided forced confessions.[117] A native of Mauritania with an engineering degree from the

University of Duisburg in Germany, Slahi, arrested in January 2000, was a case of mistaken identity; though he was believed to be a big fish, after years of harrowing torture he provided no valuable information.[118] His case ultimately was dropped for lack of evidence. Judge James Robertson granted Slahi habeas corpus and ordered his release in April 2010. The Department of Justice appealed the decision and Slahi remained in custody until October of 2016.

In 2005 Slahi wrote a Dantesque document, *Guantánamo Diary*, about his years of torture. The memoir was declassified by the US government and published with many redactions in 2015. In the same way that the historian Carlo Ginzburg "learned to read witchcraft trials as texts, *which provided direct evidence on the inquisitors and lay judges behind them*, as well as some indirect and usually distorted evidence on the defendants," Slahi's diary shows the "evidence" counterterrorist knowledge and policy is based upon—most crucially evidence of the torturers' own thoughts and fantasies.[119]

Central to Slahi's experience is, in his own words, the "endless Catch-22" in which he is unbearably caught.[120] His interrogators want information, which he does not possess. Sometimes the superior officer orders the torturer to hold off, only because is "afraid of the paperwork that would result in case of my death."[121] At one point he is taken out to sea in a high-speed boat and threatened with some kind of execution unless he tells them what they want to hear. He has to build a narrative they will find credible. Slahi explains how difficult a task that is: "Had I done what they accused me of, I would have relieved myself on day one. But the problem is that you cannot just admit to something you haven't done; you need to deliver the details, which you can't when you hadn't done anything. It's not just, 'Yes, I did!' No, it doesn't work that way: you have to make up a complete story that makes sense to the dumbest dummies. One of the hardest things to do is to tell an untruthful story and maintain it, and that is exactly where I was stuck."[122] To placate the torturers he has to frame his lie in a plausible story.

"Confessions are like the beads of a necklace: if the first head bead falls, the rest follow," Slahi notes in reference to the fact that an admission of culpability is the easy thing.[123] "I had no crimes to confess to, and that is exactly where I got stuck with my interrogators. . . . But through my conversations with the FBI and the DoD, I had a good idea as to what wild theories the government had over me."[124] Slahi had to admit that "obviously there is no way out with you guys." The torturer replies: "I'm telling you how!" Slahi gives in: "Now, thanks to the unbearable pain I was suffering, I had nothing to lose, and I allowed myself to say anything to satisfy my assailants. Session followed session since I called XXXX."[125] The interrogators are "very happy."[126] Slahi notes: "I answered all the questions he asked me with incriminating answers. I tried my best to make myself look as bad as I could, which is exactly the way you can make your interrogator happy. I made my mind up to spend the rest of my life in jail."[127]

His torturers' acceptance of Slahi's tale was made more difficult because the interrogators knew that most of the Guantánamo inmates had no terrorist past. Secretary Powell's chief of staff Col. Lawrence Wilkerson declared in a sworn statement that by the end of August 2002 President Bush, Vice President Cheney, Rumsfeld, and others knew that of the initial 742 inmates, "the vast majority of Guantánamo detainees were innocent . . . [and] there was a lack of any useable evidence for the great majority of them."[128] Still, they continued to justify keeping them prisoners because the War on Terror required it.

Slahi's false information could have been checked for corroboration, but ignorance of facts is a condition for the fantasy narrative. The torturers imposed an actual taboo about admitting ignorance: "Whenever I thought about the words, 'I don't know,' I got nauseous, because I remembered the words of XXXX, 'All you have to say is, "I don't know, I don't remember," and we'll fuck you!' Or XXXX: 'We don't want to hear your denials anymore!' And so I erased these words from my dictionary."[129] He is asked to write his answers, which receive congratulatory comments: "You're very generous in your written answers; you even wrote a whole bunch about XXXX, who you really don't know," XXXX accurately said, for Slahi didn't know the person he was reporting against, but he had to write something because he had been forbidden to use the words "I don't know."[130] There is no negative in the unconscious, Freud wrote. The difference between a factual narrative and a fantasy narrative is that there is no negative limit in the second: everything is possible in the realm of fancy. Demanding information, while forbidding the answer "I don't know," is demanding a fantasy narrative.

In the end the inevitable happens: Slahi's Catch-22 is transferred to the torturers themselves, for how can they not know that the confessed evidence is anything but the blowback fabrication of their own narrative? Thus the process will require a further stage in which they will have to keep torturing Slahi to see if they can sort out when he is lying and when he is not. "If we discover that you lied to us, you're gonna feel our wrath," they tell him.[131] When he gives false testimony against a Canadian, the torturer tells him: "I talked today with the Canadians and they told me they don't believe your story about XXXX being involved in drug smuggling into the US."[132] Two years later he is relieved to learn that the man he falsely incriminated was released.

Slahi provided his torturers the tale they wanted, but when one of the torturers "doubted the truthfulness of the story" and asked whether it was true, Slahi replied, "If you want the truth, this story didn't happen,"[133] a confession that provoked the torturers' fury: "XXXX came back . . . threatening me with all kinds of suffering and agony." To protect themselves, not only did the torturers have to believe the story they were hearing, but Slahi himself had to pretend to believe it lest "the radically intersubjective character of fantasy" be lost.[134] Slahi and his tormentors had to reach some kind of agreement by which he played the role of "the-one-who-knows," and the torturers played the role of "the-ones-who-believe." But believing and taking the fantasy for real, and then convincing the tortured man that his tale did in fact take place, was the hardest for the torturers. For Slahi the hardest was believing it *himself* in order to maintain the intersubjective nature of the narrative. After years of torture, their search for truth reached its surreal climax when they subjected him to a lie detector test. His torturers wanted Slahi's lie to confirm the *truth* of their fantasy; Slahi's truth (his innocence) was the ultimate blow to their fantasy framework. Could a lie detector get them out of their own Catch-22? The answers he provided were erased from the book.

Guantánamo Diary underwent many redactions before it was published; the one that surprised his editor Larry Siems most was seeing the word *tears* routinely deleted.[135] But such a deletion makes complete sense if we consider that any emotional expression would humanize Slahi—and that would be in stark dissonance to the way he was objectified as an animal. Slahi's captor repeatedly taunted him: "Looks like a dog, walks like a dog, smells like a dog, barks like a dog, must be a dog," to which he responded: "I know I am not a dog, but yet I must be one."[136]

In a replica of Pasolini's *Saló*, photos of tortured men at Abu Ghraib showed them naked, on leashes, made to walk like dogs. Once you have turned your prisoner into a beast, you are free to subject him to your own bestiality and fun, while others watch from a monitoring room. Slahi tells how two female officers took off their blouses and forced him "to take part in a sexual threesome in the most degrading manner," something that was "hurtful" to his genitals.[137] Once Slahi had been objectified as an animal to be hunted, tortured, and fucked, the revelation of a tear on his face shatters the indispensable fantasy of his bestiality. The censor of the *Diary* is willing to let the reader know that the torturers abused the "dog" physically and sexually but not that he could feel pity for himself and weep for his family.[138] "A tear is an intellectual thing," wrote William Blake. "A tear is a nonterrorist thing," writes counterterrorism.

Slahi's case reveals how the real *body of evidence* in the War on Terror is the counterterrorist state's delusional fantasy. As John le Carré put it with rigorous precision, it's "a vision of hell, beyond Orwell, beyond Kafka: perpetual torture prescribed by the mad doctors of Washington."[139]

The true evidence that innocent inmates were knowingly kept in Guantánamo while their interrogators put on a show of searching for "evidence" is illustrated by another Guantánamo diary, Murat Kurnaz's *Five Years of My Life* (2007). Born in Bremen, Germany, Kurnaz married a Turkish Muslim woman and decided to spend two months at the Masura Center in Lahore, Pakistan, to learn what was expected of a good Muslim husband. When he was to return to Germany on December 1, 2001, he was arrested in Peshawar, Pakistan, and taken first to Kandahar and then to Guantánamo. Like most prisoners in Guantánamo, he had been sold for a bounty of $3,000. Kurnaz writes of grisly images of inmates with legs and fingers amputated as well as people killed in Kandahar and Guantánamo as the result of American torture; he describes in harrowing detail how on several occasions he came close to death. His only hope was that an interrogator would listen to *his* evidence, for it would be easy to check the facts of his ordinary German life and verify that he was by no means a terrorist.

The truth was that, in the words of his attorney, "the US government *knew* of his innocence as early as 2002 (just six months into his detention), even as it continued, cynically, to argue that Murat was an 'enemy combatant.'"[140] During five years of interrogation the United States would pretend to be either in search of or in possession of "evidence" so they could subject him to the most extreme, life-threatening forms of torture. Survival at all costs was Kurnaz's goal, and for this he held on to his faith and hope that someone would check the facts of his life—until he realized that they had checked and "they had known everything about me from the very beginning. They weren't interested in the fact that I had never been to Afghanistan and was innocent. I didn't stand a chance."[141]

As torture requires that the pretense of a search for evidence must continue, its questioning becomes more and more absurd. "You know everything about me," Kurnaz protests as the interrogators accuse him of lying. "We have our own evidence," they reply.[142] Only after almost three years of living in a six-by-seven-foot cage, and two years after US officials knew he was innocent, was Kurnaz taken to a tribunal to determine whether he was an enemy combatant. On the basis of his former friendship with a suicide bomber whose attack took place eighteen months *after* he entered Guantánamo, the judge ruled that Kurnaz was a dangerous enemy combatant.

In January 2005, Judge Joyce Green ruled that the Guantánamo detainees were entitled to due process and could challenge their detention. She mentioned in particular Kurnaz's case, her conclusion being that his detention was unlawful.[143] But the government appealed Judge Green's decision, which was later upheld by the Supreme Court. In the meantime Kurnaz's attorney, Baher Azmy, found himself in the position of having to go to Germany in March 2005 to shame the government into negotiating his release by publicizing Kurnaz's Guantánamo torture. Although Kurnaz was born and lived all his life in Germany, he was not technically a German citizen. He discovered that the Americans had been willing to release him in 2002, when they decided he was innocent, but that "the German government apparently didn't want to let [him] reenter the country, and claimed that [his] residency permit had expired."[144] Kurnaz's innocence was a *known* fact that the US and German officials had to render into an *unknown* in order to continue their search for evidence in their show of justice. It would take another fifteen months before the new chancellor, Angela Merkel, would plead his case with President Bush and obtain his release.

How can we grasp the scandalous fact that for years the US willingly subjected hundreds of prisoners it knew were innocent to the harshest of tortures for a period of years in a charade of military justice? Why the *necessity* of Guantánamo, the prison that became an international emblem of American brutality and lawlessness and whose orange jumpsuits, in a strange overlay of fetishes, were adopted by the Islamic State to enact the execution of Westerners? The staggering military reality by which the US defense budget almost doubled within a decade after 9/11 can hardly be understood until we grasp the figure of the Terrorist as its indispensable ideological supplement. Guantánamo responds to and cements the *fundamental fantasy* necessary to provide consistency to the US counterterrorism security state.

DID THEY DO IT? YES AND NO. AND HOW DO YOU NAME IT?

The question of whether they did it—the abominable act—doesn't apply only to victims of torture. When drone operators Westmoreland and Bryant tell us they killed hundreds of civilians, while the president and his officials staunchly deny it, the logical question is: Did they actually do the killing? Yes or no? But what if, as in Hollywood's structure of inherent transgression, the answer is a simultaneous yes *and* no? Recall *Casablanca*'s scene in which Ingrid Bergman pulls a gun in the hotel room and threatens Humphrey Bogart in order to obtain letters of transit for her husband; the two characters have been lovers in the past, and he responds to her demand by telling her to shoot him as a favor. She doesn't, of course, and instead breaks down with the memory of their last parting in Paris, confessing that she still loves him. As they embrace, the camera moves away for several seconds, encircling the airport tower, before returning to the pair again, to frame Bogart smoking and gazing out the window before the story continues.

The question for the viewer is: Did they do it? Richard Maltby answers, *Yes and no at the same time,* arguing that the film "deliberately constructs itself in such a way as to offer distinct and alternative sources of pleasure to two people sitting next to each other in the same cinema . . . [so it] could play to both 'innocent' and 'sophisticated' audiences alike."[145] The codified signals (the postcoital cigarette, the phallic tower) suggest that they did it, while other signals (just a few seconds, the bed not undone, the pair having the same conversation when the camera returns) that they did not. The spectator is at once allowed to adhere to strict moral codes and at the same time allowed to imagine an alternative subversive sexual narrative. But perhaps you don't need two spectators and one is sufficient—since you are absolved from guilt by the official story, you can indulge in fantasies. The Lacanian conclusion is that the couple "did not do it for the Big Other (in this case the decorum of public appearance, which must not be offended), but they did do it for our dirty fantasmatic imagination. This is the structure of inherent transgression at its purest: Hollywood needs both levels in order to function."[146]

And apparently so does counterterrorism as reality show. The reward of such artful fantasy is that, as in the world of Hollywood and Las Vegas, you can *simultaneously* believe and disbelieve the implications of the War on Terror such as the "kill list." Do drone pilots unlawfully kill noncombatants? Yes and no. They *don't* for the big Other of the general public that will never see their president as "an assassin," yet any sophisticated reader of Jo Becker and Scott Shane's report in the *New York Times* has little doubt that "signature strikes" amount to unlawful killing.[147] But these two readers can be one and the same. The question of what "belief" is in such cases is comparable to the question of whether the ancient Greeks believed in their own myths. The Greeks often laughed at their own myths and didn't seem to believe much in them; it wasn't the myths' truth or falsehood that mattered but their conventionality, their verbal nature, the art of their rhetorical modality. The liar is not even pretending to lie, so there is no scandal. In short, concluded Paul Veyne, there are "modalities of belief . . . a plurality of programs of truth," and "the Greeks believe and do not believe in their myths. They believe in them, but they use them and cease believing at the point where their interest in believing ends . . . [for] all peoples give their oracles—or their statistical data—a nudge to confirm what they wish to believe."[148] Like the Greeks in ancient times, we today fabricate our criteria for truth and degrees of belief regarding drones.

The reader knows drones are killing innocent people but doesn't care—because there are different criteria for truth and because the president and the counterterrorism regime reaffirm our need to believe that Law and Morality are being respected. Indeed, lest anyone be confused by the seeming amorality, Becker and Shane's report, as discussed in the previous chapter, repeatedly alluded to the priest-like high moral character of President Obama and his counterterrorism chief, Brennan. Somehow, as long as public leaders pay obeisance to high principles, they and we can justify the killings, even enjoy them with the patriotic superego's "dirty fantasmatic imagination," for they represent the victory of order over terrorism. In this sense "Law itself needs its obscene supplement . . . is sustained by it."[149] The "unknown known" of the kill list is that we know they are killing civilians, but we are at war and so we are allowed to enjoy the fantasy of the "known unknown" that many of those we kill are also probably terrorists. Hollywood, Las Vegas, Dreamland, Creech. Did they do it? Yes and no. Did they kill innocent noncombatants? Yes and no. Are we guilty? Yes and no.

And how do you name this duality? To begin with, could you call the drone killings *assassinations*? Officially, it is "unknown" that drones exist, let alone that they kill innocent victims. One known that must be rendered into an unknown is that drone killings are for much of the world, and were for the US until 9/11, "assassination." This knowledge is too harsh for the media, general public, and the US governments, so it is referred to as *targeted killing*. Thus the first step toward the new conceptual paradigm is linguistic—naming it becomes inaugural. Indeed, as argued elsewhere, the rhetorical arts of naming, categorizing, defining, and plotting are foundational to the required new reality-making discourse of counterterrorism.[150]

A writer must name things, but some events are hard to name and some words hard to write. *Murder* and *assassination* are among the hardest words to write down. US journalists enforce a policy of not calling drone killings "assassination," the rationale being that the word should be reserved for the killing of politically prominent people.[151] In short, the drone victims are "prominent" enough to deserve to be included in the kill list but not prominent enough for their killing to be considered of significance and therefore an "assassination." It couldn't have been easy for the

New York Times chief Washington correspondent David Sanger to write that a targeted killing by drones is "essentially assassination, because the linkage to the attacks of September 11, 2001, more than a decade ago, has been strained by the passage of time." Sanger quoted a current official from the Obama administration involved in the debate about the legitimacy of drone strikes: "it's hard to distinguish this, in a practical sense, from targeted assassination."[152] On some rare occasions they are referred to as "quasi-assassination."[153] The use of the term *assassination* for victims of US secret agencies wasn't so restricted in the past. The CIA manual defined the term as "used to describe the planned killing of a person who is not under the legal jurisdiction of the killer, who is not physically in the hands of the killer, who has been selected by a resistance organization for death, and whose death provides positive advantages to that organization."[154]

Describing drone killings as "targeted killings" has one fundamental inadequacy: since most of these killings take place in "signature strikes," where the victims' identities, names, or activities are for the most part unknown, the victims are collateral damage rather than sought-after militants—*untargeted* rather than targeted. In the end, killing by drones is not satisfactorily described by the terms *assassination, murder, collateral damage,* or even *targeted killing,* which shows that we are facing a *new* type of killing closer to Giorgio Agamben's "bare life"—drone victims are animal-like, *zoe,* people without rights of society, citizenship, and burial, and the very naming of their killings presents a problem of description. The post-9/11 War on Terror was for President Bush "an international manhunt,"[155] and, from a hunter's perspective, terrorists are wild game, *dirty* animals whose killings don't amount to homicide, let alone assassination. If formerly the CIA had an assassination manual with clear techniques and warnings as to how to do it, now "assassination" is out and "targeted killing" is in. The predicate describing the action has changed as well—the killer is now a *targeter.*

First off, a hunter-killer, as either a drone or a pilot, needs a target. Drone pilot Martin "found himself hoping that the targets he was following would prove themselves to be insurgents so he could 'get some action.'"[156] When the US War on Terror expanded to involvement in Yemen, "there was excitement" at the CIA and other agencies, for "we'd been wanting to do strikes forever at that point."[157] The local Yemeni government was advised that the "manhunting right in their country would be shared by two US target-killing agencies, the CIA and the JSOC."[158] At the CIA, "Their focus [was] on *head-hunting* rather than intelligence."[159] Target-hunting had become a profitable business.

But one doesn't need to be a passionate hunter for the job. Drone targeting became "a career track" for "ordinary people":[160] "The bar for war had been lowered, the remote-controlled age had begun, and the killer drones became an object of fascination inside the CIA."[161] Thus targeted killing gave rise to a new profession: "Many targeters spent their entire professional lives doing nothing else, rising steadily through the ranks as they developed greater expertise at hunting people, one by one."[162] Indeed, "'targeting' came to mean something quite different for the analysts who moved into the Counterterrorist Center. It meant tracking down someone deemed a threat to the United States, and capturing and killing him."[163] And what you needed for this was skill—targeting, like archery, had turned into a form of art.

Some writers avoid the expression *targeted killing*, claiming it is nothing but a euphemism for assassination.[164] But the power of the euphemism is central to drone warfare and constitutive of counterterrorist discourse. Dropping bombs is "kinetic military action." A call to go to war is couched as a call for "all necessary measures" to *protect civilians* on the ground.[165] The rewording of "torture" to "enhanced interrogation techniques" was critical in legitimating it for public debate. Westmoreland's and Bryant's particular Slaughterhouse seemed so *nonreal* and dissonant because their killings were "targeted killings" for the general public, while for the targeters they were "assassinations."

DRONE WARFARE AS FINE ART

Thomas de Quincey's famous essay "On Murder Considered as One of the Fine Arts" examines a series of murders committed in London by John Williams in 1811 in which people were "murdered in a rapture of creative art," murder was "treated *aesthetically* . . . that is, in relation to good taste," and the murderer was "like Michael Angelo in painting . . . [who] carried his art to a point of colossal sublimity."[166] De Quincey's killer "gloried in his crime as an artist glories in the execution of an image, or a poet in a poem."[167]

In page after page of his memoir on his years at Creech, drone pilot Martin declares how deeply satisfying, even aesthetic, his experience of flying and killing was, comparing his "art" to Leonardo da Vinci's work— the Renaissance painter being "among the first to raise the specter of using flying machines for war."[168] While manhunting he "often felt more like a *spectator* . . . than an actual participant," enjoying "a fine box-seat view of fireworks," bringing along "a pair of binoculars to conduct a little sightseeing of the ground war."[169] Flying the Predator allowed Martin "the extraordinary perspective of being not only a 'combatant,' albeit from 7,500 miles away, but also an observer with a broad overview."[170] He said he had "a god's seat above it all."[171] Martin the drone pilot wants to be seen as a philosopher and an artist of national security. He describes his man-hunt as something like "watching an NFL game on TV," enjoying the "pleasures of a spectacle with the added thrill that it is real for someone, but not the spectator."[172] It's a fight between space age technology and "primitive squalor not far from the Stone Age," with Martin "a voyeur in the sky snooping on people's lives."[173] Martin, a reader of history who says he has realized we are entering a new era of warfare that poses difficult questions, wonders "what laws and ethical codes applied."[174] He is com-mitted to drone warfare as a new form of ethics and art.

But drone assassinations are above all political art. They were "a huge political upside for Obama," his chief of staff, Rahm Emanuel, recog-nized.[175] A crucial factor in the drone program is for politicians to show they are doing things "in order to generate certain political effects at home."[176] One instance of this was the long piece in the *New York Times*, quoting members of his administration, detailing Obama's eager involve-ment in the weekly Tuesday "kill list" meetings—the goal was turning the killing of thousands of unknown people into a show of presidential candi-date Obama's "toughness" to secure reelection. (See "Playing Terrorist" and the powers of narrative in the next chapter.)

Obama himself boasted that "it turns out that I'm really good at killing . . . didn't know that was gonna be a strong suit of mine."[177] He was patient, methodical, relentless, not one of those squeamish people who'd lose sleep about it. With rhetorical artistry, Obama took pride in his toughness, reassured by lawyers who told him killings in self-defense were not assassinations. Assistant Attorney General David Barron's secret memo that provided the legal foundation for killing Awlaki, an American citizen, "treated the word *assassination* as a term of art," observed journalist Charlie Savage.[178]

"War is beautiful," the Futurists wrote in their early manifesto, "because it establishes human domination over the subjugated machinery. . . . War is beautiful because it creates the new architectural form of big tanks, geometrical flight formations, smoke spirals from burning villages."[179] In his diary, Lieutenant Colonel Wolfram von Richthofen, the Nazi in charge of bombing Gernika, wrote of "marvelous effects of the bombardment."[180] Similarly President Truman, hearing the news of the effects of "Little Boy" on Hiroshima, ecstatically praised the atomic bomb as "the greatest thing in history!" The latest creation in technological marvels is the remote-controlled, pilotless drone.

Quoting the Italian Futurists, Walter Benjamin wrote that with "the aestheticization of politics" "all efforts . . . culminate in one thing: war."[181] For Benjamin, "The logical result of Fascism is the introduction of aesthetics into political life." Such command to create art unconcerned with the destruction of the world is the ultimate perfection of the aesthete's *l'art pour l'art*—its ultimate expectation being that war will supply "the artistic gratification of a sense perception that has been altered by technology." The final result of such aestheticization of politics is that humanity's "self-alienation has reached such a degree that it is capable of experiencing its own destruction as an aesthetic enjoyment of the highest order."[182] "Shock and Awe" was the name of the initial massive US-led campaign against Iraq in March 2003. Whatever it was for the inhabitants of Baghdad, for the world watching on TV, Shock and Awe was *awesome*. According to a *New York Times*/CBS poll, 62 percent agreed with the attack, even if only 8 percent thought it made terrorist retaliation less likely. It was war as spectacle, documentary drama, prime-time TV—*war as art*.

Ten thousand feet high in the sky, drones are the latest step in technological aestheticization and sensorial distancing from the targeted enemy. The enemy is no longer a real body, even for a warrior attacker, but an image seen from a screen in Creech, Las Vegas. The hunter's eye must perceive not the fatal consequences but the direction of the goal, the operational geometry, the precise execution in destroying a target. Aesthetics is needed to frame the event and monitor the viewer's perception. Then there's the added assumption of precision, *pinpointed* being the magical word for robots firing missiles from far away—accompanied with the image of hitting the needle in a haystack.[183] Drones provide the required geographical distance and technological proximity for making assassination efficient, precise, legal, and aesthetically pleasurable.

As De Quincey sets out to establish "the principles of murder," he first refers to "the kind of person" suited to carry out a perfect murder, suggesting, "I suppose it is evident that he ought to be a good man." His explanation takes us back to the aesthetic of tragedy, "For the final purpose of murder, considered as a fine art, is precisely the same as that of tragedy, in Aristotle's account of it, viz., 'to cleanse the heart by means of pity and terror.' Now, terror there may be, but how can there be any pity for one tiger destroyed by another tiger?"[184] Only a *good* man ordering the killing makes killing tragic and arouses our pity—only a man like Obama, described as Hamletian in his attempts to balance the various pressures of his administration, who voiced hope and reason, who promised to reduce violence, who countered his racist opponents with dignity, who wept openly for the US children killed by gun violence, who movingly sang "Amazing Grace" after the racist killings in Charleston's Emanuel Church. Indeed, one might imagine that Obama, while performing his duties as commander in chief, would empathize with De Quincey's self-proclaimed predicament: "my infirmity being notoriously too much milkiness of heart. . . . I am too soft. . . . In fact, I'm for peace, and quietness, and fawningness, and what may be styled *knocking-underness*."[185] The art of killing had to wait for the drone, with its "realm of video games and button-pushing murder," to truly excel in its knocking-under style, killing beautifully and with robotic precision for a Hamletian president.[186] De Quincey would have applauded.

3 Drone Wars Returning from the Future

Time is the difference between science fiction and actual reality. There is no requirement of real time in fantasy or myth. Terrorism takes place in real time, yet its discourse and policies show a tendency to manipulate the axis of time. Counterterrorist thinking has a peculiar relation to time, as threats and preemption, two of its basic components, are largely based on the unreality of future events. Waiting becomes inevitable, and actual historical temporality is subservient to the feared future. Such distortions of time are constitutive of counterterror policies and culture. If there are no violent attacks, the counterterrorist claims success in having prevented them; if the attacks do occur, the counterterrorist can say, "I told you so." In either case, impervious to historical error, counterterrorism is always right in its fear-based predictions.

SELF-FULFILLING PROPHECIES

Oedipus's father was told that his son would murder him and marry his wife. The prophecy became true because the father attempted to escape it: he left his son in the forest to die, a brutal act that prefigured another future violent encounter during which the young man's defensive reaction resulted, unknown to him, in the aggressor's, his father's, death. The communication of the prediction to those affected, and the subsequent efforts to elude it, made it become true.

"Self-fulfilling prophecy" is the sociological concept of such a "return from the future." Sociologist Robert Merton calls it "a false definition of the situation evoking a new behavior which makes the original false conception come true."[1] Terrorism foretold also turns frequently into prophecy fulfilled—a time warp at the heart of counterterrorist mythology. Counterterrorism is a discourse in the future perfect continuous "will have been" by which mostly unknown events are all of a sudden interpreted in the symbolism of the apocalyptic danger now. Thus, by returning from the future, terrorist fears become a present hallucinatory real.

Such bending of the axis of time recalls as well the pivotal role of *transference* in psychoanalysis, or the famous "time paradox" of science fiction—when a fictional subject travels in opposite directions to the past or the future and "things which mean nothing all of a sudden signify something, but in a quite different domain."[2] Unconscious transference of fears and hopes makes possible such a journey into the future, a knowledge that is an illusion but a necessary one for the subject to find its truth—when meaningless traces of the imaginary become "realized in the Symbolic" and unconscious vestiges of the past "will have been" in the future.[3] The repressed content of the symptom returns from the detour of the future, allowing the subject to bring about and change the traumatic past, and "the Truth arises from misrecognition."[4] The truth of counterterrorism arises from examining how wars return from such a misrecognized and self-propelling future.

One can find much evidence that drones are a self-fulfilling prophecy. Currently dozens of countries besides the US are developing drone technology for military robots, and drone use by terrorists "is not far away."[5] Jo Becker and Scott Shane, in addition to others, reported: "Drones have replaced Guantánamo as the recruitment tool of choice for militants."[6] A report by the Stanford and NYU law schools states: "There is strong evidence to suggest that US drone strikes have facilitated recruitment to violent non-state armed groups, and motivate attacks against both US military and civilian targets."[7] The authors add that the evidence that drone strikes increase terrorism is gathered from "many of the journalists, NGO and humanitarian workers, medical professionals, and Pakistani governmental officials with whom we spoke" and that "numerous policy analysts, officials, and independent observers have come to similar conclusions."[8] Admiral Michael Mullen, the same chairman of the Joint Chiefs of Staff who recommended obliterating an entire training camp to kill just one target, put it most clearly: "Each time an errant bomb or a bomb accurately aimed but against the wrong target kills or hurts civilians, we risk setting our strategy back months, if not years. . . . Civilian casualty incidents such as those we've recently seen in Afghanistan will hurt us more in the long run than any tactical success we may achieve against the enemy."[9]

Former colonel Andrew Bacevich argues that American military strategy since Reagan, and especially since Bush's War on Terror, "has been characterized by attempts to wish reality away."[10] He sees in the grand strategy of the National Security Council "extreme agitation laced with paranoia, delusions of grandeur, and a cavalier disregard for empirical truth . . . with just a little connection to reality."[11] Bacevich places at the source of this delusion the "causal" link between the American thirst for oil, credit, and consumer goods on the one hand and "our penchant for empire" on the other.[12] And this leads to the "contempt for international law," the "embrace of preventive war," the presumption of a "prerogative of waging war when and where [the US] sees fit" with the pretense of doing it "on freedom's behalf," imperial ambition that is "self-defeating and irrational," based on "hubris and sanctimony." Hypocrisy regarding these activities inhibits self-understanding: "The hypocrite ends up fooling mainly himself."[13] Those responsible at the highest level for the disasters that ensue are held the least accountable; "A private who loses a rifle suffers far greater consequences than a general who loses a war."[14]

How is it that military leaders are so prone to grand delusions, and how do they convince the nation to support them? In strict military thinking, Bacevich points to "the intersection of three great illusions." First is the pretense that new technologies have reinvented armed conflict so that a leader or regime can be targeted without having to go to war and without having casualties. Drones are an example of this fantasy of attack and invulnerability. Second is the belief in a set of principles based on the military dominance of the US that found expression in the Weinberger-Powell doctrine of using overwhelming force. Third is the illusion that the divorce between the military and the public caused by the Vietnam War has been patched up, that there is a renewed love affair by which support for troops is guaranteed. The wars fought in the Middle East, particularly since 9/11, with the "preposterous" prospect "of waging war on a global scale for decades," showed that the generals who believed in such "puerile expectations" were "guilty of flagrant professional malpractice, if not outright fraud" and that their views were deliberate attempts to ignore war's permanent and intractable components of uncertainty and risk.[15] All the enemy needed to bring to a crashing halt the overwhelming power of the US military were the simple improvised explosive devices, which could be built at the cost of a pizza and could easily target Americans. Bacevich mentions Reinhold Niebuhr, Obama's "favorite philosopher," to argue "the folly of preventive war"; for Niebuhr preventive war was not only "morally wrong; it was also mad."[16]

Bacevich could have quoted Hannah Arendt, when she described the links between totalitarianism and fantasy: "The elite is not composed of ideologists; its members' whole education is aimed at abolishing their capacity for distinguishing between truth and falsehood, between reality and fiction. Their superiority consists in their ability immediately to dissolve every statement of fact into a declaration of purpose."[17]

Obama took office promising to end the war in Iraq while focusing on the war in Afghanistan, from where bin Laden had staged his attack on 9/11. The Petraeus-led "surge" in Iraq created the illusion that the withdrawal of US troops was something other than a retreat. Obama appointed Stanley McChrystal to lead the Afghan war. The new general soon requested his own "surge" of forty thousand troops. Obama grudgingly accepted, tripling Afghan forces. McChrystal organized an operation coded Moshtarak ("together") to make the city of Marja a model enclave liberated from the Taliban. Soon, however, it became the site of "a full-blown guerrilla insurgency."[18] The result, writes Bacevich, was that "McChrystal's attempt to pacify just one small Afghan city . . . came nowhere close to succeeding. . . . The problem was ignorance, laced with hubris."[19] McChrystal himself admitted to "superficial understanding of the situation" and "a frighteningly simplistic view of history."[20] A major tenet of such a simplistic view of recent Afghan history is the merging of al-Qaeda and the Taliban into a single terrorist enemy.[21]

It wasn't that McChrystal was completely ignorant of these dynamics that led to his failure in Afghanistan. He himself had stated, "We're going to lose the fucking war if we don't stop killing civilians. . . . If we . . . use our technological capabilities carelessly . . . then we should not be upset when someone responds with their equivalent, which is a suicide bomb in Central Park, because that's what they can respond with."[22] McChrystal's claim was supported by his head of intelligence, Major General Flynn, who noted, "Merely killing insurgents usually serves to multiply enemies rather than subtract them."[23] Flynn was replaced by Petraeus, who doubled the number of mostly night raids, further increasing American unpopularity; under him civilian casualties and displacement dramatically increased along with American casualties, rising from 798 in the last year of Bush's presidency to 5,000 a year under Petraeus. Still, on national television, Obama declared his Afghan surge a success.

News of "success" in the War on Terror would continue, extending drone warfare from Afghanistan and Pakistan to Yemen, Somalia, and Libya in a War for the Greater Middle East but without making any real difference. Secretary Clinton's primary intervention in the War on Terror was the killing of Gaddafi in Libya—"We came, we saw, he died," she declared, echoing dictator Julius Caesar's boast "I came, I saw, I conquered" after one of his swift victories. The unconcealed imperial aspirations of the US counterterror warriors led soon to the disaster at the US embassy in Benghazi and the current Libyan chaos. The decision to go to war with Libya was taken by Obama while he was in Brazil promoting American business; the lawyers would not allow to use the term *war* because they hadn't sought congressional authorization.[24] Gaddafi had gotten rid of his nuclear ambitions in 2003 to appease the Western powers. This was the Empire's payback and a lesson for North Korea and Iran in case they also get rid of their nuclear programs.

The war in Iraq best reveals the retro-feeding aspects of the War on Terror. Bacevich explains the four Gulf Wars as follows: the first war (1980–87) was in support of Saddam Hussein against Iran; the second (1991) was to punish an emboldened Hussein for invading Kuwait; the third (2002) was to eject Hussein from power; and the fourth (from 2013 on) was to fight the Islamic State or ISIS, which had evolved from the failure of the Iraqi regime created by the US and abandoned after US forces retreated from the country. Bush's war, Operation Iraqi Freedom, with its stated goal of fighting terrorism, not only killed over six hundred thousand Iraqis but produced al-Qaeda in Iraq. Similarly with the War in Afghanistan, "While General McChrystal's counterterrorism campaign had depleted AQI [al-Qaeda in Iraq], ISIS had emerged as its successor."[25] Clearly, while the stated goal of the War on Terror is to eradicate terrorism, its result has been to generate further terror. Bacevich replies to his own question: "Why did Washington choose to reengage militarily in Iraq? Because it couldn't think of anything better to do."[26]

By 2005, American forces in Iraq were obsessed with Abu Musab Al Zarqawi, the alleged link between Saddam and al-Qaeda. They imagined that by eliminating him the insurgency would collapse. So they killed him and hung "a twice life-size matte photo-portrait of the dead jihadi in a large gilt frame that reminded some who viewed it of a hunting trophy."[27] A week later Al-Masri, his successor, was judged to be "worse."[28] The new leader who saw Iraq as part of a wider war activated suicide bombers, and attacks on Americans dramatically increased. Noting that 3,149 had died in June alone, McChrystal admitted that "Zarqawi's focused sectarian killing helped inaugurate a system of violence that was, by the time he died, a self-propelling cycle."[29] Other reports repeat similar stories.[30]

Historian Gareth Porter would find evidence of the same logic by which the obsessive targeting of Taliban "leaders and facilitators" produced "a direct correlation between stepped-up rate of raids in Kandahar Province in southern Afghanistan and the number of homemade roadside bombs reported by locals to the American forces."[31] The probability that eliminating a high-value target can lead to an even worse substitution was shown again when the killing of Hakimullah Mehsud increased the influence of his rivals the Haqqanis, later designated as "terrorists" by the US, and produced the next leader, Maulana Fazlullah, known for his calls for beheadings.

Researcher Saba Imtiaz found that for Pakistanis the drone war is "America's war" and that "the debate has now reached a point where drone strikes alone are widely believed to be one of the major causes of militancy in Pakistan."[32] Nawaz Sharif's Pakistani government advocated ending the US drone program. Peter Bergen agreed: "If the price of the drone campaign that increasingly kills low-level Taliban is alienating 180 million Pakistanis that is too high a price to pay."[33] Indeed, 94 percent of Pakistanis believe drones kill too many innocent victims. But not so the Americans, who "are almost unique in thinking that the deaths of foreign civilians are largely insignificant in relation to national security concerns."[34]

"The one civilian that you killed has now turned an entire village against you," law professor Greg McNeal notes, and that "has to be part of the calculus if your military or strategic goal is to win hearts and minds."[35] Ibrahim Mothana concurs that the US "drone program is leading to the Talibanization of vast tribal areas and the radicalization of people who would otherwise be America's allies."[36] "The drone undermined us," Brigadier Abdullah Dogar, a commander in North Waziristan, concluded; "Each drone strike puts my men in jeopardy."[37]

In his groundbreaking book *Dirty Wars,* journalist Jeremy Scahill concludes that, "from my experience in several undeclared war zones across the globe, it seems clear that the United States is helping to breed a new generation of enemies in Somalia, Yemen, Pakistan, Afghanistan and throughout the Muslim world. Those whose loved ones were killed in drone strikes or cruise missile attacks or night raids will have a legitimate score to settle."[38] The book ends with these words: "The war on terror has become a self-fulfilling prophecy."[39] And this is William Arkin's conclusion regarding the large Data Machine with its counterterror masters of software: "Their world is a self-contained and self-generating society within itself, not the real world."[40]

Robotic technology exacerbates time pressures. Robots will react with such speed, an army colonel wrote, that the decision cycle will be reduced from minutes to microseconds. The apocalyptic scenario increasingly predicted is one in which, "as the loop gets shorter and shorter, there won't be any time in it for humans."[41] is the war on terror will no longer be the perversion of the axis of time in waiting for terror but the very elimination of human time—the perfect fantasy by which humans not only will not have to fight and die but also will not have to make the tough decisions or carry the burden of consequences. The "human baggage" will be sidelined to avoid faulty senses such as human eyes.

A crucial issue in the application of robots to military use is robotic *autonomy,* prompting the question of who will make the final combat decisions, humans or robots. Whether or not man will be "in the loop" of a final decision is "the Issue-That–Must-Not-Be-Discussed."[42] The strength of emerging robotic weaponry, we are told, consists in "their ability to see and think."[43] Drones can program a destination, can fly themselves, and from the invisible altitude can follow a target for days, while a faraway operator is never in danger of being killed from below. Flying robots will soon be "in the position to take the initiative against the enemy on a battlefield," and that "pressure to let robots take the shot will be very hard to resist."[44] Some consider the requisite that man should be in the loop "a line in the sand"—that is, they consider the outsourcing of killing to machines to be unacceptable. As John Kaag and Sara Kreps argue, "The distinction between militants and non-combatants, between licit and illicit targets, is a normative one that machines cannot make—now or in some brave world."[45] But Peter Singer disturbingly adds that the constant repetition of this mantra betrays how the more you affirm something the less you believe it. It helps only to "keep people calm that this isn't the Terminators."[46]

Although the initial assumption is that humans will delegate tasks to robots but will need human permission for final decisions to act, "the problem is that it may not prove workable in reality," for "there has to be an exception, a backup plan for when communications are cut and the robot is 'fighting blind.'"[47] Robotic autonomy simply means robots don't have external remote controls or signals that humans can jam. Robot designers' goal is to increase robot autonomy, for "there are combat situations where there isn't time for the human operator to react."[48] A robotic pilot needs less than a millionth of a second to respond to a stimulus, where a human pilot takes several seconds to choose. Devices such as the countersniper automatically fire back at any shooting enemy, enabling robots to fire independent of human intervention. Singer quotes various high officials who admit that new weaponry "will be too fast, too small, too numerous, and will create an environment too complex for humans to direct" and that these new technologies "are rapidly taking us to a place where we may not want to go, but probably are unable to avoid."[49] A 2005 report by the Joint Forces Command entitled "Unmanned Effects: Taking the Human Out of the Loop" suggests that in a few years autonomous robots will be the battlefield norm. Singer's conclusion is unambiguous:

"Autonomous armed robots are coming to war."[50] The human warrior, with *no time* for decision, will obey the split-second reactions of robots.

The consequences of the drone campaign might have been expected: the number of terrorist attacks in Pakistan rose sharply, in a wave of anti-Americanism, for Pakistanis "overwhelmingly believe that most of those who die in the attacks are civilians."[51] Given the fact that drone strikes "have had a particular affinity for hitting weddings and funerals, and appear to be seriously fueling the insurgency," it is no surprise that Taliban recruits increased.[52] A UN report concluded that air strikes motivate suicide attacks, and surveys show direct links between family members killed and survivors joining or supporting the insurgency.[53] Faisal Shahzad, the Pakistani American known for the failed bomb in Times Square in May 2010, declared at his trial, "Until the hour the US . . . stops its drone strikes in Somalia and Yemen and in Pakistan, we will be attacking US, and I plead guilty to that." When the judge asked him, What if he had killed children?, Shahzad replied, "When the drones hit, they don't see children."[54] "I'm avenging the attack" for the "drones [that] kill women, children . . . everybody. . . . I am part of the answer."[55] A suicide bomber who in March 2008 targeted a CIA compound in Khost, Afghanistan, said that the suicide attack would be "the first of the revenge operations against the Americans and their drone teams outside the Pakistani borders."[56] Similarly, Najibullah Zazi, who plotted an attack against the New York subway system, spoke of "a new desire for revenge, and more recruits for a militant movement that has grown exponentially even as drone strikes have increased."[57]

Colin Powell's former chief of staff, Lawrence Wilkerson, explained succinctly how drones help terrorist groups swell: "From their point of view, this is not war, this is murder, and that's the way they look at it. It [drone killing] is recruiting terrorists all over the world. It's making young men and young women make the decision that the United States is their enemy and therefore worthy of their jihad."[58] But the simple fact that this is "murder" from the victims' perspective is the first thing counterterrorism must ignore.

A long list of US officials have acknowledged the self-fulfilling nature of drone warfare. Former US ambassadors Anne Patterson and Cameron Munter tried to veto drone strikes over Pakistan but were unsuccessful.

President Obama's national security adviser Tom Donilon also questioned the blowback produced by drones. Former commander in Afghanistan McChrystal expressed concern that the drone campaign might be compromising US interests, saying: "What scares me about drone strikes is how they are perceived around the world. . . . They are hated at a visceral level, even by people who've never seen one or seen the effects of one."[59] McChrystal's former intelligence officer, Michael Flynn, admitted before his retirement in 2014 the frustrating results of such targeting: "We kept decapitating the leadership of these groups, and more leaders would just appear from the ranks to take their place."[60] Obama's first director of national intelligence, Dennis Blair, cast doubts about drone efficacy, considering its long-term damage.[61] John Brennan acknowledged that the US was "establishing precedent that other nations may follow."[62] People most knowledgeable about the effects of drones had misgivings, aware that the new technology could come back to haunt the US. What nobody can ignore is that the US drone policy has established a precedent that "provides an easy template for other empowered actors to deploy drones for targeted killing in multiple contexts with limited adherence to core legal principles and perhaps with even less transparency."[63]

The counterterrorist position regarding the self-generating use of drones is in the end a cynical one: they know what they are doing, they know they are promoting further terrorism while forcing wars to "return from the future," but they don't care. Should anyone be surprised about the latest data stating, in a study by the Center for Strategic and International Studies, that after almost two decades of a war on terror whose costs are measured in trillions and in hundreds of thousands of lives, the number of Salafi-jihadists combatants increased 270 percent from 2001 to 2018?[64] And so it goes.

THE TERROR FACTORY

If you want to show US counterterrorism's constitutive need for terrorists and the use of narrative fantasy to manufacture them, there are dozens of cases from which to choose. A typical one is the one known as the Liberty City Seven,[65] the alleged al-Qaeda operatives arrested in Miami on June

22, 2006. With "Terror Raid" or "Terror Arrests" flashes to the public on the screen, the alarming news was that these Muslim terrorists were going to blow up the Sears Tower in Chicago and the FBI office in North Miami Beach. Since the FBI and the media were certain there were terrorist sleeper cells in the US, all disbelief was suspended, and there was no question about the veracity of the plot. The day after the arrests, Attorney General Alberto Gonzales held a news conference confirming that the arrested plotters had been about to wage "a full ground war against the United States." Then Alex Acosta, US attorney and later secretary of labor with President Trump, added that the terrorists had hoped their attacks would be "just as good or greater than 9/11."[66]

The reality of the plot was something else, however. As Trevor Aaronson, journalist and director of the Florida Center for Investigative Reporting, concluded, "The only terrorist involved in the case was an *imaginary* one on the FBI payroll."[67] All the media had to do to assess the nature of the plot was to read the eleven-page indictment, where they would have learned that the terrorists, allegedly about to repeat 9/11, had, in fact, no weapons or explosives and that their only link to al-Qaeda was an FBI informant posing as a terrorist. It took more than four months before any journalist interviewed the primary defendant's wife. By then the news was off the front pages. Aaronson delves into the story of how the FBI fabricated the plot. Its central character, Narseal Batiste, a street preacher who "was a natural-born bullshitter and hustler,"[68] was having problems paying rent on his warehouse and was promised $50,000 by an FBI undercover agent posing as al-Qaeda. James J. Wedick, a former FBI agent whom Batiste had hired to review the case, later told Aaronson, "These guys couldn't find their way down the end of the street. . . . They were homeless types. . . . They only cared about the money. When we put forth a case like that to suggest to the American public that we're protecting them, we're not protecting them. The agents in the bullpen, they know it's not true."[69]

For years now, we have become used to these plots routinely fabricated by the counterterrorist state and the media. Aaronson describes the sequence of events that regularly end up in the evening headline news:

> Informants report to their handlers on people who have, say, made statements sympathizing with terrorists. Those names are then cross-referenced

with existing intelligence data, such as immigration and criminal records. FBI agents may then assign an undercover operative to approach the target by posing as a radical. Sometimes the operative will propose a plot, provide explosives, even lead the target in a fake oath to Al Qaeda. Many times the target hasn't shown any inclination to commit crime, whereas the informant leading the plot has a long history in crime. Once enough incriminating information has been gathered, there's an arrest—and a press conference announcing another foiled plot.[70]

In March 2009 a report by a national coalition of Islamic organizations expanded on "several high-profile cases in which informers have infiltrated mosques and have helped promote plots."[71] The rationale for the Justice Department to prosecute these cases, which normally end in a thirty- to forty-year prison sentence for the guys caught in the sting, is "preemptive prosecution"—conspiracy charges for what the plotters *would have done* had they not first been prompted and then busted by law enforcement. Ana Jhones, attorney for Batiste, told the jury: "This is not a terrorism case. This is a manufactured crime."[72] One of the informants earned $85,000 and another, $21,000. For the FBI and Justice Department the Liberty City Seven became a test case for what post-9/11 law would allow regarding terrorism cases in court; it proved that the government "could win terrorism prosecutions even when no evidence linked the defendants to actual terrorists."[73] It sent a message to lawyers that the Justice Department could win these cases and played a role in winning guilty pleas in almost all terrorism stings. The juries, it seems, don't buy the defense's argument that the FBI informant came up with the idea and moved the plot forward. By 2011 Aaronson found approximately *fifty* terrorism cases in which the informant was an agent provocateur who provided the plan and means for the terrorist plot; the defendants argued entrapment, but none was successful.

What else but fantasy and playacting could be decisive in the making of these would-be-plotters? The alleged terrorists often would not distinguish fact from fiction, as in the case of James Cromitie. US district judge Colleen McMahon admitted during sentencing that Cromitie was "bigoted and suggestible, one who was incapable of committing an act of terrorism on his own" but who "created acts of terrorism out of his fantasies of bravado and bigotry, and then made those fantasies come true." Before sentencing him to twenty-five years in prison, McMahon added, "Only the government could have made a terrorist out of Mr. Cromitie, whose buffoonery is positively Shakespearean in scope."[74] Judges know they are sending suspects to decades of prison for their playacting, a charade of justice they tolerate because in their own counterterror frame of mind they themselves believe Terrorism is the most real Thing.

Not surprisingly, several rank-and-file officers confessed to Aaronson that "chasing terrorists is like chasing ghosts—you'll only see them if you're willing to let your eyes play tricks on you."[75] On the premise that "we're at war with an idea," leading to the motto that "one man's terrorist is another man's fool," Aaronson concludes: "The FBI currently spends $3 billion annually to hunt an enemy that is largely of its own creation. Evidence in dozens of terrorism cases—involving plots to blow up synagogues, skyscrapers, military recruiting stations, and bars and nightclubs—suggests that today's terrorists in the United States are nothing more than FBI creations, impressionable men living on the edges of society who become bomb-triggering would-be killers only because of the actions of FBI informants . . . [thus] creating what a federal judge has called a 'fantasy terror operation.'"[76] Such "FBI creations" are a form of narrative art and make-believe for both counterterrorism and the media; while producing the illusion that the public is protected from terrorism, they increase the media's ratings and justify the billions of dollars counterterrorism receives from the government.

According to a Heritage Foundation report, the US foiled sixty terrorist plots during the decade after 9/11.[77] Theresa May, then home secretary, on November 2014 claimed that British security services had foiled forty terror plots since the 2005 London attacks.[78] Only later did it turn out that plots that were known as the Washington Metro bombing plot, the New York subway plot, the plot to blow up the Sears Tower, the plot to bomb a Portland Christmas tree lighting, and dozens more were organized and led by the FBI, but this information has barely registered with the general public.

Aaronson, having examined all the high-profile terrorism plots of the decade from 2001 to 2011, concludes that "of the 508 defendants, 243 had been targeted through an FBI informant, 158 had been caught in an FBI terrorism sting, and 49 had encountered an agent provocateur.[79] With the exception of three cases, most of them were small-time criminals, people who made some false statement (72 cases) or were prosecuted for immigration violations (121 cases).[80] "Of the 508 cases, I could count on one hand the number of actual terrorists."[81] Attorney Eric Holder argued that sting operations have "proven to be an essential law enforcement tool in uncovering and preventing potential terror attacks."[82] But his claim doesn't take into account the extent to which sting operations are actually *creating* terrorism. Sting operations are about the intentionality of potential terrorists; they illustrate counterterrorism's need to act before the crimes are committed—its primary evidence mere clues about future possible events. Aaronson concludes by stating the most elementary, inaugural fact: "The organization responsible for more terrorist plots over the last decade than any other is the FBI."[83] As one defense lawyer put it, "They're creating crimes to solve crimes so they can claim a victory in the war on terror."[84]

The 9/11 events were preceded by a previous terrorist attack on the Twin Towers in February 1993; six people were killed and more than a thousand injured. A key protagonist behind the plotting of the 1993 attack was identified as Omar Abdel-Rahman, also known as "the Blind Sheik."[85] He was imprisoned for life after that attack, on the grounds of informer Emad Salem's stories, including an alleged fatwa by the Blind Sheik—a charge never proved in court. The *New York Times* reported on the trial that Salem "began his testimony by admitting that he had lied to just about everybody he ever met," that he was "always ready with another believe-or-not exploit," and that his testimony sounded *"like sheer fantasy."*[86] An editorial added that the indictment of the Sheik "only required to prove *the intention* to wage a terror campaign," adding that "only the sketchiest connections [were] established between Sheik Omar Abdel-Rahman and the alleged mastermind of that crime, Ramzi Ahmed Yousef."[87]

Aaronson's discoveries on the manufacture of imaginary terror and on the manipulation of the courts in terrorism cases bring an added question mark to the reality of the testimony "like sheer fantasy" on which the Blind Sheik was condemned to life in prison. Many Muslims, including Osama bin Laden, who had been supporting his stay in the US, and Ayman al-Zawahiri, who had been tortured with him in an Egyptian prison, considered the Blind Sheik their supreme spiritual leader and legal authority.

Salem's "fantasy" was not just his; the counterterrorism industry had recruited Salem and was monitoring his every step. According to John Miller and Michael Stone, the infiltrated "Salem was offering to restart the paramilitary training that had lapsed in the year since Nosair's [Al Khifa's former leader's] arrest."[88] Salem was the one who secured "a warehouse in which to build bombs."[89] Not surprisingly, there was concern within the FBI that "the Bureau was training potential terrorists, holy warriors who may not be breaking the law now, but who might one day turn the skills they were acquiring against the US."[90] Robert Friedman showed that the CIA's involvement with the first attack on the World Trade Center was, through setting up jihad offices such as Al Khifa across the country, "far greater" than the general public knew and that by 1985 "the CIA had inadvertently managed to do something that America's enemies have been unable to: give terrorism a foothold in the United States."[91]

Salem had tried unsuccessfully for months to record on tape the Blind Sheik's fatwa to act against US interests. Soon after the Sheik's life sentence, his sons were plotting to hijack planes and distributing plastic-laminated cards of their father's photograph and "will" for a fatwa calling for America's destruction. Journalist and CNN terrorism expert Peter Bergen, who interviewed bin Laden and many other al-Qaeda jihadists, insists that the plastic cards are "a key to understanding why some three thousand Americans lost their lives on the morning of September 11, 2001."[92] Much as Aaronson found in other plots, the FBI planted someone in the Blind Sheik's circle to activate illegal paramilitary activities, including renting a warehouse for them to start making bombs. The premise was preemptively to push potential terrorists into action to find out how far they would go. The counterterrorist informer was *playing terrorist* in order to catch the real terrorists, and in the process promoting terrorism and promoting himself.

The latest twist in the self-fulfilling prophecy of friends turning into archenemies and their reversal when convenient has to do precisely with al-Qaeda, whose elimination, we have been told ad nauseam, was the entire rationale for the War on Terror after 9/11. By branding any adversarial combatant "al-Qaeda," US counterterrorism extended its drone warfare to various countries of the Middle East. Prior to 9/11, during Reagan's anti-Soviet insurgency in Afghanistan, there was a well-established alliance between Osama bin Laden (founder of al-Qaeda), the Blind Sheik, and their jihadist group with the CIA. Former friends later turned into deadly enemies. But now, after two decades of an all-out War on Terror on which we have spent trillions, isn't it time to make of al-Qaeda an ally again? This is in fact what a recent AP report is claiming: now that the Houthis have gotten rid of al-Qaeda in Yemen, the US and the Saudi-led coalition have cut secret deals and recruited al-Qaeda fighters in Yemen in a military alliance to battle Houthi rebels.[93] Old friends turned archenemies may now be allies again. And so the terror factory keeps thriving.

PLAYING TERRORIST: FORMLESS POWERS AND ARTFUL NARRATIVES

Terrorism is the subversion of the explicit, regulated structure of normal politics in organizational, legal, and social terms. Given the invisible and illegal nature of revolutionary/terrorist action, its abrogation of form in all aspects is quintessential to it, expressed in its logic of chance, disregard for stable rule, ritual bluff, and contagious taboo. By its very nature, it is an underground politics, informal, disorderly, and ritualistic in that it enacts disorder. The militant subject formed in this type of action relies, not on parliamentarian or representative politics, but on the charisma of revolutionary martyrdom—the antinomian persona discussed in the previous chapter of being at once "a priest and a murderer."[94] One dimension of such *formlessness* is the difficulty of ending a terrorist type of war, as there are no established protocols for such unstructured action;[95] the lack of formal structures makes "the war on terror" essentially endless and unwinnable.

Underground groups are characterized by breaking through norms into anomaly, in an ontological dynamics between form and formlessness that is also intrinsic to the metaphysical powers and dangers of magic, pollution, taboo, and ritual in general.[96] At the level of the imaginary, fantasy replicates the chaotic vagrancy of anomalous unconstrained forms. Such "formless" states in actual cultural institutions and political behavior, as in fantasy formations, are empowered with simultaneous notions of the sacred and the exceptional. Key to anthropological understanding is

how "ritual recognizes the potency of disorder."[97] Anomaly is not an oddity in the history of social and political movements when one thinks of
revolutionary periods, millennial cults, or infamous massacres. In general,
"A paradoxical relation and a dialectic tension . . . exists between taxon-
omy and anomaly."[98]

Counterterrorism tends to replicate terrorist anomaly by mimetically
adopting similar principles and tactics. In the case of the War on Terror,
the formlessness of terrorism begins with the question of whether such
war is in fact *war*. "Are drones engaged in something readily recognizable
as war?," Hugh Gusterson asks.[99] He echoes the conclusions of three UN
special rapporteurs that "the disparate targets attacked by US drones in
various countries . . . fail to rise to the standard of a single armed group . . .
with which, under international law, the United States could be said to be
at war."[100] Gusterson finds the liberal theory about war "somehow askew"
because it is the very notion of "war" that we should question—in drone
warfare in particular.[101]

Another dimension of such dissolution of form has to do with the *borderless* nature of the War on Terror. Inherent to the hunter's pursuit is the
violation of any boundary by the prey. Counterterrorism's approach to
finding and eliminating its target creates also a borderless territory in
which all boundaries fixed by nations, laws, or conventions disappear
when the target is a runaway terrorist. In classically colonial settings, as
described by Franz Fanon, occupation meant establishing clear boundaries and internal barriers to control the natives on the basis of the premise
of reciprocal exclusivity.[102] Drones eliminate reciprocity by technological
means and thus can dispense with territorial boundaries. The "formlessness" typical of anything touched by terrorism is displaced to territoriality.
Drones are displayed in the "in between" of civilization and barbarism—
they exemplify the antistructural "liminality" of being between countries
and established national boundaries, as well as between legal and illegal
actions and animal and human categories. "Terrorism" is the name for the
imperial superpower's license to dissolve any national border or political
category for the sake of fighting an enemy conceived as a prepolitical animal to be controlled only through hunting via satellite. Like the hunter,
the drone imperial power is not interested in the takeover of a territory; it
cares only for the hit-and-run operation—the killing that proves who is

sovereign. If all modern armies have recognized the command of aerial space as the hallmark of military power, the drone projects sovereignty by collapsing territorial boundaries with impunity.

A logical consequence, leading to questionable legal claims, is that the terrorist battlefield is everywhere—thus the US should have the right to act against terrorists anywhere it deems necessary. This justification emerges from the view that the very form of international law can be abrogated in the fight against terrorism, given the formless nature of the enemy (total disrespect for any law, morality, or politics), in a war without end. Thus terrorist lawlessness gives ground to state lawlessness. Drones have turned the US Empire into a borderless counterterrorist geography dubbed "the first post-territorial empire, a nation whose power and influence have enabled it to transcend traditional concepts of territory and frontiers to exert its influence on a global scale."[103] The drones create a new supranational military theater of operations, a territory equipped with its own maps, rules, and politics, extended over a dozen Middle Eastern and northeastern African countries. Concepts such as "nations" or "citizens" or "territorial sovereignty" do not apply. The result of these eliminations of borders and international legal structures in a "Predator empire" is that "drones are an imperial border-control technology for the age of late capitalism . . . [that] can be used against countries that lack the technological sophistication to shoot down the slow-moving planes."[104] Not surprisingly, the idea of a borderless battlefield against terrorism is "rejected almost universally" outside Washington.[105]

Also grounded on the dynamics between form and formlessness is the key notion of *play,* an activity ruled by the premise that "all the statements in this frame are untrue."[106] To see how "This is play" applies to terrorism, one need only consider the case of the Unabomber, who wrote a letter to the media stating his deadly threats were a "prank."[107] We might say of the Unabomber that he was simply playing terrorist and that so were the counterterrorist FBI agents and informants who posed as radical Islamists to snare potential terrorists, or drone pilots who describe their work as "playing Nintendo." If in general "war is a lie," terrorism as military strategy is close to the concept of stratagem—a class of ploys that implies play-like

trickery, disinformation, bluffing, threat, betrayal, deception, ambush, surprise, feigned attacks and retreats, sophistic treaties, and more.[108]

On the edge between "This is war" and "This is play," between the real
and the fantasy, terrorism produces violent *copycat* events. Frequently
there is a mimetic duplication between terrorism and counterterrorism.
Begoña Aretxaga has argued that the state may engage itself in such terrorist playacting with violent results. She examined the response of the
Spanish state terror to ETA's terrorism as mimetic terrorist desire, namely,
"an organized mimesis of terrorism as the constituting force of the state as
subject."[109] State officials even decided to organize an extortion system
similar to ETA's to kidnap French industrialists and levy a "revolutionary
tax." In what we might call a case of terrorism envy, Aretxaga observes that
what mattered to state officials was "the power emanating from mimetic
action, the enactment of the desire to be a terrorist." For the state, "fantasy
cannot be separated from the calculated objectives that originally triggered the actions of terror. Indeed, it is through the enactment of fantasy
in mimetic performance that terror becomes real and the state powerful."[110] If terrorists can kidnap and torture and kill, why can't our powerful
state?

As in play, in ritual the meaning of certain actions does not denote what
they stand for. A bite means aggression, but a ritual bite between two playing dogs does not mean aggression. Many terrorist acts can be seen as
ritual bluff within symbolic discourse. Ritual simulation compensates for
military disadvantages. By definition, what a threat denotes is different
from what may actually happen. Bluff is one thing and combat quite
another, yet military strategy is notorious for the use of bluff and stratagem. The detection of bluffs and false threats is central to counterterrorism. Not chess, but poker, where cards are unpredictable and bluffing is an
essential tactic to the game, might be the best model for the kind of systemic knowledge needed for this type of warfare.

The abrogation of form typical of terrorism leads ultimately to its categorical confusions between the frames of "war," "threat," "play," "ritual"—
frames that contain internal paradoxes of the type "I'm lying."

A central dimension of terrorism, and one that is crucial to its retro-
feeding quality, has to do with *threats* and their perception, and the

reactions they provoke. A threat plays with the sign as representing a future event, while we never know for certain whether the issuer actually means it. Counterterrorism is a prime example of what Merton labeled "the Thomas theorem": "If men define situations as real, they are real in their consequences."[111] Once the situation is defined as one of inevitable terrorism and endless waiting, what could happen weighs as much as the actual case; once a threat, whose intention or possibility is unknown to us, is taken seriously, its reality requires that we act on it. What is most defining and terrifying about contemporary terrorism is the "not if but when" of nuclear terrorism. Nothing has been more consequential in the War on Terror than the Bush administration's doctrine of preemption that was first tested in the war in Iraq. By definition, "the logic of pre-emption entails action *before* the event, and relies upon an imaginary of extreme threats, which justify otherwise unthinkable actions."[112]

Knowing when threats are real and when they are bluffs, the intentionality inherent in them, is central to managing terrorist crises. Remember that the US went to war with Iraq in part because it didn't know Hussein was bluffing. Whether you become "terrorized" by a threat, and thus give validity to it, will depend in good part on your reaction to it—based on the right or wrong guess regarding the intentionality behind the threat. Hence the relevance of John Mueller's question: "Which is the greater threat: terrorism, or our reaction to it?"[113] The critical policy task becomes, in Richard English's title, "how to respond" to terrorism.[114]

Dimensions essential to terrorism such as its fantasy framework, play-acting, or the above-discussed "terror factory" underline one key component of the entire phenomenon: the power of a well-crafted *narrative* turned into reality TV. Like a news story, terrorism is an action with a plot and a narrative sequence, a discursive and political construct in which "the event is that which can be narrated."[115] As with any storyteller or historian, the writer of terrorism must select a narrative form. No matter how "real" the facts being described, the writer cannot escape the shadow of the "tropes" of narration (metaphor, metonym, synecdoche, irony): that is, "the process by which all discourse *constitutes* the objects which it pretends only to describe realistically and to analyze objectively."[116] We must inquire to what extent the discourse on terrorism borrows from the art of rhetoric and fiction—not that the information provided is feigned but that the *crafting* of the story shapes and molds the narrative. Rhetoric becomes pivotal to the phenomenon; it shapes and responds to the public interpretation and reaction to the terrorist strategy, for as in literary art "the response . . . becomes the primary persuasive vehicle for the terrorists."[117]

Terrorism stories turned into reality shows can be made part of a long tradition of American humbugs and hoaxes by which fake Indians and con men belong to the national narrative—in particular to the American obsession with fabricating "wild" men such as the hoaxer P. T. Barnum's "Wild Men of Borneo" and "the Wild Australian Children," along with Ishi, the "last wild Indian," as anthropological exotica. Terrorists are the most recent fillers for this fantasy of wildness, the new villains of bunk stories fabricated by politicians or television newscasters, whose ratings benefit from a culture of foreign omnipresent threat. "The hoax warns us without warning and informs us without informing," like the failed terrorist plots manufactured by the FBI; "it welcomes us into its arms, where . . . it gives voice to our fears and fantasies as unremittingly real."[118]

We know of various well-publicized cases of terrorism hoaxes, such as Lara Logan's *60 Minutes* episode "Embassy House," in which she encouraged Dylan Davies's false claims that he had been a hero during the terrorist attack against the Benghazi embassy, when in fact he was not even present during the attack; or Judith Miller's series of stories on the front page of the *New York Times* on Saddam Hussein's WMDs that could end up in terrorist hands. Another example of a semihoax narrative is how the White House portrayed the killing of bin Laden to the media, given what Seymour Hersh later found out.[119]

Hoaxes are believed "because they confirm what we suspect—but cannot know or, better yet, prove."[120] They cater to voters' or audience's prejudices. The hoaxer's art derives from the knowledge that a hoax is "a fantasy in search of a fact."[121] Once a fantasy, the looking glass through which we see our most intimate fears and wishes, is made real by the evening news, who can prove that it is largely counterterrorist fabrication? In an era of fake news and postfact journalism, the hoax fools us with its revelations "not of what's true but of what we truly believe."[122] By the time they turn into "news," narrative hoaxes are solid political reality.

Narrative is also a pivotal weapon in the counterterrorist tool kit. If any critical view of the culture of counterterrorism is soon confronted with its constitutive components of myth and bluff, the counterterrorist's task is to create the reality effect by which the public can never forget the threatening evils out there—"the world as it is." Obama's main spinmeister and assistant, the speechwriter Ben Rhodes, entitled his memoir *The World as It Is* to reflect his "mind meld" with his boss. Both saw that their main job at the White House was a "restructuring of the American narrative."[123] Narrative is what Obama and Rhodes, both writers, are very skillful at and what they practiced in order to sell their various deals through a cascade of social media posts and tweets. A qualitative change has taken place in the news business having to do with platforms such as Facebook and the fact that 40 percent of newspaper professionals have lost their jobs; the average reporter now is "27 years old," Rhodes observed, and "they literally know nothing."[124] It was the spinmeister's "real mastery of an art" turned into "war room" that, by using the latest tools in the way information moves, and by mixing policy, politics, and messaging, would manipulate and when necessary mislead public opinion to the administration's advantage.

Obama himself had tried successfully the power of narrative in his memoir *Dreams from My Father.* The last thought that comes to the dazzled reader while following Obama's journey to his father's Kenyan land is that *Dreams* is, in the words of literary scholar Pierre-Marie Loizeau, less a true memoir than "an exercise in self-invention."[125] As an instance of the narrator's freedom with the facts, Obama conflates three of his girlfriends into the figure of a single woman that only fleetingly appears in the book, while he presents in the book passages that were copies of letters he had written from Africa to one of them. As novelist Jonathan Raban put it, Obama's book "is less memoir than novel," some characters are "composites with fictional names," its "total-recall dialogue is as much imagined as remembered," and "its time sequences are intricately shuffled."[126] Biographer David Garrow's conclusion is that "*Dreams From My Father* was not a memoir or an autobiography; it was instead, in multitudinous ways, without any question *a work of historical fiction* ... [which] employed the techniques and literary license of a novel, and its most important composite character was the narrator himself."[127] In short, Obama's book is partly autofiction, an obfuscating genre it shares with many other autobiographies and memoirs, and whose genealogy and history has been recently studied by Kevin Young under the rubric of *bunk.*[128]

One certain thing about *Dreams* is that it's the book of a man who was weighing a political career: he published right before he ran for the Illinois State Senate and fashioned his self-representation to that end. It's not that Obama ignores the boundaries between lying and telling the truth. His attitude as the author of this allegedly factual autobiography is more like that of Harry Frankfurt's *bullshitter*, so typical a character among politicians—someone who "does not reject the authority of the truth, as the liar does, and oppose himself to it. He pays no attention to it at all. By virtue of this, bullshit is greater enemy of the truth than lies are."[129] And bullshit ultimately is not unrelated to the hoax, in the sense that "the hoax is bullshit that believes its own bullshit, so much so that it starts to act like it doesn't stink—or worse, knows that in our current overwhelmed state, misinformation and information feel the same."[130] Bullshit "doesn't care if it's real or not—it just expects you to accept it."[131] This is one more expression of an era in Washington in which "fact and fiction are blurred not only by writers eager to score but also by presidents and their attorneys, spinmeisters and special prosecutors."[132] By practicing the deliberate blurring of fact and fiction in his writing, the "crime" of composing an autofiction that could be taken as autobiography, Obama was preparing himself for this new information environment in which people "elect who they're going to believe" and in which factual blurring is part of the narrative.[133]

This political pattern of deceptively blurring fact and fiction had Obama say that the civilians killed by drones during his administration were between 64 and 116. For those on the left disturbed by drone signature strikes, Samuels writes that according to Rhodes they "are a result of Obama's particular kind of globalism, which understands the hard and at times absolute necessity of killing. Yet, at the same time, they are also ways of avoiding more deadly uses of force—a kind of low-body-count spin move."[134] It takes the power of narrative to turn the several thousand people killed extrajudicially by drones into a low body count.

"THE ONLY GAME IN TOWN"

Former CIA director and defense secretary Leon Panetta's characterization of drones as "the only *game* in town" became a mantra in counterterrorism.[135] It likens drone warfare to science fiction, or to "playing the computer game Civilization";[136] it provides the illusion that killing is a play, a game, a skill, an artful performance. To begin with, drone pilots are "as if" pilots; they don't fly over enemy territory and endure the risks of war but sit at a control station in the Nevada desert, watching a screen. Then they press a joystick trigger—as if playing a Nintendo game.

It was General McChrystal who led the troops' surge in Afghanistan when Obama took office. He put in effect the counterterrorist unit Joint Special Operations Command (JSOC), an organization at the disposition of the president involved in lethal targeting operations across the globe, working alongside the CIA and described as "an almost industrial-scale counterterrorism killing machine."[137] It is not part of the conventional military or akin to the CIA but "a highly secretive military organization with a record of human right abuses, possibly resulting from a distinctive culture and dubious relationship to international humanitarian law."[138] A former senior military official characterized JSOC to Hersh as "a group of childish men who take advantage of their operational freedom to act immaturely. 'We're special and the rules don't apply.' . . . McChrystal [who commanded the JSOC while working closely with Vice President Cheney from 2003 to 2008] was not paid to be thoughtful. He was paid to let his troops do what they want with all *the toys to play with* they want."[139] Killing is a hunt, a game, a play.

McChrystal later described the surge and the prominent role of the JSOC as "an artful shift in strategy." It was an approach that showed the influence of social network analysis: "Thanks to such studies, the business of assassination, or targeted killing, could move beyond a crude fixation with killing an enemy network by killing carefully selected individuals whose elimination would make the entire structure more fragile and thus easier to disrupt."[140] To kill everyone on the ground is a mop-up operation; drone warfare's selective targeting of a few dozens or hundreds of targets, thus disrupting entire countries, requires thoughtful precision—it proves it's indispensable for national security.

Targeting, as in hunting, is a *skill*—a "distinct career track" pursued by one in every five intelligence analysts. A former agency official explained: "We spent years getting the bureaucracy to approve it as a career track, and it came in just in time when we needed people to spot targets for strikes. It was the same skills. We're not thinking about bloodthirsty butchers. . . . These were ordinary people, soccer moms, who would come in to work on their vacations because they felt they were 'saving lives.'"[141] Nothing is more disturbing for the drone pilots than the public perception that "we were a bunch of bloodthirsty, video game-playing, missile-slinging cowboys who indiscriminately shot up a town and then went for a beer."[142] It takes conceptual acuity and verbal camouflage to turn assassination into "targeting," assassins into "soccer moms," and killing into "saving lives," all done, as Brennan observed frequently, via the artistry of using drones as "a scalpel, not a hammer." Israel, an exemplar in counterterrorism, "has turned targeted preventions into an *art form.*"[143] Artful killing by drones demands swift action; whereas in aerial bombing the time between the intelligence and the missile's impact was forty minutes or more, drones "shrink the kill chain almost to zero."[144]

At the end of the Cold War the United States emerged as the only superpower. Fears of nuclear holocaust waned. But with 9/11 a new enemy under the figure of the Terrorist gave ground to a reality whose fantastical menace requires more resources than those against the Soviet Union during the Cold War's nuclear arms race. In only one decade, according to Dana Priest and William Arkin, a vast new security bureaucracy created some 1,200 government organizations and 1,900 private companies working in more than seventeen thousand locations across the country. In the Washington area alone, they occupy the equivalent of nearly three Pentagons or twenty-two US Capitol buildings.[145] By 2011, Americans with top-secret clearances numbered over 850,000; the number of private contractors working on counterterrorism was more than 250,000. By 2016 the total bill of the War on Terror was according to one estimate close to $5 trillion;[146] this figure rivals the $5.8 trillion spent in the nuclear armaments race during the Cold War.[147] In such "asymmetric warfare," the United States spent in the War on Terror the equivalent of its enemy al-Qaeda's total financial resources in just one hour in Iraq.[148] Who is really playing "the only game in town," counterterrorism or al-Qaeda?

And can such a confrontation between the greatest military power in history and an underground group whose main success was an attack by nineteen suicide bombers armed with box cutters be considered a real war among equals? Or is such futuristic war once again, as in the case of that most American of heroes, the Great Gatsby, the product of "colossal fantasy"? In the words of Singer, "Many commented on the oddity of a war where many of the forces still rode to battle on horses, and yet robotic drones were flying above. In the words of one US officer, it was 'the *Flintstones* meet the *Jetsons*'"[149]—a 1960s TV sitcom about a *Stone Age* working-class man's world with machines powered by dinosaurs, versus a *Space Age* animated sitcom also from the early 1960s depicting a world of elaborate robots and futuristic inventions. While devoting trillions to combating him, counterterrorism knows that the Stone Age Terrorist on horseback and with box cutters is no match against a US military whose budget is as large as those of the next eight to twelve countries combined—except in the terrifying black hole of terrorist desires and counterterrorist fantasies of atomic devices in terrorist hands.

All US involvement in the Greater Middle East, from President Carter to Obama, the very premise of "American dominance" of the region, "was a chimera," argues no less an authority than Bacevich. He examines documents such as Bush's second inaugural speech and sees "the unmistakable imprint of self-indulgent fantasy . . . [in which] expectations of ending tyranny by spreading American ideals mirrored Osama bin Laden's dream of establishing a new caliphate based on Islamic principles."[150] Counterterrorism seems unable to see how its fantasy structure often becomes terrorism's best ally for perpetuating an unending struggle. The crucial issue is how to conceptualize the dynamic of mutual denial and mutual constitution between the terrorist/counterterrorist couple that leads to drone wars returning from the future.[151] It displays the qualities of *the edge*—"a duality that has nothing to do with the dichotomies between complementary oppositional terms. . . . The edge is the thing whose only substantiality consists in its simultaneously separating and linking two surfaces . . . a duality that simultaneously constitutes the cause, the advent, and the consequences of the Real."[152] When waiting for terror becomes the basic political culture and real terror cannot be detected (as in the intelligence failures leading to 9/11), it is the duality of the terrorist/counterterrorist edge, their mimetic retro-feeding between past and future, that we must grasp in its radicalness—an intimate relationship that takes place at the edge of its "nonrelationship," yet constitutes the double-faced phenomenon of terror and guarantees its future replication.

4 Trauma

THE KILLER AS VOYEUR

Was it all just a game or was it real? The drone pilot, who spends the days at Creech and the nights in Las Vegas, has difficulty distinguishing fact from fiction, map from territory, patriotic killing from murder. Was it a terrorist he killed or was it a bystander? "We are saving lives," he is told. His eyes suggest something else: Isn't this Slaughterhouse-359?

Distance should protect the pilot from the traumatic effects of the Catch-22s intrinsic to the soldier's battlefront experience, except that technology makes distance evaporate—the drone's Eye in the Sky allows the pilot an intimate gaze over the lives to be eliminated on the ground. He presses the button at Creech and in seconds the Hellfire hits the target in Afghanistan—the "time-space compression" produced by drones makes the instant hit a killing not only *from* Las Vegas but *in* Las Vegas.[1]

Add to the collapse of time-space and visual barriers the asymmetry of the situation, the pilot hunter's invulnerability to retaliation and enemy reciprocity, and the moral dilemmas of the *bugsplat* resulting as his actions pile up. Traditional military values, such as courage and honor, are obsolete in drone warfare, a mockery, more a play-like shooting of fish in a barrel than actual war. The various levels of paradox and dissonance begin with the inability to know for sure what the targets are, whether the pilot is hunting real beasts or just metaphors, whether he is combatting enemies or creating them. The double-binding tangle of these messages playing against each other at various levels of abstraction—hunting, warfare, patriotism, morality, witnessing, murder—leads the pilot to experience confusion and potential pathology.[2] Trapped in a constellation of unsolvable Catch-22s, he is thrust into either the breakdown of trauma or (as we will discuss in the next final chapter) the breakthrough of creativity and resistance.

FARAWAY TARGETS, CLOSE-UP KILLS

Drones are unmanned aircraft, and the killing is done by robots at a distance. The old symmetry between the two contending face-to-face parties no longer applies. If we define "war" as involving real risks and casualties, the implication of the new technological asymmetry is that the experience is war for *them* but is like a Nintendo encounter with no real risks or casualties for us. The drone strikes that have resulted in the killing of several thousand people are "something that would have previously been viewed as a war" but now are "not being treated like a war" and hence don't require any debate or votes in Congress.[3]

Counterterrorists take full advantage of such legal and practical distinctions. Until 9/11, "the idea that state-sponsored killing would become a normal part of American policy would have seemed unthinkable."[4] For example, the US has routinely condemned the targeted assassinations carried out by Israel. The infamous shoot-to-kill policies practiced by some European governments against suspect terrorists during the 1980s created an international scandal.[5] In the past there were heated discussions in the Clinton White House as to the right method to kill bin Laden so as to not violate the ban on assassination; at one point the Clinton adviser Sandy Berger, enraged at the prospect that some type of killing might amount to assassination, lashed out: "So, you guys are perfectly OK if Bill Clinton kills bin Laden with a Tomahawk missile, but if Bill Clinton kills him with a 7.62-millimeter round in the middle of the eyes, that's bad? Could you tell me the difference between killing him with a Tomahawk and an M16?"[6] The obvious difference was *distance.* Similarly, the former

Counterterrorist Center officer Hank Crumpton "found it puzzling that the United States still seemed to make a distinction between killing people from a distance using an armed drone and training humans to do the killing themselves."[7]

There are legal complications about killing someone face to face in cold blood, but it is entirely legal to kill from a drone's technological distance. "We can kill them from the air," a commander observed, "but the lawyers say, 'No, you can't just'—the source put his hands together, stretched out his index fingers, stiffened his arms, and pointed his invisible pistol at my forehead—'blow someone away like that—pow!'"[8] Drones provide the required spatial and linguistic distance—the technologically mediated, aestheticized, robotically subject-less component—for killing to be "legal" and accepted as "normal."

It is a simple fact of war that the greater the distance the easier it is to kill. "It is considerably easier to impale a man with a twenty-foot pike than it is to stab him with a six inch-knife," wrote the military historian Dave Grossman.[9] A corollary to the advantage of distance engagement is that "it is far easier to deliver a slashing or hacking blow than a piercing blow . . . [for] the piercing of the enemy's body . . . is an act with some of the sexual connotations we will see in hand-to-hand combat range."[10] Faced with the soldier's Catch-22—damned if you kill the enemy, damned if you don't—a primary reaction is to distance yourself from the battlefront. From space, to time, to weapons systems, to categorical differentiations, the various means of achieving distance are strategies to avoid the traumatic impact of the tabooed killing. Unlike the shoot-to-kill actual assassination of one man by another, in drone attacks from the sky there is no direct eye-to-eye or body-to-body contact but only a subject-less plane—a "predator," a "hawk," a "raven"—eliminating a perceived animal-like target below, a terrorist suspect of whom almost nothing is known and about whom everything can be fantasized.

Grossman's well-documented conclusion is that "the closer the soldier draws to his enemy the harder it is to kill him."[11] The resistance to killing is strongest in hand-to-hand combat. Taking a man with a knife "is often experienced with sexual excitement," for "there is total possession in such killing."[12] Killing with a knife is harder than with the bayonet, and there is a world of difference between killing with a bayonet or a bullet. Bayonet fights could drive soldiers into delirium and nightly hallucinations that they were "in the act of pulling their bayonets out of the bodies of men they have killed."[13] Bayonet killings had an intimate brutality that horrified soldiers and an "enormous potential for psychological trauma."[14] It is when the enemy is retreating, and from the back, that most killings by hand take place, because of the so-called "chase instinct" and because the killer cannot see the enemy's face. The psychological distance sought by blindfolding or hooding the prisoners to be executed by a firing squad explains its practice, as does the greater risk of death of kidnapped victims kept hooded[15]—distancing devices that have direct implications for the effect of drones in military behavior.

There is physical distance and mechanical distance in combat. At the "Home of the Hunters" another key distance is categorical: the enemy is an *animal*. Drone pilot Matt Martin wrote: "The man wasn't *really* a man."[16] It is the age-old premise that, since the victim is not human but categorically inferior, you are allowed to kill him. The real of drone hunting is that the enemy is not really a man, a distinction intrinsic to most political killing. Martin admits he "found it easier and easier to justify bombing barbarians like these,"[17] for it was a given that "terrorists didn't *have* hearts."[18] Similarly Saddam Hussein, when he was taken out of his hole, "appeared more animal than human."[19] The racist prejudice against Muslims further facilitates the killing. As a sample of such prejudice for killing, a researcher found that the 44 percent of American soldiers in World War II would "really like to kill a Japanese soldier" but only 6 percent expressed a wish to kill Germans.[20]

Modern warfare has increased the physical distance to the enemy target. During World War I, body-to-body confrontation bloodied the trenches. Midrange rifles, long-range artillery, bombers, and missiles changed our relationship to killing. In the post-Vietnam era a paramount aim of the US military was nonexposure of soldiers to danger, known as the Powell Doctrine of overwhelming military force and rapid victory. The first Gulf War was a model of such wars: the US led a massive coalition and obtained its military goals with minimal casualties. Drones, managed from a trailer in the Nevada desert seven thousand miles away, bring a new dimension with their distance, a kind of ultimate solution to warfare—a war without casualties. The attack is unidirectional, and bat-tlefield reciprocity is lost—it's "almost like a computer game."[21]

But there is a paradoxical counterpoint to the presumed distance and invisibility of the hunted subterranean prey—the faraway pilot hunter actually *sees* a full and continuous image of his victim, involved in daily social and family life. The pilot is physically distant, yet thanks to the sur-veillance technologies he couldn't be visually closer to his victims. The faraway target turns into a close-up kill. It is this intimacy that is so peril-ous to the pilot. This was the genesis of Cian Westmoreland and Brandon Bryant's traumatic problems.

The distancing game by which drone operators are "just watching" doesn't work because there's no perceptual distance. The drone's "eye in the sky" shows the Creech pilot the reality of his victims in sensational and excruciating detail in the faraway theater of operations. The result of such a "combination of physical distance and ocular proximity" is that the vio-lence is no longer "more abstract or more impersonal." On the contrary, it is "more graphic, more personalized."[22] Creech commander Colonel Pete Gersten said, "We're closer in a majority of ways than we've ever been."[23] One particular moment continued to plague him—the instant that an old man had appeared, walking before him on the screen, at exactly the same moment that Gersten pulled the trigger.[24] On another occasion a ten- or eleven-year-old boy with a younger one balanced on bicycle handlebars had showed up. Martin and his copilots, with kids the same age, screamed "No!" but it was too late. They'd hit the joystick. Martin and his colleagues were "in shock over what [they] had just witnessed."

But they were not just witnesses, they were the *authors* of the killings. The pilots entered a kind of paralysis. Bobby, more detached, called them back to action: "What's done is done. No good can come from obsessing about it. It'll only distract us from doing our job."[25] Martin protested it wasn't a Nintendo game.[26] Pilot Falisha said tearfully: "We are as bad as terrorists if we laugh off the deaths of those kids." But Martin invoked McNamara's words: "You must sometimes do evil in order to do good." They assured each other that "we were right" and that they had to pay with "the darkness that crept through our souls" for doing the right thing.[27]

Martin describes himself as a sky sniper capable of "stealthy aerial assassinations."[28] The voyeur is no longer just watching. His instructor told him, "[Now] you're *in* the airplane, Captain Martin. *Feel* it."[29] His wife worries how someone can be so personally invested in the action thousands of miles away.[30] But Martin explains, "I was no longer a spectator. . . . You couldn't get much closer to war than this."[31] He says he knows about the men he is watching almost as much "as I knew about my wife."[32] He is hunting. For her. Once Martin asks her forgiveness—not for pulverizing some casual bystander with a Hellfire missile, but for not killing *more*. "Trish, I almost killed a man today," he tells her regretfully. "I'm sorry I didn't kill him."[33] It takes a man to be a killer; that's why his wife will love him.

THE TRAUMATIC COLLAPSE OF FANTASY

"We're the ultimate peeping toms," said Bryant to an interviewer.[34] And in another interview he stated, "I got to know them [the Taliban]. . . . I saw them having sex with their wives. They were good daddies."[35] Bryant became a pilot at Nevada's Creech Air Force Base just after high school graduation. The drone pilot watches his victims in their daily intimate lives, as if it were a reality show. But Bryant was a special kind of voyeur, expected to follow orders through the chain of command and fire when told to. During free time he'd play video games or World of Warcraft. But this "game" was different. He felt the horror of the now fatherless children.

"What would you do?" Bryant asked us in Las Vegas after we had seen *National Bird* and heard the testimonies of former drone pilots like himself. "These people are just like you, not angels, not demons," he said. He'd pleaded with his Creech superiors for another job: "Sir, we didn't sign for this job. Please, sir, could we do another job?" What would you do? He answered himself: "Experience the trauma by which your body gets shut down. . . . That's what happened to me."

Pulling the trigger and firing the Hellfire at a mud house in Afghanistan was something mechanical. It was watching the results from the drone's hovering eye in the sky that was the hardest part. He had circled the hut with a Predator and, when he received the order to fire, had pressed a button with his left hand while marking the target with a laser. Then the pilot next to him pressed the trigger on a joystick, and the missile was launched. There were sixteen slow-motion seconds until impact. With three seconds left in the countdown, a child walked out from behind the corner of the house.

"Did we just kill a kid?" Bryant turned to his copilot.

"Yeah, I guess that was a kid."

But maybe they were wrong. They entered the question into a chat window on the monitor. "Was that a kid?"

Someone wrote back: "No. That was a dog."[36]

Was it a kid or was it a dog? Once again reality was getting blurry. They reviewed the video. A dog on two legs? Bryant had been following orders; he'd marked a roof with a laser and pushed a button; it was the copilot on the joystick who had pressed the trigger. The ensuing report said enemies had been killed in action. Why should Bryant be concerned? Maybe it was a dog after all.

Bryant had been told President Obama was involved in the operation: "We got direction from some higher-up that the President would call our GCS [Ground Control Station] and would issue the order directly to us as a crew if we needed to shoot. That's a little bit thrilling." The only thing left was "if President Obama would've come down himself and pulled the trigger."[37]

But the last thing Bryant expected was that he'd vaporize a child. He had been advised repeatedly not to allow war to become personal. His job was just to look for the enemy. His looking should not extend into a voyeuristic gaze—where human intimacy was involved. A drone pilot must grab the action from the hunter's distance, always keeping at bay any proximity with the object—he should see, not a kid, not even a dog, only a *target*. The difference between public and private domains had to be preserved at all costs. But "war somehow becomes personal," Colonel William Tart, a drone operator, said.[38] "Targeting with RPAs [remotely piloted aircraft] is more intimate. It is war at a very intimate level," a pilot told Daniel Rothenberg.[39] While he was following the Taliban from his drone in the sky, Bryant's eyes could not avoid *seeing*—the gaze that led him to his ultimate mistake: "I got to know them."

"I never thought I would kill that many people," Bryant said. "In fact, I thought I couldn't kill anyone at all."[40] His scoreboard award stated he had killed 1,626 enemy combatants.[41] At 359, Westmoreland's score was a fourth of his. The first time Bryant fired a missile, he killed two men instantly, then watched a third twisting in mortal agony. He had to be strong, show he had the mettle not to feel remorse for the fatherless children. Bryant "felt disconnected from humanity."[42] This was no longer a video game. Now it was the real. It had never crossed his mind that society would require him, a teenager, to become a serial killer.

Caught at the crossroads between duty and horror, Bryant watched himself become insane. He had had no idea that "killing comes with a price, and . . . soldiers will have to spend the rest of their lives living with what they have done."[43] He thought of seeing a therapist, but if he did, his security clearance would be taken away. He went to see a chaplain, who assured him that killing is "part of God's plan."[44] There was no escaping his terrible military double bind of experiencing himself at once as soldier and murderer.

The child was not a dog. The fantasy that he was hunting actual terrorists couldn't hold. Distance was what in theory defined Bryant's moves and shielded him from trouble in the Nevada desert—except that drones, "even if they increase the distance to the target . . . also create proximity."[45] Since his job required that he keep looking for enemies, he became a voyeur of his victims and of himself—of his killing. Bryant saw again and again the little boy before he had vaporized him, a vision that burned his eyes, short-circuited his brain, haunted his very being. His girlfriend found that he had become a stranger in a strange body. Frightened, she left him. It was as if something in Bryant too had been vaporized with no way to switch back to his former life. "I wish my eyes would rot," he said.[46]

One day Bryant collapsed at work, spitting blood. He was ordered to stay home. But he was trying to be brave. Six months later he was back in the cockpit, flying drones. "Hey, what motherfucker is going to die today?," he heard himself say to his coworkers. He was diagnosed with PTSD and released from the job. Drone pilot Christopher Aaron described a similar experience: "The distress began with headaches, night chills, joint pain. Soon, more debilitating symptoms emerged—waves of nausea, eruption of skin welts, chronic digestive problems."[47]

Bryant was nineteen and had just graduated from high school when in 2007 he joined the army to avoid college debt. Four years later he was utterly broken and homeless, wondering what he could do now with his life. Perhaps he should tell his story—the short-circuit between the finger that pushed the button, the eye that saw the child disappear, and the recurring nightmare. That's why he was in Las Vegas that evening, and why he would join the group of antidrone protesters at Creech the following day. Bryant had gone through the crucible: either the pathology of paralyzing trauma or the empowerment of resistance and breakthrough. "I lost my fear and gained myself back," he says in the documentary film *Drone*.[48] "The fire that had been gone, my soul, made its triumphant return." He was a war criminal with a soul—the emblematic embodiment of drone warfare America.

There are, however, different ways of watching and seeing the drone killing's *bugsplat*. To grasp what is specific to the traumatic gazing of the drone pilots, one has to contrast it in particular to the live screening known as "Predator porn." A black box, by which Predators transmit ROVER (remotely operated video enhanced receiver) or motion imagery, brings "the extended eye everywhere and [makes] the job of targeting even more individual and intimate."[49] Drone operations from Creech Air Force Base are thus transmitted to hundreds of US officials. The video feeds go to more than a dozen remote intelligence hubs in the US, Europe, and Asia, where the CIA, the NSA, the Pentagon, and the White House are linked in their voyeuristic watching. On any given occasion, "senior officials all the way up to the president might . . . be watching."[50] According to one major general, the demand for the real-time Predator porn feed by "our higher-ups" was such that "we eventually had to evolve rules . . . to make sure the president didn't call the Predator pilot up."[51] In his memoir Stanley McChrystal writes how by 2007, linked to the large plasm screens of "Kill TV," "the O&I [operations and intelligence] was a worldwide forum of thousands of people associated with our mission."[52] This secret warfare, whose very existence is officially denied, is so much *fun* that those involved in the planning and action of the manhunt can't stop watching it.

The audience enthralled by these videos of drone strikes includes soldiers deployed in Iraq and Afghanistan. David Kilcullen, who later became a critic of drone use, was the architect of using drones to boost troop morale: "When people can see a bad guy carrying a weapon, acting like a bad guy, getting blown up, it's enormously satisfying for some Humvee guy who goes out and spends all day driving around Baghdad getting shot at. He comes back and he fires up some gun camera footage from an Apache or drone strike footage and says, 'Well, at least we got some guys today.'"[53] Many in the ranks appeared to have "an insatiable appetite for videos of drones and other aircraft carrying out success strikes." And not only the troops: "The media too had a strong appetite for 'Pred porn.'"[54] By 2012 there were well over ten million viewers of war porn.[55] Sex and killing have historically been linked in the battlefront experience, and now, with virtual sex, free porn, and drone feeds so easily accessible, all of these could be vicariously enjoyed. It was the spectacle of war as entertainment, almost as pornography, for "looking at pictures of dead bodies is like looking at pornography, trying to see more of what is there."[56]

The task of imagery analyst illustrates the vulnerability to trauma that derives from simply seeing through the drone's eye in the sky. Heather was a college student in her early twenties when, following her boyfriend, she enlisted in the air force and became an imagery analyst and screener for the drone program. In the film *National Bird* she explains that her job was "to watch what was happening in the video drones—the live videos of course—and identify everything. In another remote station [there'd be] the pilot who was flying the actual aircraft and the sensor operator who is moving the camera around; they were the ones that actually push the button. I didn't push the button. I just identified what necessitates the button-pushing." Lives of people on the other side of the world depended on her identifications. If on her computer screen she saw a sixteen-year-old rather than a twelve-year-old boy, the fate of the boy was sealed. Heather was so alarmed by her work, she became suicidal. A psychologist recommended that she leave the drone unit so as not be exposed to constant death. But the military was understaffed and would not let Heather quit, despite her being on suicide watch. She was ordered not to talk to anyone about her work, not even her therapist or her mother.

What traumatized her was seeing it all, "*like slow motion*, and it was like, you are watching someone just drag themselves across the field, when you watch someone in those dying moments . . ." Heather can't find words to describe what she saw on a daily basis: "it's so primitive, it's really raw, stripped-down death, it's what it is, this is *real*. . . . I have specific memories of many of them that I know I killed. . . . Maybe we killed our objective, maybe we killed the guy we thought was our objective, we don't know." After the missile hits the target, her task is not over yet, for she has to follow through the results of the strike. "The bomb hits and you get down close and you can see the body parts . . . and sometimes you will stick around and watch a family come in and get them and like pick up the parts and put their family member in a blanket and a couple of people hold on to the corner of the blanket and carry them back to the compound."

It was the brutality of the vision that undid Heather, not some ideological objection, for "I can't say whether our drone program is wrong." What bothers her is that she was forced to take part in the action of killing and that "I don't know how many people I killed. After a strike I'd ask for a break and let it go, and go outside and smoke a cigarette, and just think, and try to decompress, and push the idea that I was killing people out of my mind, try not to think about it. Sometimes if I just couldn't get out of the situation for very long, I'd just go to the bathroom, just sit there in my uniform and just like cry and just think about what I was doing." Heather is now in search of healing by doing massage. "I have lost friends to war, I have lost friends to suicide that were part of that unit, and I have seen a lot of people die in the war. So I brought to the massage table pain and just absolute despair and horrible memories, and along with that, an anxiety disorder and a sleep disorder."

How you see the images and react to the live streaming of drone videos determines whether you are a real "hunter;" if you are not, then hunting will subject you to trauma. Carla was one of the drone operators watching Predator porn, she recounted for me in my office, when something happened that changed her life. "I remember vividly once watching the video feed, and that everybody was very excited about it. And it wasn't when I was working. But I'd seen it, I think, a day or two afterwards. It was a large-scale bombing that the video had from our feed. It had been called in and approved and then bombed, and everybody else was 'Yeah! we got them!' The whole male . . ." They were two or three hundred people shouting. "It was like we were watching a sporting event as opposed to we just killed all those people. They were at least a dozen killed. I think that's when my politics started to change, that this was perhaps not where I wanted to be." She decided to quit the air force and go back to college.

Carla (a fictional name) had forgotten that as a "hunter" she was supposed to enjoy the kill. She had stepped out of the war frame by realizing that the targets they were killing were actually people. I asked whether she was comfortable talking about her experience with the drone program. She said that she was not and that she had signed a form promising that for seventy-five years she would not disclose anything about her work. "Did your experience with drone warfare leave you with trauma?" "It left an indelible mark, it put a stamp on me, it changed my politics." She could no longer enjoy the videos of drone hits as Predator porn. Suddenly she was seeing something else. She sensed she was caught in the Catch-22 of a patriotic calling that seemed to turn her into an accomplice to murder. She was facing an alternative: staying in the air base and experiencing traumatic stress or returning to college and creating a new life for herself.

The problem for Bryant and Westmoreland (and for the hundreds of pilots currently working at Creech, each drone having a crew of about 170 operational people) is that they saw too much—in detail and intimacy—while watching their victims play at home, laugh, or cry. They could no longer hold into the idea that the thousands of people they were helping to hunt and kill, whose names they would never know, were the embodiment of Evil. Daily intimacy with their victims had undone them—they were like the executioner who, having watched the condemned man for months and years, becomes friends with the walking dead. Out of a sample of 141 intelligence analysts and officers involved in drone operations, "three-fourths reported feeling grief, remorse and sadness."[57] Many of them, like Westmoreland and Bryant, must have tried to look at their victims through their ideological screen by which they *were* terrorists. Yet what many of them began to see was no longer "bugsplat" but horrified family members collecting what remained of the body parts. In one case a strike killed a "terrorist facilitator" but not his son, who "walked back to the pieces of his father and began to place the pieces back into human shape."[58] It was too much to preserve the pretense that their inhuman monstrosity deserved it. *And once the fantasy failed, trauma took over,* a sense of an apocalyptic "coincidence of opposites" by which *their* Evil was *our* Evil. "What would *you* have done in our shoes, what will *you* do now?," Westmoreland and Bryant were asking us in Las Vegas.

Killing is the Thing that the soldier or the drone pilot cannot stop thinking about, the unspoken presence ubiquitous in everything the military does. Psychoanalysts write about the "fantasmatic supplement" for sex: "It is the real sex itself which, in order to be palatable, has to be sustained by some fantasy."[59] Killing similarly requires the help of fantasy— as when pilot Martin saw himself acting as General Patton or even God, or Begin claimed that destroying Arafat was like eliminating Hitler.[60] Fantasy is not a substitute for desire but constitutive of it. The fantasy factor is needed for the soldier to *want* to kill the enemy. Drone warfare creates the coordinates of fantasy and desire by which the Enemy is made something so loathsome that only killing can quell it and thus provide meaning and order to the subjective world of the counterterrorist. Outside the fantasy frame, the killing is nothing but brutal, meaningless cruelty. And the hard truth is that the soldier's mental health "is totally invested in believing that what he has done is good and right."[61] The unbearable question for the pilot facing the fatal consequences of his action is: Did I *have* *to* kill the victim, or was it really an act of murder?

For understanding this process one might refer to what psychoanalysts call "traversing the fantasy"—accepting its inconsistencies, shattering its foundations. That's what happened to Westmoreland and Bryant and so many other drone operators. The psychoanalytic cure for the traumatized subject consists in awakening the subject from the spell of fantasy: "the experience of the fact that the fantasy-object, by its fascinating presence, is merely filling out a lack, a void in the Other. There is nothing 'behind' the fantasy; the fantasy is a construction whose function is to hide this void, this 'nothing.'"[62] Traversing the fantasy means identifying with the Enemy one has just killed, submitting "to that effect of the symbolic lack that reveals the limit of everyday life. . . . [It means] being brought into an ever more intimate relation with that real core of the fantasy that transcends imaging."[63] Under the effects of the violent intrusion of the Real of killing, the collapse of the fantasy frame of the Enemy leaves the drone pilot with the catastrophic doubt of how to categorize his killings and himself.

THE BODY'S BETRAYAL AND THE MYTH OF INVULNERABILITY

I met Matthew (a fictional name) during a flight from New York to Reno. He is a veteran who served in Afghanistan after he joined the Marines at eighteen. He has PTSD. I was interested in knowing more about his experiences as a Marine, and, during the several times we met, he described some of his memories: one was of the family he had killed by calling a drone strike. Another was of the face of the man he had killed because of how he had looked back at Matthew. As the man looked at him directly and smiled, Matthew gave the order to "light it up" and his men killed him on the spot. Another man ran to where the first man had fallen, and they killed him as well. Later he was told the men he had killed were on reconnaissance for the Taliban, that they were Taliban. But Matthew cannot free himself from the image of that man's face. That man was his first kill, and he thought it was the end of himself; he thought it wasn't right, that he might be jailed. The next day he killed another guy on a motorcycle. He has killed "many, many people," he told me casually.

But the worst memory was the family. He called for a drone strike and the missile killed everyone in the family of six except for the mother. She ran from the house screaming at him, making him feel responsible for the drone that had killed her husband and children. Matthew will never forget that. Her face. He is sitting at the other side of the desk in my office, his right leg shaking compulsively, when he tells me this. Matthew is matter-of-fact, says that that memory is the most important event in his PTSD. A week after he saw that mother's face, all the tough Marine could do was weep. "PTSD ruined my career," he laments. He had wanted to go up to JSOC, "the real killing machine," he says. He wanted to kill more, but his body *betrayed* him, he confesses. He felt like a "murderer" and a "terrorist," he repeats. He lives with his wife and two daughters, is clearly intelligent. But recently he lost his job—because of PTSD, he says. He doesn't expect any breakthrough, doesn't see any good ending for his trauma. Matthew doesn't wear a weapon because it is too easy for him to fire. "Numb," he tells me, is the one word to describe the experience of the killer. "Killing makes one numb." The one word to describe how he feels now, he says, is *rage*. It's a rage similar, perhaps, to what anthropologist Renato Rosaldo found among the Ilongot headhunters in the Philippines, a rage he could not understand until his wife died in a mountain accident doing fieldwork.[64] A Filipino sniper soldier told psychiatrist Theodore Nadelson: "Talking . . . words, that is nothing. Only killing eased the hurt and then gave the satisfaction. I'm angry, I've been so angry all the time."[65] Rosaldo concluded: "This anger . . . is irreducible in that nothing at a deeper level explains it."[66]

The laws of warfare establish a categorical difference between a soldier's killing of the enemy combatant in the battlefield and an assassin's killing of an arbitrary target. "The basic aim of a nation at war is establishing an image of the enemy in order to distinguish as sharply as possible the act of killing from the act of murder," wrote Glenn Ray.[67] The distinction between killing and murder requires first of all a clear line of demarcation between enemy combatants and noncombatants. This is not always easy. A state labeling someone "terrorist" solves the uncertainty—killing a terrorist should never be murder.

The soldier risks his own life while following orders, and this justifies his killing in self-defense. It is not just his right, it is the duty of the soldier to kill the enemy on the battlefield; if he refuses to do so, he is liable to harsh punishment, including execution. This leads to the soldier's essential double bind: "He is damned if he does [kill], and damned if he doesn't [kill],"[68] and he has no way to avoid the combat situation. The ultimate catastrophe for the soldier is to feel that, no matter what his army says about the Enemy, his killing was an act of murder. Such fear of "remaining a combatant and not becoming, in his own eyes, an assassin" explains, in part, the many reports of soldiers who refuse to fire against an unarmed soldier or who prefer to spare the life of the enemy.[69]

A history of ethics in warfare says you cannot kill if you are not ready to die. Authors Michael Walzer and Grégoire Chamayou argue that the drone, by supplanting real combat, "destroys the very possibility of any clear differentiation between combatants and noncombatants."[70] If in the past the soldier's potential to be the victim of another soldier killer was the condition that justified killing in battle, the current drone pilot's remote-control engagement changes all that. The moral justification for killing changes when the ones doing the killing are not bodily present, when there's no risk to their own lives as they carry out their enemies' killings. This only adds to the drone pilot's double-binding dilemmas.

"The robot is our answer to the suicide bomber"[71]—this statement sums up the current struggle between terrorists and counterterrorists. Against the vulnerable self-destructive body the drone fosters the myth of invulnerability. If the suicidal component is indispensable to the latest wave of terrorist strategy (self-immolation establishes at the outset that there will be no negotiation and no way out—a decision not to be reduced to religious fanaticism), counterterrorism's solution is to shoot Hellfire missiles at potential suicide bombers from thousands of miles away.[72] Death instinct versus drone magic. Mythical figures of invulnerability such as Achilles, Siegfried, Hercules, or Ajax are now replaced by techno-logical invulnerability—even though "the great myths of invulnerability are almost all accounts of failure."[73] The belief in warfare without risk, warfare without warfare, is based on illusion. Wrote Michael Ignatieff: "We see war as a surgical scalpel and not a bloodstained sword . . . We need to stay away from such fables of self-righteous invulnerability."[74] These "fables" are now the dominant counterterrorist culture.

So are drones really invulnerable? Chamayou replies: "A far cry from the all-powerful image that they wish to convey, drones are fragile weapons, riddled with faults and deep contradictions."[75] But drone vulnerability is not just technical. The dronization of the armed forces and withdrawal of the soldier from the battlefield implies other strategic weaknesses. The assumption that, in the era of drones, no American soldier should be a casualty of war ends up empowering the enemy, becomes the Achilles' heel by which the killing of one soldier, rather than an ordinary war event, is considered an intolerable failure. Moreover, whereas the burden of risk was traditionally placed upon soldiers, thus providing a certain protection for civilians, a casualty-averse military displaces the burden of danger to civilians as targets. Drones are the best example favoring nationalism over international law developed after World War II.[76]

Along with the pretense of invulnerability comes the false premise of total safety exemplified by the "Cheney doctrine" against Saddam Hussein: "Even if there's just a one percent chance of the unimaginable coming due, act as if it is a certainty."[77] Such inflexible invulnerability may render a sys-tem most vulnerable. Just consider the policy of the so-called asymmetric warfare by which "the United States [has] so far spent $1.4 million *per dol-lar of AQ [Al-Qaeda] investment in the attacks.*"[78] Such an unsustainable show of safety and strength can only be the overreaction of traumatized vulnerability.

Fascism thrives on the "illusion of invulnerability," thought Walter Benjamin.[79] A kind of armor, safe from fragmentation and pain—that's how fascist aesthetics depicted the body.[80] The supposed success of unmanned technological drone warfare is also built on the illusion of invulnerability. It is the body reduced to the armor of a drone guided from Creech thousands of miles away.

But antiwar writers and artists have also used the image of body-as-armor to cope with its traumatic reconfigurations in war. After World War I, soldiers' bodies were commonly depicted as weapons and war machines, their abject impersonality juxtaposed to the humanistic cynicism of the military-politico elites that produced the war: "Our rage had to find some expression somehow or other. This we did quite naturally through attacks on the foundations of the civilization responsible for war."[81] The machine penetrates the soldier's body, and a gun is like a metallic phallus. Max Ernst was one of these artists; in his *Petite machine* "the (male) body has become an instrumental camera or gun," which "suggests a defensive shield, perhaps even a machinic substitute, for a damaged ego."[82] It was art's defensive armoring against the body's betrayal and mental illness—the "degenerate art" hated by the Nazis.

Warfare has always involved spells and magical weapons.[83] Arthur Clarke thinks that "any sufficiently advanced technology is indistinguishable from magic."[84] Drones echo and further such fantasies of magical invulnerability, as the fighting bodies remain remote in the Nevada desert while their decisions are conveyed by the robots' flying armor. Adorno's warning to Germany after the war—that fascism was not a past momentary fall into barbarism but a present threat—remains true for drone warfare.

In an influential essay on artwork in the era of technical reproducibility, Benjamin wrote of "the crisis in cognitive experience caused by the alienation of the senses that makes it possible for humanity to view its own destruction with enjoyment."[85] What Benjamin demanded from art was to undo the corporeal alienation of the senses, "to restore the instinctual power of the human bodily senses for the sake of humanity's self-preservation, and to do this, not by avoiding the new technologies, but by passing through them."[86] This is the experience of drone operators, whose senses, beyond the myths of the Terrorist, force them to actually *see* the people they are killing.

A FATHER AT WAR: THE TRAUMA OF KILLING

In one of our antidrone protest weeks at Creech during the spring of 2017, as we were about to take action and close the traffic to the base, next to me was Frank Pauc. I introduced myself to Frank and we struck up a conversation. He is a veteran, he told me, a graduate of West Point, and he had served six years, five as a helicopter pilot. While serving in the army in Germany, he had met and married a woman whose father had fought with the Nazis. He found that his in-laws were not the vilified German enemy. He became a pacifist. Against his wishes, his son had joined the army in 2009 and fought in Iraq. Frank told me how "my kid" had survived one of the reconnaissance missions, thanks only to the intervention of his dog, who had jumped at the enemy's throat. At Creech Frank had been wrestling with the idea of getting arrested when he heard Ray, another veteran standing next to him, say, "Frank, I am glad that you're here." Frank decided right there he would stay on the road with Ray when the group was ordered to disband. He was arrested and taken to the Las Vegas county jail. When I saw Frank the following day and asked him what he did for a living, he said he was a writer. I asked him one of his titles. *A Father at War*, he replied.

I read his self-published book and saw how little exaggeration there was in the title. *A Father at War* begins with goodbyes. Frank's son Hans is leaving home, deployed to Iraq. Frank and his wife Karin thought they had prepared themselves for this moment, but they found they were never going to be ready for what Hans had to endure. For days Frank had thought about what he would say to Hans, but when the moment of departure arrived there was nothing to say. Karin asked her son for a hug, but Hans would only shake her hand. She told him how much she loved him. As he drove away she went into the house and cried. "Hans shouldn't have to go to war. He shouldn't be going to Iraq. No American soldier should be in Iraq," Frank writes out of his heartache.[87]

Months passed, and Hans returned to Texas on a two-week mid-deployment leave. Frank and Karin hoped he would visit them, but he didn't. One Wednesday, as Frank came home from work, his wife told him that Hans had called that morning and told her, as a parenthesis in small talk, that he'd shot a dog in Iraq and that then "he had told her that he had shot somebody, but that it hadn't bothered him that much."[88] She said maybe she hadn't heard him correctly. Frank shrugged it off and took a nap.

But when the phone rang again that Wednesday evening Frank picked it up. It was Hans. They talked about the truck and the weather. Then Frank asked:

"When you were in Iraq, did you shoot someone?"

Hans replied without hesitation: "Yes." Frank took a breath.

"Did he die?"

"Well, yeah, I guess so . . . I must have pumped thirty rounds into him."

"Aaaaw fuck."

"There was an ambush . . . they bombed the first vehicle . . . we fired back."

"I'm sorry, Hans. I'm sorry that had to happen. I'm sorry that you were in that situation."

"It didn't really bother me," Hans replied. "I slept okay that night. I'm all right."

Frank didn't believe that all was "okay." He understood why Hans hadn't come home to visit: it was hard enough to admit it over the phone. He couldn't say it in person. Frank talked to his priest, who counseled Frank to be patient, to "be there for Hans." But Frank just wanted to pray for Hans, for the man who had died, "for us all." He could barely accept what had happened. He kept thinking, "Maybe I heard him wrong."[89] A few years later Hans would leave the army with PTSD. He was suicidal. Frank told his second son, Stefan, who also wanted to join the army, about Hans's killing. "He needs to understand what is real," he said.[90]

I'm only on page 11 in Frank's narrative. There isn't going to be much really new afterwards—just afterthoughts, reverberations of an explosive confession. Hans tells Frank that there are things he can never tell him, since Frank has never killed someone. Frank agrees: "I really can't understand."[91] They go together to a grocery store and Hans makes racist remarks about a man from the Middle East—he looks like the ones who tried to kill him. Frank thinks it's pointless to talk about it with his son, "because he has been hurt in a deep place where words and logic never go. Something inside of Hans is scarred. . . . Hans knows that his feelings are irrational, but they are also terribly real."[92] There is now "an invisible wall" between father and son. "When Hans came back to us after a year, I looked into the eyes of a stranger. The boy we knew is gone, and he is never coming back."[93] At one point Frank sees Hans again as a little boy, wants to take him in his arms and hold him, scare away the monsters. But you can't make the monsters go away. They are a churchgoing family but Hans refuses to go to mass because "There is no God. If there was a God, He wouldn't have let me see all that fucked up shit in Iraq."[94] Several of Hans's army buddies have died in suicides and accidents. Hans himself has had three motorcycle accidents. He was homeless and jobless for more than a year. At the time Frank was talking to me, Hans had settled down, owned a house, was engaged. Later Frank would send me photos of Hans with his newborn son.

There is no sentimentality, escape to moralism, or utopian pacifism in Frank's bare text. Frank has no tolerance for protesters ignorant of military culture, shouting at drone operators to refuse the order to kill, as it goes against a soldier's training. As a veteran, Frank finds it difficult to sustain moral outrage against soldiers who obey orders. The first lesson at West Point is that the army is "a place where people are expected to be both gentlemen (or gentlewomen) and would-be killers. It is a set of contradictions."[95] Not moralism but Zen helps Frank understand his son. He knows that "a young man needs a rite of passage, and in a perverse sort of way, the military provides that."[96] He knows that playing with military toys is fun and that the sense of solidarity and belonging with comrades is attractive.

It is the militarization of America that pains Frank. Hans's experience drove Frank to make the long trip from Wisconsin to Nevada to be arrested at Creech. At a meeting of Voices for Creative Nonviolence, led by Kathy Kelly, the discussion was on how to oppose drone warfare. When he was asked to comment on his letter to the *Catholic Herald* in which he had argued for loving one's enemies, Frank found himself talking about Hans: "Hans's trauma had very little to do with drones per se, but it had everything to do with war and the suffering that comes from it. A person cannot kill without being wounded himself." And in fact, Frank added, a drone pilot's wounds take longer to heal, because "Hans killed in order to survive. The drone operator does not."[97] In addition to knowing of Hans's trauma, it was Frank's hearing a vet with PTSD tell how he lost his family and everything else when he returned from the war and spent a year in a mental institution, that made him "feel that tidal wave of his agony sweeping over me and filling my ears, my eyes, and my mouth. Standing in front of this veteran, I drowned in pain, I drowned in Hans' pain. I couldn't breathe."[98] Frank woke from a dream in the night screaming "No!"—"the same interior voice that cried out when Hans told me that he killed a man. I felt the same racing heartbeats and the same panic."[99] I asked Frank what would hurt more, having his child killed in a war or having him kill another person; his response was immediate—your child killing another person hurts more.[100]

It is the killing that changes everything in the experience of the soldier—a "lifelong sentence to contemplate the nature of one's own character, endlessly asking, 'Am I good, or am I evil?'"[101] As he was sending thirty thousand more troops to Afghanistan, a somber Obama mused, "They're so young." [102] But "young" was perhaps an overstatement; they were more like Kurt Vonnegut's "children's crusade," eighteen- and nineteen-year-olds suddenly asked to kill. The high school kid who joins the army ready to kill does so "for my family,"[103] to make the parents proud of his willingness to serve. Much as in the rituals of manhood in primitive societies, the kid must relinquish personal identity and agonizingly become a killer. In many cases family members have already joined the military—"My pops always told me it's my duty to serve my country as a young American. . . . He was killed when I was twelve, so I figured I'd do what he told me to do."[104] The child will try to square his duty to be a "good kid" as his parents wanted—by killing. Once these children see their lives have been ruined, they will feel the rage of having been betrayed by politicians and military commanders who forced them to do what was against their sense of morality and humanity. As First Lieutenant Thomas Saal put it, "It's Bush and Cheney that were criminals, not these Marines."[105] And for the killings done by Westmoreland and Bryant, who was responsible?

Tens of thousands of veterans say they are haunted by their own killings. In a hierarchical military culture, a basic premise is that soldiers

shouldn't feel responsible for killings that were not their personal decision. But something goes wrong. A comrade is dead and the soldier feels
the rage. "It was more than rage," says Shelton, describing his experience.
He is a veteran who sobs inconsolably while remembering what happened
twenty years before: "I never want to feel that way again. It was animalis-
tic. . . . You get angry and you want to kill. The rage is just incredible."[106]
Or take the case of Saal. Upon the death of his platoon lieutenant, he
became commander. When he saw a man running across a rice paddy, he
ordered his men to shoot. When they retrieved the lifeless body, they
found he was a North Vietnamese Army officer; they also found something else, photographs of his wife and children. Saal suddenly realized,
"We had killed a human being."[107] Vietnamese were "slopes" or "gooks,"
but those silent images in the pocket of the man he had ordered his men
to kill, rather than let him run, shattered the fantasy that it was a sort of
wild animal they hunted. Saal would never erase from his mind the image
of what his platoon subordinates did to the dead body: they crucified him
naked on a cross they assembled from nearby bamboos. "Take him the
fuck down!" Saal screamed. When one replied that the enemy would do
the same in a reversed situation, Saal shouted back, "We are not them!"
But of course they were. Saal would never recover from what they had
done: "I knew that's where I left my soul. . . . I lost my humanity. I saw it
fly over my head. I'm sure there's a lot of souls like mine."[108] Soldiers who
served in Vietnam confess they regularly found among the dead photos
that were "a crack in the veil of denial that makes war possible."[109] "The
dead soldier takes his misery with him, but the man who killed him must
forever live and die with him"[110]—their ultimate brotherhood.

Twenty percent of the annual forty-five thousand suicides in America
are of veterans.[111] "Almost everyone thinks daily of suicide," says psychiatrist Dr. Jonathan Shay of veterans. "It seems to sustain them as a bottom
line of human freedom and dignity. Having touched that talisman every
day, they continue to struggle."[112] But, as journalist Kevin Sites learned
from experience, it is not only the killers who get PTSD. On one occasion
he walked away from an Iraqi man who was dying. On another, Sites
watched the Marines execute, point blank, wounded Iraqis in a temple,
only to discover when he was left alone that there was one injured survivor
who, arms outstretched, was pleading for his help. Sites would later

discover that the injured man he didn't help was later murdered. "I have carried its burden ever since," admits Sites.[113]

To kill or be killed. Military culture is founded on the imperative to deny the brotherhood between killer and killed. The Enemy is categorically different, typically turned into some type of metaphoric animal to permit the killing. And yet, at times, the unthinkable happens and the brotherhood between killer and killed becomes so apparent that the horror of killing is revealed in all its traumatic and unforgettable real. Could there be anything as hard as looking another human being in the eye and killing him, face to face? Anthropologist David Marlowe found that, among combat veterans of the First Gulf War, killing an enemy soldier or witnessing one getting killed caused more distress than being wounded oneself.[114] This makes soldiers' resistance to killing a significant even if controversial topic of research. S. L. A. Marshall observed in World War II that many of his comrades didn't shoot and wrote a study on the soldiers' reluctance to kill.[115] Marshall's methods have since been questioned, but the conclusion that soldiers often will not shoot is still largely accepted.

Combatants talk of the hunter's initial excitement in killing. Having heard stories of Vietnam veterans, Nadelson concludes that "many veterans experienced satisfaction in killing and, through memories of killing and slaughter, rekindle some of the pleasure of the event."[116] Not that combatants saw themselves as "born killers," except for a 2 percent who sought out opportunities to kill.[117] Yet, having experienced the intoxication of killing, combatants also describe themselves as "tortured by memories of what they have done or witnessed. They are shocked by the electric thrill, or what has been called 'satisfaction' felt in killing."[118] At least 50 percent of Vietnam veterans "are still burdened with varying degrees of psychological distress," and one estimate found that twice as many veterans died prematurely after returning home as those killed in war. It is the burden of war's trauma, for "war is inherently traumatic because it dehumanizes its participants."[119] Animal metaphors and fantasy are the required ingredients for dehumanization—until they collapse under the weight of the real, and trauma sets in.

Typically, after the initial euphoria of killing comes guilt, frequently resulting in physical revulsion. It's a common event in war narratives, historians tell us. The killer fatally shoots his victim, then asks forgiveness from the soldier he has killed, then vomits.[120] Here is William Manchester: "I shot him with a .45 and I felt remorse and shame. I can remember whispering foolishly, 'I'm sorry' and then just throwing up. . . . I threw up all over myself. It was a betrayal of what I'd been taught since I was a child."[121] At close range you can hear the screams and cries of the dying enemy: "Men, dying in battle," reported Major General Frank Richardson, "often call upon their mothers. I have heard them do so in five languages."[122] There can be no comparable love to the one experienced by the dying soldier in that last breath. Then the surviving soldier awakens to the obvious fact that the feared Enemy was just a desperate kid like himself. The killer may even find himself comforting the man he has shot, as was the case with Harry Stewart during the Tet offensive in 1968: "I charged the VC [Viet Cong], firing my M-16. He fell at my feet. He was alive but would soon die. I reached down and took the pistol from his hand. I can still see those eyes, looking at me in hate. . . . I put a blanket over him and rubbed water from my canteen onto his lips. That hard stare started to leave his eyes. He wanted to talk but was too far gone. I lit a cigarette, took a few puffs, and put it to his lips. He could barely puff. We each had had a few drags and that hard look had left his eyes before he died."[123] Deadly antagonism has given way to the ultimate trauma: the brotherhood of killer and killed. Only now can he see behind the mask of his much-feared and fantasized Enemy an all-too-human soldier like himself.

How to turn teenagers into killers without producing trauma—that's the fundamental issue for any modern military. With the new collective mirage of an army of autonomous robots that will do the killing without trauma, drones provide the latest false promise.

"NOW I AM BECOME DEATH"

Creech Air Force Base and the Nevada Test Site are two paramount symbols of martial America, forty-five and sixty-five miles away from Las Vegas, experienced as a single apocalyptic site by the antidrone resisters regularly protesting in the southern Nevada desert. There is nothing as alarming as the vision of nuclear holocaust for these pacifist militants. But it was the scientists who built the Bomb who were the first ones to be traumatized by what they had created and to raise their voices to demand international control of nuclear energy, predicting that without a change in thinking a doomsday scenario was inevitable. J. Robert Oppenheimer and the Manhattan Project scientists who developed atomic bombs were described as the "most exclusive club in the world," who possessed "a spirit of Athens, of Plato, of an ideal republic."[124] These were the greatest minds of the century—yet they also engaged in meetings hosted by Oppenheimer to establish criteria for the selection of "target" cities to be obliterated, such as Kyoto, Hiroshima, Yokohama, or Kokura.[125] It all began in August 1939 when, prompted by the physicist Leo Szilard, Einstein wrote to the president of the United States warning him of the possibility of Nazis setting up a nuclear chain reaction in a large mass of uranium, which could lead to an extremely powerful bomb. Einstein received a thank-you note from the president. Einstein, unwittingly, had launched the nuclear armaments project.

By the end of 1944, Einstein had heard from the physicist Otto Stern, secretly working on the Manhattan Project in Chicago, that the nuclear reaction would be successful. What Stern said upset Einstein. He felt compelled to write to Niels Bohr, working for the Manhattan Project in Los Alamos. A worried Einstein wanted to let Bohr know about the need to control atomic weapons because "the politicians do not appreciate the possibilities and consequently do not know the extent of the menace."[126] He argued that a world government must prevent an atomic armaments race and that scientists should pressure the political leaders of their countries "in order to bring about an internationalization of military power."[127] Bohr shared his friend's desire for internationalization, an approach he had advocated in his meetings with Churchill and Roosevelt. Was it justifiable to use the bomb against Japan when it might not be needed to win the war? (It was known by 1944 that there was no German nuclear program.) Einstein agreed to write another letter to Roosevelt telling him about the scientists' concerns. But Roosevelt would never read the letter, which was passed to President Truman after Roosevelt died.

Einstein was taking a nap when the Bomb was dropped on Hiroshima. When he awoke and was told about it, "Oh, my God" was all he said.[128] No matter who else's, it was surely *his* bomb. Three days later was Nagasaki. The following day the Smyth report was published by Washington officials, assigning great weight to Einstein's intervention for launching the project. "Had I known that the Germans would not succeed in producing an atomic bomb, I never would have lifted a finger," Einstein lamented.[129] A traumatized Einstein became the evangelist of the creation of a "supranational" world government and opposed national sovereignties holding armaments secrets.[130] His efforts were fueled, he admitted, "by his guilty feelings about the role he had played in encouraging the atom bomb project."[131] In May 1946, he became chairman of the Emergency Committee of Atomic Scientists and gave speeches and chaired meetings in this role. He urged Washington officials to try harder to enlist Moscow in arms control. The "realists" would consider his politics naive. "If the idea of world government is not realistic, then there is only one realistic view of our future: wholesale destruction of man by man," Einstein wrote in 1948.[132] He offered a dire warning: "The secret of the atomic bomb is to America what the Maginot Line was to France before 1939. It gives us *imaginary* security, and in this respect it is a great danger."[133] The imaginary presented the greatest danger.

Truman was exultant after news of Hiroshima's annihilation: "This is the greatest thing in history." Fleet Admiral William Leahy, President Truman's chief of staff, disagreed: "The use of this barbarous weapon at Hiroshima and Nagasaki was of no material assistance in our war against Japan. The Japanese were already defeated and ready to surrender."[134] Dorothy Day, in rage, responded in her *Catholic Worker* weekly column: "Mr. Truman was jubilant. . . . Truman is a true man of his time in that he is jubilant. . . . We have killed 318,000 Japanese. . . . We hope we have killed them, [says] the Associated Press. . . . It is to be hoped they are vaporized, our Japanese brothers—scattered, men, women and babies, to the four winds, over the seven seas. Perhaps we will breathe their dust into our nostrils, feel them in the fog of New York on our faces."[135]

In 1956 the University of Oxford granted Truman an honorary degree. Eminent British analytic philosopher Elizabeth Anscombe opposed the degree and wrote a pamphlet that echoes Day's rage: "For men to choose to kill the innocent as a means to their ends is always murder, and murder is one of the worst of human actions."[136] Not a pacifist, Anscombe specified that for her, when unintended, "killing the innocent . . . is not necessarily murder."[137] But Hiroshima and Nagasaki were in no way "a borderline case," and she thought a "bad joke" the question as to where to draw a line. Facing the fact that weapons are manufactured "whose sole point is to be used in massacre of cities," the philosopher who had a seminal influence in contemporary ethics left this verdict: "The people responsible are not murderous because they have these weapons; they have them because they are murderous."[138]

Day never bought into the need for nuclear deterrence, or the theory of "just war"—contrary to the Catholic bishops' position during the Cold War. For her Catholic Worker movement, the unprecedented destructiveness of nuclear technology made any notion of self-defense meaningless and a violation of just-war principles. She had no compunction about blasting scientists, army officers, great universities, and captains of industry; for them Day had one word and one word only: "murderers." "God is not mocked," she added.[139]

The first detonation of an atomic bomb occurred in the early morning of July 16, 1945. Oppenheimer code-named it "Trinity"—apparently inspired by John Donne's poetry.[140] Twenty years later, Oppenheimer recollected that moment: "We knew the world would not be the same. A few people laughed, a few people cried. Most people were silent. I remembered the line from the Hindu scripture, the Bhagavad Gita: ... 'Now I am become death, the destroyer of worlds.' I suppose we all thought that one way or another."[141] A *New York Times* reporter described the scientists' euphoria of the moment: "A loud cry filled the air. The little groups that hitherto had stood rooted to the earth like desert plants broke into dance."[142] Oppenheimer and his team were now celebrities, no longer scientists working in furtive secrecy. The evening of Hiroshima's annihilation they assembled in Los Alamos, and Oppenheimer made a dramatic entrance, raising and clasping his hands together "like a prize-winner boxer."[143] He told his cheering crowd that it was too early to know the effects of the Bomb but that "the Japanese didn't like it" and that he regretted only that they were too late to have done the same to the Germans. The hollering of the crowd of scientists was such that it "practically raised the roof."[144] It wasn't only Truman that was jubilant. These scientists were the greatest minds in America—the new Athens.

But a week after the detonation Oppenheimer looked depressed, not triumphant, as if he were thinking: "Oh God, what have we done! All this work, and people are going to die in the thousands."[145] Later Oppenheimer acknowledged, "The atomic bomb is shit."[146] By November 1945, most scientists were opposing an armaments race and the development of the hydrogen bomb (the equivalent of about seven hundred Hiroshima bombs), whose use "would be a betrayal of all standards of morality."[147] Before using the bomb, 72 percent of scientists had thought that it should be demonstrated to the Japanese before being dropped on a city. The knowledge that their work had killed tens of thousands of people undid any remaining enthusiasm; they now had to attempt to justify those deaths. "Few of us could see any moral reason for dropping a second bomb," recalled Otto Frisch.[148] There was in fact an increasing "revulsion" in Los Alamos against the bombings following Nagasaki; even for those who thought the bombs were justified they brought "an intensely personal experience of the reality of evil."[149]

By then it was too late for the scientists. Government officials had taken hold of the Bomb as the fetish that was going to secure their country. One can take their predicament as another instance of "dual power" structure in the aftermath of the development of the atomic bomb. Roosevelt wanted the scientists' advice regarding the technical aspects of the bomb but "reserved solely to himself the right to make policy."[150] The power to develop the weapons belonged to the scientists; the power to decide their deployment was a military matter belonging to politicians. In the debate over the hydrogen bomb's development, the scientists were overruled.

Far from projecting a figure of evil, Oppenheimer would strike people for "his priestly style."[151] In a talk he gave in the summer of 1959, he admitted his anguish over the lack of ethical discourse regarding weapons.[152] He was open to accepting evil in oneself. Similarly Fermi, as the completion of the Bomb was in sight by March 1945, "began to be very worried" and felt "a growing sense of panic."[153] At its initial stage, "the success of the Manhattan Project [had] depended almost entirely on Fermi's ability to achieve a self-sustaining reaction."[154] He had been "the last holdout" against any use of the Bomb.[155] Fermi was one of the scientists who in 1949 was vehemently opposed to the hydrogen bomb, calling it "evil";[156] but, inexplicably, by the summer of 1950 he was working on it intensively.[157]

These were not wicked men. Oppenheimer, Bohr, and the rest of the scientists, aware of the monstrosity in which they were taking part, including the human experiments linked to the Manhattan Project, urged an international agreement to prevent nuclear war and proposed a policy of openness for sharing information for the sake of "the enlargement of human welfare."[158] They also indulged in the fantasy that "the shock of seeing just how powerful the Bomb was would be so great that the people and governments of the world would demand international cooperation to end war."[159]

Oppenheimer visited Washington to try to convince Truman that a nuclear race had to be averted. He was so dejected that Truman asked Oppenheimer what was the matter. "Mr. President, I feel I have blood on my hands," replied Oppenheimer.[160] Truman became furious and ended the interview right there. Earlier the president had asked him when the Russians would develop their nuclear bomb; to Oppenheimer's reply that he didn't know, Truman added that he did know the answer: "Never." Two days later in a public address Truman said that the United States had to keep secret the possession of the nuclear weapons as a "sacred trust," deriding the scientists' assumption "that the 'secret' of the bomb was an illusion" and rejecting their premise as a treasonous plot by influential people in Washington.[161] At a talk in New York's Waldorf Astoria Hotel on March 14, 1946, Truman said to thunderous applause that the United States didn't need to worry about the Russians because "those people can't even make a jeep."[162] It was the invincible force of fantasy.

A MODEST PROPOSAL FOR COLD WARRIORS

In the spring of 1961, President Kennedy addressed the Joint Chiefs of Staff with a simple question: "If your plans for general [nuclear] war are carried out as planned, how many people will be killed in the Soviet Union and China?"[163] Their answer: between 275 million and 325 million. What about the totality of global death? Answer: roughly 600 million deaths.

It was a number not for the faint-hearted. But they were men of the Greatest Generation planning the Greatest War ever, tough cold warriors willing to ride the horses of the Apocalypse while facing the modest proposal of absorbing 600 million deaths.

As Defense Secretary McNamara concluded in 1965 the Vietnam War to be unwinnable, General William Westmoreland issued a report with an arresting idea: "Short of a decision to introduce nuclear weapons against sources and channels of enemy power, I see no likelihood of achieving a quick, favorable end to war."[164] Westmoreland had constantly been requesting more troops, but they were never enough. The potential of a recourse to atomic weapons was, in fact, present throughout the war, beginning with McNamara's signals during the escalation of 1965 and his reference to President Eisenhower's statement that the armistice in Korea was obtained by bringing up the prospect of nuclear attack, suggesting the same for Vietnam.[165] During the Nixon administration, both Nixon and Henry Kissinger frequently mentioned the option of nuclear weapons to end the war. According to the North Vietnamese leader Le Duan, the US had threatened to use nuclear weapons on thirteen different occasions.[166]

McNamara later had a change of thinking regarding his own conduct during the Vietnam War and his support for nuclear weapons. At the end of the documentary *The Fog of War*, having admitted that "reason has limits" and that the nuclear holocaust had been avoided by sheer luck, a sobbing McNamara quotes T. S. Eliot: "We shall not cease from exploration, and the end of all our exploring will be to arrive where we started and know the place for the first time"—the place where the antinuclear objectors had been from day one.[167] He concludes his autobiography by quoting Sakharov: "Reducing the risk of annihilating humanity in a nuclear war carries an absolute priority over all other considerations."[168]

McNamara was echoing what George Kennan had long been advocating after his own change of mind. No other figure articulated more insightfully the thinking, fears, contradictions, and retractions of the Cold War than diplomat and historian Kennan. He is universally known as the man who provided the theoretical basis for the strategy of "containment" of Soviet expansion, and yet he was also the one who later would most abhor the militarized interpretation given to his thinking. Kennan mercilessly attacked the "fantasy world" of the armament race: "It has no foundation in real interests—no foundation, in fact, but in fear, and in an essentially irrational fear at that. It is carried not by any reason to believe that the other side *would*, but only by a hypnotic fascination with the fact that it *could*."[169] The nuclear arsenals were "fantastically redundant," the leaders were hypnotized "like men in a dream,"[170] and there was now no other priority but to reduce or even eliminate nuclear weapons. Already in his

1951 book *American Diplomacy: 1900–1950,* Kennan's thesis was "short but shocking: the insecurity the United States faced resulted less from what its adversaries had done than from *its own leaders' illusions.*"[171]

In his 1980 speech at the Second World Congress for Soviet and East European Studies, addressing the leaders of Washington and Moscow, Kennan spoke in words not that different from Dorothy Day's: "For the love of God, of your children, and of the civilization to which you belong, cease this madness. You have a duty not just to the generation of the present—you have a duty to civilization's past, which you threaten to render meaningless, and to its future, which you threaten to render non-existent. You are mortal men. You are capable of error. You have no right to hold in your hands . . . destructive powers sufficient to put an end to civilized life."[172]

By the mid-1970s Kennan saw his own country, not the Soviet Union, as the real threat to international relations. During the Ronald Reagan administration and the emergence of Gorbachev, Kennan's criticisms would focus mainly on the "simply childish, inexcusably childish" Washington government that in his opinion was deliberately destabilizing the nuclear balance. Powerful elements in the US needed an inhuman enemy "as a foil for what they like to persuade themselves is their exceptional virtue."[173] The extraordinary reversal in the two superpowers' positions was such that "now, Kennan seemed to be saying, Gorbachev in his dealings with Reagan was facing an American Stalin."[174]

The Joint Chiefs of Staff's answer to Kennedy's 1961 question had been 600 million deaths as the result of a nuclear war. Daniel Ellsberg, at the time special assistant secretary of defense to McNamara, had drafted Kennedy's question. But it became clear by 1983 that those numbers were a gross underestimation. Nobody at the time knew that the phenomena covered by "nuclear winter" and "nuclear famine"—the smoke and soot produced by firestorms from hundreds of burning cities, which would be lifted to the stratosphere, blocking most sunlight, preventing rain, and lowering temperatures to the level of the last Ice Age—would destroy all harvests and cause universal starvation. Nuclear war would kill nearly *all* human and large animal life on earth.

Ellsberg became a whistle-blower in 1969, famously delivering war secrets known as the Pentagon Papers to the *Washington Post* and the

New York Times. He had been informed by Morton Halperin, a deputy to Kissinger, that President Nixon had threatened to escalate the Vietnam War "to achieve a quasi-victory." Warnings to the Soviet ambassador "had implied a readiness to use nuclear weapons if Nixon's terms were not met."[175] Nixon wrote in his memoirs that what prevented him from testing his "madman theory" were not leaks or Vietnamese compliance but the fact that on October 15, 1969, two million Americans demonstrated against the war.

How much better off are we today than in 1962, when the Cuban Missile Crisis brought the world to the brink of war? Ellsberg, the man who drafted the above questions for President Kennedy, has a nonambiguous answer: "Tragically, I believe that nothing has fundamentally changed."[176] As Ellsberg looks back to the documents he wrote during his Cold Warrior period, his comments are unsparing: "I am talking about the madness of the strategy and the planning I personally laid out in the spring of 1961: my draft adopted word for word by Secretary of Defense McNamara as his official guidance to the JCS for their operational planning for general nuclear war."[177]

Ellsberg's recent book faces the reader with the existence of an actual Doomsday Machine in both the United States and Russia—the system that was portrayed in Stanley Kubrick's *Dr. Strangelove.* "These two systems still risk doomsday: both are still on hair-trigger alert . . . susceptible to being triggered on a false alarm, a terrorist action, unauthorized launch, or a desperate decision to escalate."[178] This is still true thirty years after the Cold War ended. These Doomsday Machines can be dismantled relatively easily within a year, but there is one major obstacle: "it would mean—and here's where institutional resistance would be strong—giving up certain infeasible aims and illusory capabilities of our nuclear forces: in particular, the notion that it is possible to limit damage to the United States (or Russia) by means of a preemptive first strike."[179] If for Einstein atomic weapons give us only "*imaginary* security," for Ellsberg dismantling them is not achievable until we dismantle the *illusion* that we can win a nuclear war.

Few could grasp the dangers endured during the Cold War as well as William Perry, or reflect more dramatically on the transition from the "old thinking" to the "new thinking" regarding nuclear weapons. People familiar with the US security state acknowledge that nobody has more technical expertise and political experience than Perry, US secretary of defense from 1994 to 1997, to assess the nuclear conundrum.[180] In 2015 he published *My Journey at the Nuclear Brink*,[181] a book that one can read as both a counterpoint and a complement to the work of radical militants protesting at the gates of the NTS. Despite all we have learned about past risks, and despite the end of the Cold War, Perry clearly states, "Today, the danger of some sort of a nuclear catastrophe is greater than it was during the Cold War and most people are blissfully unaware of this danger."[182]

Perry has a long career in the development of smart weapons going back to Jimmy Carter's presidency. He directed the improvement of battlefield conditions by inserting smart weapons, stealth systems to evade radar, GPS, and intelligent sensors to locate enemy forces. While serving as undersecretary of defense and secretary of defense during the Carter and Clinton administrations Perry had to deal, he writes, with defense proposals that were "a bizarre piece of fantasy," products of "an old, familiar mode of thinking," or "farcical comedy."[183] The deterrence power of the US nuclear arsenal is so secure that Perry regrets "that I let myself be stampeded by the prophets of doom."[184] But Perry is no less critical of the current situation, which is only in appearance stable.[185] His memoir is an anguished cry that "we should never underestimate the ability of a country to act against its own self-interests, especially when passions are high."[186] Perry ends his memoir invoking a "new vision" for nuclear disarmament. Throughout the book he can't emphasize enough the catastrophic danger of the "unthinkable surreal 'overkill'" during the Cold War; he supports the Reykjavik proposal to dismantle all the nuclear forces as a historical necessity—something that for Perry amounts to the imperative to commit to "*radically new thinking.*"[187]

Perry, who believes that "time is not on our side," ends his book with a tormented confession that he has "a special responsibility" to dismantle nuclear weapons.[188] His book is a cri de coeur, a supplication to the reader to help him achieve that goal. At a seminar convoked by George Shultz to commemorate the twenty years of the Reykjavik Summit, Perry proposed a step-by-step reduction of nuclear weapons until reaching the goal of zero. In collaboration with former secretaries of state Shultz and Kissinger and former senator Sam Nunn, on January 4, 2007, Perry's op-ed in the *Wall Street Journal*, "A World Free of Nuclear Weapons," called attention to the great dangers of nuclear arms. It had an enormous impact and was endorsed by other former Cold Warriors—McNamara, Colin Powell, and George H. W. Bush. It seemed that the converted Cold Warriors had made common cause with the pacifists. This was before they heard President Trump threaten the nuclear destruction of North Korea during his address to the United Nations in September of 2017 and before they read in October 2018 of Trump's intention to pull out of the landmark Intermediate-Range Nuclear Treaty with Russia, signed by Reagan and Gorbachev in 1987 after the Reykjavik Summit. One cannot escape the historic irony that Perry and his Cold Warrior colleagues, their average age past eighty, having spent their entire lives building and defending the Bomb, were traumatized enough by the nuclear predicament they had pushed their country into that they were compelled to embrace a radical change of thought and convert to the ranks of the antinuclear movement.

THE WESTMORELAND ALTERNATIVE

William Westmoreland, "the general who lost Vietnam," and Cian Westmoreland, the drone operator who introduced himself to us in Las Vegas as a war criminal, are both men from the same extended family with lives defined by service to their country.[189] But the two combatants couldn't be more fundamentally opposed in their thinking and their subjective response to their actions and responsibilities. William Westmoreland was the field commander in Vietnam from 1964 to 1968. Handsome, upright, craggy, he was hailed as 1965 "Man of the Year" by *Time* magazine when the Johnson administration was creating an all-out war in Vietnam. An emblematic figure of his generation's military ambitions and failures, Westmoreland is key not only to understanding the Vietnam War but also to grasping in its full force the historic alternative presented by the younger Cian Westmoreland, an equally emblematic figure in the failures of drone warfare, who, as he told me, "was raised at the knee of General Westmoreland," his family hero.

General Westmoreland was known for his search-and-destroy tactics in a war of attrition where body count was the measure of success. As if nothing had changed since the campaigns of World War II, he considered that the meat-grinder ratio of ten Vietnamese killed for each American was good enough. Fascinated with statistics, he created a "command data system" in order to have "some type of crude measure for everything."[190] In his conduct of war Westmoreland committed basic errors, beginning with the most glaring– conducting a conventional search-and-destroy war against an enemy fighting a guerrilla war and willing to absorb enormous casualties. His bosses in Washington allowed Westmoreland to develop his own strategy of a war of attrition. In the view of H. R. McMaster, the strategy of attrition and graduated pressure "was, in essence, the absence of a strategy."[191] McMaster concludes that the failings were many and self-generating: "arrogance, weakness, lying in the pursuit of self-interest, and, above all, the abdication of responsibility to the American people."[192] In McNamara's own words about US failure in Vietnam, "We misjudged. . . . We exaggerated the dangers to the United States of their [the adversaries'] actions . . . Our misjudgments of friend and foe alike reflected our profound ignorance of the history, culture, and politics of the people in the area, and the personalities and habits of their leaders."[193]

Cian Westmoreland's primary task was also to set up a relay data system for battlefield command and control. He served with the 606 Air Control Squadron in Germany and the Seventy-Third Expeditionary Air Control Squadron in Kandahar, Afghanistan. It was a far more sophisticated system than General Westmoreland's statistical counting, maintained over 240,000 square miles of "persistent data, radar, and radio transmissions."[194] The younger Westmoreland's world was the Data Machine that William Arkin described in his book *Unmanned.* Compared to a military general of the Vietnam War, the young Westmoreland was one of the counterterrorist "x-men," sharing the terrorist's fundamental duality of being assassins as well as a new class of warriors whose hallmark is to cross the lines between soldiers and covert operators, without borders and conventional laws, armed with new technologies as weapons.[195]

There are striking difference between Cian and William Westmoreland. Just look at their attribution of responsibility regarding their military actions. "General Westmoreland had a trait that was repulsive," said the much-decorated general Ellis Williamson. "He *always, invariably,* had someone between himself and anything unpleasant. If it was the slightest bit tenuous, it was always somebody else's fault or responsibility. He was just unbelievably agile at that."[196] The tragedy of My Lai, as an instance, took place on Westmoreland's watch and was a measure of "a failure of leadership on Westy's part" due to "a permissive attitude" and "an almost total disregard for the lives and property of the civilian population."[197] He never owned it.

Cian Westmoreland was the antithesis of the general. He was directly responsible for the killing of 359 civilians, he told us in Las Vegas, repeating what he had written in blog postings. He had arrived at that number after researching reports by the air force, the UN annual report, and the London-based Bureau of Investigative Journalism. A central point in his talk concerned *diffusion of responsibility*. He wrote an essay with that title in which he devises concrete scenarios to show the extended network of different agencies interacting in a single drone air strike. If "formlessness" permeates every aspect touched by terrorism, "diffusion" is a similar notion when it pertains to responsibility. Westmoreland couldn't help but question where responsibility lay—"Was it with the battlespace commander? Was it the pilot? Was the intelligence analyst choosing targets based on reconnaissance imagery? . . . Am I responsible for building the network to facilitate all of this as was Oppenheimer for building his H-bomb?"[198] Westmoreland was twenty-one when he was congratulated for a job well done in "killing bad guys." In the best Orwellian tradition of Newspeak ("War Is Peace"), in training Westmoreland had been told, "We are going to save lives," a claim that Obama also stated and that made Westmoreland sick.[199] Snowden's revelations in June 2013 played an additional role in alerting him to what was really happening.

General Westmoreland and Secretary of Defense McNamara never accepted personal responsibility for having engineered a war that killed tens of thousands of Americans and two to three million Vietnamese. Drone operator Westmoreland's self-blame is unrelenting: "I hold myself personally guilty as an accessory to murder in Afghanistan and Pakistan. . . . It's not just the pilot who is pulling the trigger. Everybody has a part in making this happen. It is volunteering . . . for excessive force and unlawful killing of civilians."[200]

General Westmoreland's failure was rooted in his involvement in a systematic campaign to get the public to believe that the US was winning the war. The field commander had become a propagandist and, in effect, "a spokesman for the administration in the domestic political arena."[201] The evening Cian Westmoreland was addressing the audience at the Las Vegas Law School, one could sense he needed a loudspeaker big enough to awaken the public to the murders he had committed. The American public, so willing to believe General Westmoreland's deceptions, was hardly interested in Cian's confession.

By late 1965 Secretary McNamara had concluded "that the [Vietnam] war could not be won militarily"[202]—and yet the war would continue another decade, killing over fifty thousand Americans and two to three million Vietnamese. General Westmoreland could never acknowledge that the US had lost the war. Defeat was simply unacceptable. Coaching his memoir ghostwriter Charles MacDonald, Westmoreland told him: "Never a defeat of a US unit of battalion size or larger. Some hard knocks, yes; no defeat."[203] Compare that with what Cian Westmoreland told us in Las Vegas: "I don't think drones win a war. What we are essentially doing is we're fueling hatred."

Cian Westmoreland had joined the air force when he was eighteen to be with his father in the family's military tradition. When Cian was a child, his father had been stationed in Armenia, working as a linguist for the Defense Intelligence Agency after the Soviet collapse. When later his father was stationed in Kuwait doing logistic work during the post-9/11 Afghan war, Cian remembered asking, "Dad, did you kill anybody?" and his father's reply: "No, I didn't kill anybody personally, but I ordered all the parts for the bombing in Afghanistan." The father told the son stories about officers hollering and giving each other high fives when they killed somebody. When he returned from Kuwait, his father "became more quiet and distant. He was affected by the bombings." Cian had to also be in Afghanistan before he could understand "the heaviness he must have felt."[204] Father and son knew intimately their own defeat by "winning."

For General Westmoreland, who could never contemplate defeat, the only solutions to the conflict were military—even if this implied having recourse to the nuclear arsenal. Pacification meant defeating the enemy, and defeating the enemy meant killing it. Ghostwriter MacDonald spoke of Westmoreland "being inured to casualties. I don't think he was emotionally affected by heavy losses."[205] The general's autobiography says "so little about the pain both his troops and the Vietnamese people endured," wrote journalist George Wilson.[206]

Cian Westmoreland's reaction to killing couldn't have been more differ-ent. He wasn't simply affected, he was severely traumatized by his memo-ries of the people he had helped kill. He told us that one day he had watched a woman in Afghanistan walk out onto a bridge with her kids, lift and drop them over, then jump herself to death—and that "[he] didn't know how to process that," that he was in therapy, struggling to get by. In his nightmares he found himself standing in a village being bombed with his system's help, while he was desperately trying to save people. He had nightmares of a child standing next to a body covered with ash and look-ing at him. Another time Westmoreland "dreamt that there was an air raid, and that there were something like 50 children staring at the sky in terror. I ran for them, and would try to save them, but when they saw me they would scream and run away. The bombs dropped. I blacked out. Then I found myself standing amongst them in a rubble field, and they were all dead." In another nightmare, Westmoreland saw a village burning and "I run toward it, and saw a small girl crying over a body on the ground. I looked down, and it was a woman. Instinct made me get down and try to give her CPR, but I hesitated to give mouth to mouth because it was caked in blood. I looked at the girl, and told her I was sorry. . . . I looked at my hands and . . . they were covered in her mother's blood. Then she turned around and ran away. I reach for her, then I hear the same whistle I heard during a rocket attack I experienced in Kandahar, there was an explosion, and I woke up."[207]

Unable to sleep, Westmoreland sank deeper and deeper into depres-sion. He became ill with mononucleosis and nearly died of dehydration. His girlfriend broke with him. Feeling that he was a war criminal, he determined that his life was no longer worth living. He flipped a coin to decide whether or not to kill himself. At this period he stumbled into Brandon Bryant's video for Democracy Now! They both knew what was meant by "moral injury." They decided to organize a conference on drone warfare. When someone from the audience called Bryant a hero, he responded: "I am not a hero and you should know that. I'm a murderer and an international war criminal,"[208] The two of them agreed to be will-ing to stand trial at the international criminal court for having partici-pated in an illegal war—a gesture unthinkable for General Westmoreland. But in fact McNamara had told Errol Morris that, had they lost World

War II, he and his boss, General LeMay, might have been prosecuted as war criminals, making McNamara wonder how winning or losing changed a deed's character. It did not present a quandary for Cian Westmoreland: "I know myself to be a war criminal by international standards," he wrote. The old Westmoreland would have been appalled by such an admission. Young Westmoreland thought differently: the signing of the Nuremberg Principles by the US after World War II "set the norm that 'just following orders' is not a valid excuse for human rights violations."[209]

Cian Westmoreland is not a pacifist unable to understand the principle of killing in self-defense. "However," he adds, "the very reason one is sent to war is also a social construction based on decisions a handful of leaders have made to expend the lives of otherwise peaceful individuals to meet a political objective." He demands that the country first examine the reasons for going to war, for "we are still fighting for things that are only as real as people make them, and are figments of our imagination supported by generations of evolving thoughts that we must be aware of to make decisions based off of them."[210] And there is always an escape that permits the diffusion of responsibility, one that "distances people from the moral weight of their decisions," that "allows people to live in their collective fantasies by limiting their exposure to the actual injustice of taking another person's life." The old Westmoreland would be appalled to hear the young man claim that the problem was not the enemy but rather "these illusory structures that we have built for ourselves, these structures that guide our actions . . . which we have mistaken for reality." Nor was drone warfare determined by national security, but rather by decisions a few leaders took that allow "us to live in illusionary worlds where we are deprived of the exposure to our own personal violent consequences."[211]

Social construction, figments of our imagination, collective fantasies, illusory structures, illusionary worlds . . . Cian Westmoreland had the lucidity to realize that, as with other issues such as racism and colonialism, with terrorism too the foremost political question is to see its fantasmatic frame. In psychoanalytic terms, Westmoreland has had the courage to act a subjective destitution by which he has *traversed the fundamental fantasy* of US militarism during its War on Terror—awakened from its spell, accepted its inconsistency, identified with the killed Enemy, dissolved its discourse, seen the void behind imperial desire.

The Westmoreland alternative forces on the American public a confrontation with radical choice: either the old general's self-aggrandizement of "victories" that were lies (a pattern we see in the wars in Iraq, Afghanistan, Syria, and Yemen, and the War on Terror in general), or the young drone operator's traumatized breaking through the fog of military fantasy. Integration of the two Westmoreland positions is impossible—between the two exists an unbridgeable gap. But will the same public that was so ready to accept the general's deceptions bring itself to confront the radicalness of such alternative choices in thinking and politics? In chapter 2 we discussed Hollywood's structure of inherent transgression of simultaneous yes *and* no: Did they do it in *Casablanca?* Did we murder innocent civilians? Yes and no. The breakthrough of Cian Westmoreland, Brandon Bryant, and other whistle-blowers is that, in such public indiscernibility between the yes and the no, their traumatized bodies force open a new situation of accountability. They are the *event* deciding the undecidable for the country. Hence their trauma. Hence, beyond the yes and the no, our obligation to choose—for *or* against.

5 Resistance

A HARSH AND DREADFUL LOVE

It was the morning after Donald Trump won the presidency, promising in his victory speech to "renew the American Dream," that a dozen of us gathered in the predawn darkness around a ceremonial fire across from Creech Air Force Base in the Nevada desert. Smoke from the burning of cottonwood and cedar rose in the air as shoulder to shoulder, facing the fire, we stepped first one direction, then the other, circling to the rhythm of Shoshone chief Johnnie Bobb's chanting and drum. Soon a rooster crowed. A hawk took flight. Johnnie touched the flame with his deer skin drum and, facing the mountains to the east, lifted his arms toward daybreak, praying for the cleansing and renewal of the earth, for protection for the desert and the life it holds, and for our courage that day and always.

We were there to protest drone killing, prepared to be arrested at Creech for doing so. I had joined the protests that spring as I was writing a book on drones; my goal was to study protesters' resistance, but soon I felt I couldn't just observe them without participating in their protest, including being arrested in order to know of their experience. Johnnie gave each of us a cedar twig to throw into the fire as we spoke our thoughts. One by one we gave thanks, asked to be cleared from error, to be healed, and to find strength. Next to me was Nico, who was filming the gathering.

He spoke of his five-year-old son Zidane, the light of his life, who a month earlier had suddenly died. Johnnie's chanting created bonds of mourning and commitment between us.

We were on Shoshone land occupied by the US military. The government's appropriation of Western Shoshone land has its own history of unilateral decisions, misunderstandings, and legal deceptions, all of which favored the occupiers. The Shoshone never ceded their rights to the land, and, according to Johnnie, the 1863 Treaty of Ruby Valley, a treaty of "peace and friendship" that confirmed Indian title to specific territories and "safe passage" for immigrants traveling through Shoshone lands, remains in effect.[1]

At sunrise we drove to Creech Air Force Base to meet personnel of the 6 a.m. shift with our banners and signs. It was ritual: our circle at the fire pit, our facing the guards and police that blocked the gate, our holding a twenty-foot banner "Shut Down Creech," and then five of us being arrested in handcuffs and taken to jail. But these gestures, the only things left to us, were more than gestures, they were actions against what goes on daily at Creech and, twenty miles to the north, at the Nevada Test Site. "There's something profoundly American about getting arrested at the Nevada Test Site," wrote Rebecca Solnit; "land, war technology, apocalypse, Thoreauvian civil disobedience, bureaucratic obscurity" warrant it.[2]

Standing on Shoshone land, as we turned ritual into action, Christian read our statement through the bullhorn loudly enough for the base's pilots and support personnel to hear: "As global citizens we are part of the International Peace Patrol. Creech AFB, through its participation in the US drone assassination program, is in direct violation of the United Nations Declaration of Human Rights, articles 3, 7, and 10. As an active member of the US Air Force, your duties indirectly support the illegal activities taking place on this base. Therefore you are complicit in the crimes against humanity being committed here." The line of policemen and guards faced us. We stepped into them, over the line, and were arrested.

Our hands cuffed behind our backs, body-searched and identified, we were taken in police cars to Clark County Jail at 330 South Casino Center Boulevard in Las Vegas. Unlike me, my companions had been arrested many times. When we reached the jail, they stripped us of everything except our pants and T-shirts, provided us with plastic sandals, and recuffed our hands behind us. Later we would be shackled at our waists. Michael, Christian, and I were taken to a holding room with an open toilet and an acrid stench of urine, packed with twenty other men, most of whom were African Americans or Latinos. Linda and Toby were taken to a different room. We were soon moved from this room to another, then brought back before being moved again for fingerprinting and mug shots. By 1 p.m. all of us, except Linda, who was kept longer because of an unpaid fine from a previous arrest, were released. In a later arrest I would spend thirty hours in Clark County Jail, enough to have a small taste of the helplessness and anxiety experienced by the inmates, who were of course the truly jailed there, the homeless and defenseless, the poor of Las Vegas, the wretched whose freedom is uncertain at best.[3] Compared to their jail time ours was ritual, but it was also real, as it was for me real to be arraigned in the Las Vegas Court months later and to declare in front of the judge that "*I believe the drone pilot* when he says he helped kill 359 civilians."

CAMP JUSTICE

It's not only Marines and drone pilots who are traumatized by drone warfare. Many Americans watching its consequences—killings, starvation, displacements—are shocked by what is going on. Some of them experience what a third-century convert to Christianity, Lactantius, wrote regarding the killing of Christians as sport and entertainment in the Roman colosseum: "Now, if merely to be present at a murder fastens on a man the character of an accomplice; if barely to be an spectator involves us in one common guilt with the perpetrator: it follows, of necessity, that, in these murders of the amphitheater, the hand which inflicts the fatal blow is not more imbrued in blood than his who passively looks on . . . nor that man seem other than a participator in murder who gives his applause to the murderer and calls for prizes on his behalf."[4] Christians were the subversive outsiders to the Roman Empire; now the Afghani and Yemeni and other Middle Eastern combatants enemy terrorists for the American order. Many Americans feel, as Lactantius did, that they are accomplices in crime and that resistance to this state-sanctioned murder is the only way to address the guilt they share with the killers. Some of these resisters bring their protest to Creech Air Base.

The Code Pink organizers have been demonstrating at Creech twice a year since 2009. Most of us travel from other states and park our cars on both sides of the road running perpendicular to Highway 95. On a typical day of protest, between 6 and 7 a.m. and between 4 and 5 p.m. there's a rush of cars getting in and out of the base, heading toward Las Vegas, forty-six miles away. Drones fly around and above us, then land a mile away. A banner, "Camp Justice," names us. The protesters are mostly Veterans for Peace, Code Pink activists, and members of Dorothy Day's Catholic Worker movement. They hold banners, "US drone warfare is terrorism"; "Muslim lives matter"; "Drones fly, children die"; "'I have a dream' (King) 'I have a drone' (Obama)"; "Stop killing for capitalism;" "There is no flag large enough to cover the shame of killing innocent people."

The day after I arrived, on March 31, 2016, eight elderly members of Veterans for Peace were arrested and taken to a Las Vegas jail. In a mock funeral staged the next morning at 7 a.m., six children and eight adults dressed as angels represented the "double tap"—the procedure by which drones attack first responders. At the head of our procession a ballerina laid roses on the road; in silence the children carried a casket to the gate and set it down before forty policemen, some of them mounted on horses, who were blocking the gate. A drone strike was reenacted with the tossing of baby dolls and mannequin body parts into the air. Activists blocked an entrance to the base, delaying operations for an hour. Others blocked the highway. Twenty-five were arrested.

Activists carried caskets with the names of nations targeted by drones: Pakistan, Afghanistan, Syria, Somalia, Yemen, Iraq, Libya. A woman was singing John Lennon's "All we are saying is give peace a chance." A cemetery was built alongside Highway 95 with placards naming children killed by drones: "RIP. Salman. 12 years old. Pakistan." "RIP. Noor Aziz. 8 years old. Iraq." "RIP. Salma. 4 years old. Yemen"—more than eighty of them. Sitting on the asphalt of the road to Creech's gate, their voices distorted by emotion, their bodies dragged by the guards who were arresting them, the antidrone protesters kept shouting the names of the dead children— Salman! Noor! Abdulrahman! It was the only grace the victims could find in the desert from where the missiles had been fired at them.

Who are these people with families and jobs who once or twice a year travel to Creech Air Base to engage in antidrone protests? Toby Blomé is one of them; a Code Pink organizer for Shut Down Creech, she is a dedicated and fearless sixty-something arrested and jailed dozens of times for protest. A teacher and medical therapist for years, she is married to a physician and had a disabled child with a neurodegenerative disease who died at age seven. She told me, "It is the mother in me that drives me." For years she went to Washington to lobby legislators, but, she said, the great majority of them show no interest in ending the war. "When I see victims of the drones, I see my dead child in those pictures. In one child in particular I saw my own child." She could barely whisper her child's name, "Denise."

Ann Wright is another independent-minded protester. She served twenty-nine years in the US Army, rising to the rank of colonel and earning the State Department's Award for Heroism in 1997 for work during the civil war in Sierra Leone. But in March 2003 she resigned from the military because, she wrote, she could no longer ignore the lies and illegality of the war in Iraq. It was she who introduced Cian Westmoreland to the audience at the panel on drones at the University of Nevada, Las Vegas, and who read the letter that he and other young drone pilots, Brandon Bryant, Michael Haas, and Stephen Lewis, had written to President Obama: "We came to the realization that the innocent civilians we were killing only fueled the feelings of hatred that ignited terrorism and groups like ISIS, while also serving as a fundamental recruitment tool similar to Guantánamo Bay." The letter told the president of their trauma: "When the guilt of our roles in facilitating this systematic loss of innocent life became too much, all of us succumbed to PTSD." They said they could no longer "sit silently by."

Wright was arrested at the Creech entrance the day after she introduced Westmoreland. She spent the day in a Las Vegas jail, then returned to Camp Justice, decrying the conditions of those without the means for bail. She wore a T-shirt on which was inked: "I HATE WAR as only a soldier who has lived it can, as only one who has seen its brutality, its futility, its stupidity (General Dwight Eisenhower)." She was carrying a banner that read: "Paris. Boston. San Bernardino. Brussels. Drone Strike Blowback." With Susan Dixon, Wright is the author of *Dissent: Voices of Conscience*,[5] a book that explains the history of her resignation the day before the US bombing of Iraq began. She, a decorated colonel, calls the invasion of Iraq "illegal" (as did UN secretary general Kofi Annan) and a "war crime."[6] After she resigned she received nearly four hundred emails from her State Department colleagues telling her how proud they were of her. Her boss, Colin Powell, who, weeks earlier on February 5, had delivered his infamous speech at the United Nations in front of the reproduction of Picasso's *Guernica,* said nothing.

If Westmoreland is shell-shocked by his Slaughterhouse-359, Wright cites her own number in the first page of chapter 1 of her book: 655,000 Iraqis killed by the war her army conducted in Iraq, a number ascertained by a 2006 Johns Hopkins University study.[7] Name by name, report by report, Wright states the facts, events, lies, and crimes leading to and produced by the war in Iraq, revealing American politicians, military, media, and the public's withdrawal from and betrayal of basic international codes of ethical behavior in war, in favor of self-serving nationalism. It is the collective mythmaking inherent to the War on Terror that makes stating the bare facts so difficult and shocking. Now it is the facts of drone warfare, a continuation of the same military deceptions and illegalities of the Iraq War, that concern Wright and bring her annually to Creech.

Don Kimball is another veteran and Creech protester who joined the military in 1977 because the GI Bill would pay for his college education and who spent four years in the US Air Force. He served at the Strategic Air Command base, dealing with bombers carrying nuclear weapons. One Sunday morning, November 9, 1979, something happened that changed Don's life, the reason he would lead Veterans for Peace in Las Vegas. Training was taking place at his Pease Air Force Base in Portsmouth, New Hampshire, when the air traffic controller alarm sounded. He knew they didn't do drills on Sunday morning, so the unusual alarm meant they could be under nuclear attack. Soon the bombers and pilots, kept on twenty-four-hour alert, were ready to leave on their mission before the base was attacked. A missile fired from the Soviet Union takes only twenty minutes to reach US mainland. The windows were rattling with the engines of the six bombers, each one carrying one or more nuclear bombs. He looked at his wife in bed, and said, "Maybe this is it." The "it" of nuclear war.

Computers at the NORAD headquarters inside Cheyenne Mountain had determined that a massive missile attack had been launched from submarines and sites within the Soviet Union and would hit American targets within minutes. At Strategic Command Bases nationwide missile crews were put on alert. Air traffic controllers prepared to clear American airspace for military flights. Minutes passed, but no missiles with warheads arrived, and soon it became clear that it had been a false alarm. As part of a training exercise with war games, a technician had put the wrong tape into one of the computers.[8] (The following year another false alarm on June 3, 1980, had national security adviser Zbigniew Brzezinski ready to call President Carter at 2:30 a.m. with news of a nuclear attack launched by the Soviet Union.) Don said that experience was his "epiphany": "It changed my view on nuclear war and everything right then and there." His time in service was almost up, and soon he was discharged. He had been a Republican, a Christian, a military man; he was no longer any of it. He got involved in the antinuclear and anti-Creech movements because, he said, he felt he had a duty to make the world aware of the perils of the military-industrial complex and of the drone program and its blowback effects.

One of the people I met at Camp Justice was Linda Sartor, a quiet woman with a master's degree in environmental studies and a PhD in integral studies. She told me her story after we had both been arrested at the Las Vegas jail on November 10, 2016, for protesting at Creech. When the US had started bombing Afghanistan in October 2001, Linda felt she must do something. She became a member of a group of sixteen international peacekeepers. Her memoir describes her experience, the ten years she spent in Israel/Palestine, Iraq, Afghanistan, Sri Lanka, Iran, and Bahrain as a peacekeeper and unarmed civilian witness.[9] She got her inspiration from the nonviolent action of Dr. King. In Iraq she joined fourteen Code Pink women from the US and another thirty-nine Iraq Peace Team representatives from across the globe. They went to various sites, presenting banners that read: "Bombing this site is a war crime." Media from all over the world, except from the US, interviewed them. In live interviews from Baghdad, she criticized any justification "that war is inevitable" and concluded that "the US government seems determined to create the very conditions that will promote what they say they are trying to avoid." Linda was acting on the proposition that "protesting and educating aren't enough anymore, I need to take a stand with my body that as a US citizen my life is not any more precious than anyone else's life."[10] It was that same determination that brought Linda to the Las Vegas jail.

Another protester I met was JoAnn Lingle, an eighty-year-old woman with osteoarthritis who asked me to help her sit on the asphalt of the entrance road to Creech as she was about to be arrested. For the police to handcuff her, they had to lift her from the ground. She was born and raised in Savanna, Georgia, during the Jim Crow era, and she had one story in particular to tell me. She was nine when she was taking a segregated bus through a black neighborhood—blacks in the back, whites in the front. As the bus filled up, all the seats were taken by the black people except the bench she was on, with two empty seats next to her. But the blacks could not sit next to her. JoAnn noticed an old black woman standing uncomfortably and told her that she could take her seat. As the old lady sat down, the driver stopped the bus, stood up over JoAnn, and shouted at her: "Little girl, sit down, don't ever give your seat to a nigger!" JoAnn sat down crying. "I never forgot that. That injustice followed me all my life. I was a powerless child, like now the children attacked by drones."

That experience attracted JoAnne to the civil rights movement led by Dr. King during the 1960s when she was a housewife taking care of her eight children. Two of her sons were gay and died of AIDs at ages thirty-four and thirty-nine. "They were beautiful young men," JoAnn tells me, her voice quivering while talking about how they died and how they now accompany her wherever she goes. After her children grew up and her son Robert died in 1991, JoAnn sold her house and joined a spiritual community of Mennonites who were antiwar. In 1995 she began working on Central American issues, protesting against the School of the Americas. In 1996, someone from the Christian Peacemakers Teams (CPT) who worked in Palestine came to talk to her community. She liked what he said: "if we believe that the cross is stronger than the sword, why are not we willing to risk what soldiers risk? They are willing to risk their lives for their country. Aren't we willing to go to places of conflict unarmed for what we believe in?" She began visiting Palestine as a member of CPT. The members are volunteers and they pay their own way. They don't do humanitarian work, don't go to solve problems, and don't want to be known as members of NGOs. "Palestine is my other life," JoAnn sums it up. Once a year she goes with a tourist visa for as long as three months. Her stays in Palestine over twenty-one years add up to about five years. "I know families so well there that they are like my second families. I love their villages." The kids call her grandma. One of them is studying medicine in a US university and hopes to return to help his people. CPT is too small to help Palestinians economically. Creech is one more antiwar activity for JoAnn. She also works with Code Pink and has been connected to the Catholic Worker movement. Dorothy Day's books had a big influence on her. She has been arrested about thirty times. Isn't she concerned about going to jail at age eighty? She has the privilege of her white skin, and now being old is nothing but "an inconvenience," she says.

John Amadon is a member of Veterans for Peace who lives in New York, protests the drone program at Hancock Field Air National Guard Base, and also comes to Creech. He served four years as a Marine before he quit the army in 1969, went to college, and got involved in protests against the Vietnam War. Later, under the influence of a Maryknoll priest, he became active against the Central American wars. He became close to the Quakers and to the Franciscans of New York. Now he is active against drones. John says his duty is to the US Constitution, which allows only defensive wars; the US as signatory of the Charter of the United Nations; the Universal Declaration of Human Rights; and the Nuremberg principles. "We are engaged in war crimes . . . double tapping, bombing funeral parties and weddings." His ideas of civil resistance are inspired by Martin Luther King's writings, "Letter from Birmingham Jail" and "Beyond Vietnam" in particular. John's activism comes from seeing people's suffering, the Pakistani peasant who lost his child, the Guatemalan peasant gunned down from a US helicopter. "We protest to create [awareness of] a moral crisis." If we don't want an environmental collapse, John concludes, "we have to stop the wars, and not prepare for wars—it's that simple."

Kathy Kelly, one of the Creech 14, was arrested and tried in Las Vegas in September 14, 2010. Born to a working-class Catholic family in Chicago, she joined Catholic Workers and became a volunteer on the soup line. She met and married Karl Meyer, a tax resister like herself, and became aware of the links between militarism and poverty; when the IRS can't collect anything from you, you come to understand, she said, how "freedom's just another word for nothing left to lose." She was sentenced to one year in prison for planting corn on nuclear missile silos. In 1990 she volunteered to join the Gulf Peace Team during the First Iraq War and stayed in Iraq for six months. Upon her return to the US, reports began to emerge about the severe humanitarian crisis in which half a million Iraqi children under age five were dying of hunger caused by the economic embargo imposed by the United Nations under US pressure. For Kelly this wasn't vague news lost among other facts in the news cycle. Headquartered in her own Chicago apartment, she helped found Voices in the Wilderness, a group willing to oppose the economic sanctions and bring medical supplies to the children and families in Iraq—an act that risked penalties of twelve years in prison and a $1 million fine.

In May of 1996, Lesley Stahl from CBS's *60 Minutes* asked then US ambassador to the United Nations and later secretary of state Madeleine Albright, "More than 500,000 Iraqi children are already dead as a direct result of the UN sanctions. Do you think the price is worth paying?" Albright responded: "I think this is a very hard choice but the price—we think the price is worth it."[11] Implicit in her response was that keeping Iraqi oil off the market was more important than hundreds of thousands of children. That exchange defined the Clinton era for Kelly, as well as the political and media world of indifference to the massive murder of children.

The US Treasury Department fined Kelly $20,000 for her crime of delivering medicines and toys to the dying Iraqi children. The group's actions were dismissed by the media as naive and ineffectual. The *New York Times* published a stream of op-ed columns about the potential crimes of the UN's Oil-for-Food Program, "while there has been no mention of the crime of child sacrifice through sanctions of war in Iraq."[12] Footage of their hospital visits by Reuters and Associated Press was broadcast in several European countries, but none in the US. Some UN officials, seeing the horror they themselves had created, resigned their posts to give talks and educate the public on the "genocidal" effects of the sanctions, as one of them put it.

The *Wall Street Journal* voiced what many American journalists must have been thinking: the children's silent massacre was all Hussein's fault. In 2005, Kelly published a book to tell the US public, in the words of Jeffrey St. Clair and Alexander Cockburn, "a history of the US war on Iraq that never appeared in the pages of the *New York Times* or in the news stories on CNN."[13] This time the *passion for ignorance* was not about a few thousand drone victims but about half a million children starved to death. "I couldn't claim I am ignorant," Kelly told me. "Once an individual like myself knows this is going on your options are very, very limited. . . . I think most people didn't really know. Had they known, there would have been more concern." Once she knew about it, Kelly had to follow the Catholic Worker tradition of Dorothy Day and Daniel Berrigan; upon release from Danbury prison in 1972, Berrigan wrote: "There is no issue comparable to the deaths of innocent children—neither the economy, nor good fellowship with China, nor cancer, nor pollution, nor taxes, nor political campaigns."[14] And James Baldwin wrote, "The children are always ours, every single one of them, all over the globe," and "I am beginning to suspect that whoever is incapable of recognizing this may be incapable of morality."[15] Similarly, once Kelly found about the drone killings from Creech, she had to be there, in Camp Justice and in the Las Vegas jail, in defense of the children whose faces she had seen on her many trips to the Middle East.

In the fall of 2018, haunting images of Yemeni children dying of hunger emerged in the US media; eighty-five thousand children had already died. It was estimated that fourteen million of the country's twenty-six million were on the brink of famine. It was all déjà vu for Kelly, who wrote on November 29 about the "death row for infants" she knew from Iraq: "starvation . . . being used as a weapon of war" while "children died amid an eerie and menacing silence on the part of mainstream media." The media's response was now more positive, she told me on the phone. As an instance, in the Sunday *New York Times* on December 9, 2018, Nicholas Kristof wrote an op-ed article about Yemen entitled "Your Tax Dollars Help Starve Children." Kelly added in her blog: "The US and its allies built up permanent warfare states to secure consistent exploitation of resources outside their own territories."[16] In city after city her group, now named "Voices for Creative Non-Violence," was organizing events to raise awareness of the Yemeni humanitarian crisis.

BLOOD WEDDING AT CREECH

Almost any day features headlines such as this one: "Yemen: Strike Kills at Least 20 at Wedding, Officials Say."[17] So one fall morning in 2017,

during Code Pink's annual Shut Down Creech protest, we staged a ceremony to draw attention to US drones' repeated bombings of weddings. I'd
driven down from Reno for the weekend event, and there at the gate I was
cast as the Groom. Eleanor was to be the Bride. As we stood by the Creech
gate early in the morning, Celine read from the list of some twenty cases
of weddings bombed with Hellfire missiles. Then I was asked to speak to
the Creech operators on the other side of the wire fence. I called out to
them through a megaphone: "Today," I began, "the Nobel Peace Prize was
given to an organization that seeks the end of nuclear arms. We are here
at the Nevada Test Site, the place where those nuclear arms have been
tested more than anywhere else. Taking as witnesses the Franciscan
priests and nuns who began protesting here, and moral leaders such as
Dorothy Day and Martin Luther King and Daniel Berrigan, and poets
such as Alan Ginsberg—and taking as witness all the hundreds of millions
of people who want a denuclearized world, we declare here the end of the
war, the victory of life over death." Then, as in a wedding procession,
silently we walked down Highway 95 toward Las Vegas. The military
police watched as we turned back to the gate where we stood once again
while some were arrested and taken to jail.

During the ceremony I kept thinking of Federico García Lorca's play
Blood Wedding (1933) and Truman Capote's novel *In Cold Blood* (1966).
Both are based on murders described in the news of the day, and both are
tragedies for modern times about a culture of blood in which fate appears
to decide people's actions. *Blood Wedding* opens with the murderer's
weapon, the knife—"Knives, knives . . . Curse them all"—and ends with its
exorcism: "With a little knife / that barely sits in the hand, / but penetrates
deep / through the startled flesh / to reach the point / where trembles
enmeshed / the dark root of a cry."[18] A friend of Lorca's said of the play: "I
didn't feel that [*Blood Wedding*] was a symbol, even less a fantasy, but a
lyrical reality more authentic than reality itself."[19] His words describe our
feelings at Creech that morning as well: as we watched the drones flying
over our heads, which would carry weapons that "penetrate deep through
the startled flesh," and raised our voices in exorcism against the killings of
thousands of civilians, our ritual had the sense of reality.

We were facing the nexus of US culture and murder, both sanctioned
and illegal: the faraway murder of civilians in war; the confused, copycat

murders of children in schools by other armed children; the murder of men by frightened police officers; or the ceremony of execution for the condemned on Death Row. They could all be felt at our Creech "blood wedding" in Indian Springs. As if we needed a reminder, eight miles away from Creech toward Las Vegas was a state prison with four thousand inmates, including the brother of Vera, a young anti-Creech activist who had been arrested and taken to the Las Vegas jail earlier during the year.

Capote's narrative describes Perry Smith, multiple killer and Nevada native, whose recurring dream, he told Capote, was that he was performing as "Perry O'Parsons, The One-Man Symphony" in a Las Vegas night club, singing "You Are My Sunshine" and wearing a white top hat and white tuxedo:

> "At the top, standing on a platform, he took a bow. There was no applause, none, and yet thousands of patrons packed the vast and gaudy room—a strange audience, mostly men and mostly Negroes. . . . Suddenly he knew that these were phantoms, the ghosts of the legally annihilated, the hanged, the gassed, the electrocuted—and in the same instant he realized that he was there to join them, that the gold-painted steps had led to a scaffold, that the platform on which he stood was opening beneath him. His top hat tumbled; urinating, defecating, Perry O'Parsons entered eternity.[20]

Perry Smith and Richard Hickock, *In Cold Blood*'s two protagonists, were arrested in Las Vegas for their murders. Since Capote wrote his novel, about a million people have died in the United States from gunshot wounds. None of this produces any sense of threat to national security; Capote is describing *normal* homegrown American murder as opposed to terrorist anomaly. Capote's novel terrifies because of the banality of ordinary people's murder by ordinary people. While Smith the murderer awaits the gallows, his fantasy whisks him away to Las Vegas. At Creech, boys kill by day in cold blood and visit Las Vegas by evening. Aristotle "made tragedy the centerpiece of education for citizens in a democracy";[21] in the America of drone warfare, he'd stage that tragedy at Indian Springs.

During our wedding ceremony at Creech, drone personnel drove through the gate for one more day of work. They would not be watching Predator porn, as those in Washington's offices would. At Creech they would be engaged in real action and fatal intimacy with their victims in faraway lands. Westmoreland's and Bryant's testimony helps one imagine how these drone operators driving by us at Creech will soon be "seeing" their victims too closely, even coming to "know" them—and the dangers to them of that knowing, as with the executioner who, for watching the one he is about to kill, suffers the consequence of such proximity.

That was the case for Donald A. Cabana, an executioner at the Mississippi State Penitentiary who, for the sake of his sanity, had hardened himself to his Death Row inmates. But then the hardening broke in the case of Connie Ray Evans, a twenty-seven-year-old ex-drug addict who, at nineteen, killed a cashier while robbing a store, a crime that netted him and his partner $140. Perhaps Cabana imagined a son in the man he was about to execute. Whatever it was, he couldn't help feeling for him. As Evans asked Cabana if the execution would hurt, Cabana told him to "breathe real deep" so the gas would make him unconscious in seconds— "Just look at me," he added, "I'll be standing in front of the window."[22] When Evans crawled into his bunk and curled up into a fetal position, sobbing, Cabana wanted to console him but didn't know what to say. Cabana watched the forever too-short goodbye between the helpless mother and son: "They just stood in the lobby, clinging tightly to each other in a long, final embrace. . . . 'Don't cry, Mama. I'll always love you.'"[23] Cabana didn't know what to say; maybe he should say "I'm sorry" but it sounded too trite. Before he could say a word, she put her hand on his arm and asked quietly: "Mr. Cabana, do you have children?" He opened his mouth but no words came out. He just nodded. Her voice trembling, she pleaded with him: "Please, sir, please don't kill my baby. Don't take my child away from me." A sinking feeling overcame Cabana. "Please," the woman repeated tearfully, "you don't have to do this, do you? Don't kill my baby."[24]

Like Westmoreland and Bryant with their victims, Cabana had made the fatal mistake of violating "my rule of never getting too close to an inmate."[25] If Evans was such a monster deserving execution, "why did I feel so bad about it, I wondered."[26] Cabana tried to persuade the governor to postpone the execution, arguing that Evans's partner in crime had cut a deal with the prosecutors and was out of prison after five years. But the governor had politics and Mississippi's public opinion to please. With the denial of clemency and midnight near, Cabana gently took Connie's arm, and with himself on one side of Connie and the chaplain on the other, the three men walked that "last mile," an eternity, what was left of them together. Other inmates from their cells were calling out their final good-byes, a sympathetic officer said, "Hang in there, Connie," and one inmate was softly humming "Amazing Grace," as the three men passed by. Evans was trembling. Cabana felt he was holding the arm of a frightened child. "We have to walk every step together, even the last one," Cabana told him.[27]

A culmination of their intimacy occurred when the condemned man asked to speak privately with Cabana, his executioner. "He gazed at me, as if in shock," Cabana says of Evans.

> His eyes were wet, with a glassy appearance that conveyed a chilling accept-ance of his impending death. Connie spoke quietly, haltingly. He wanted to whisper his final words to me privately, he said, and I leaned down so I could hear him. He thanked me for being his friend. I started to speak, but he asked me to wait, and then told me softly, "From one Christian to another, I love you." I wanted to respond, but no words would come. Now I was the one in shock, shaken to my very soul. . . . What does one say to a man who has told his executioner that he loves him?[28]

Trembling himself now, the executioner told him, "You are my friend, Connie. I won't forget you."[29] The door to the chamber was then opened and Cabana led him inside, arm around his shoulders. Within a minute Evans lapsed into unconsciousness. But eight minutes later Cabana was horrified by a loud and guttural noise from the chamber. Postmortem muscular reactions. Evans was dead.

One sees a similar climax in the film *National Bird* when Lisa Ling, a former sergeant on a drone surveillance program, returns to Afghanistan to face the people she bombed with Hellfire missiles. Ling was given a Medal for Outstanding Achievement for having identified 121,000 insurgent tar-gets in support of operation Iraqi Freedom, each one of them potentially a drone target. The bomb explodes, "and then what?" she asks. "Does some-body go down there and ask for somebody's driver's license?" The break-through in Lisa's testimony is her resolution to return to Afghanistan and face the people she bombed. "I lost part of my humanity working in the drone program," she said, but perhaps something could be healed by "seeing these people as human beings," even if "there is no way that I can make amends or change anything that I participated in but if there is any way that I can somehow give back to that country, that's what I want to do."

Ling meets with the survivors of the February 21, 2010, Creech-guided drone attack that targeted and killed twenty-three family members—the operation whose declassified radio transcripts we saw in the chapter on hunting. The survivors recount for her in detail how things unfolded. After the first group was struck, they lifted the children to the sky so the pilots could see they weren't fighters, but the bombing continued. Ling tells how the survivors told her that "they forgave me for the part I played in what happened to them. And that's amazing . . . you can see people's hearts. I just want people to know that not everybody is a freaking terrorist and we just need to get out of that mind-set. We need to see these people as people, families, communities, brothers, mothers, and sisters because that's what they are. Imagine if this was happening to us." It was the traumatized executioner facing her victims in horror.

Ling and her Afghan victims, like Cabana and Evans, were reenacting the rites of the "execution's covenant" during the Middle Ages, when "the condemned were expected not only to forgive the executioner but at times to physically embrace him. Execution was punishment but also a kind of marriage: two humans joined under a bond that both understood and transcended the actions they were about to take."[30] Asked what Cabana felt when he killed Evans, he replied: "I felt compassion and mercy at the moment I asphyxiated him. In fact, I felt love. I don't know if that makes me an innocent man."[31] It was a kind of marriage, a blood wedding.

Cabana's wife was waiting for him when he walked out of the building. "No more," he told her. "I don't want to do this anymore."[32] He couldn't get Evans's mother off his mind. (Three months later she died of a heart attack.) As his wife remarked, at the night of the execution, how bright the moon was, Cabana found solace in Evans's words earlier that, after his execution, it was "going to be like a sunrise on a whole new life. A midnight sunrise."[33] Death and the moon. Evans, Lisa, Cabana, Lorca in *Blood Wedding*: "Ay, sad moon! / Leave the dark branch to love."[34]

"I believe that more than one person dies with each execution," says Watt Espy, America's foremost executions historian.[35] This was also what Truman Capote's friends said after he witnessed the executions of the murderers Hickock and Smith—that three people died that day, the two murderers and the writer. Capote had also committed the "mistake" of identifying with Smith the killer, to the point of seeing that he "wasn't an evil man."[36] The effects of witnessing executions can have deep impact— "There's a marked and very disturbing trend for young witnesses of executions to kill themselves."[37] Cabana himself was living a kind of death: "Three coronaries. Quadruple bypass. . . . I know a thing or two about death sentences."[38] Solotaroff describes the devastation to the executioners' physical and mental health, their anxiety, depression, sleeplessness, heart attacks. "I died in Vietnam" is a common saying among veterans of that war;[39] we don't know how many of the hundreds of drone pilots "die" at Creech every day—"people who feel stuck," in the words of Bryant and Westmoreland, who talked to us about being suicidal and about having colleagues who had committed suicide. Solotaroff quotes Sophocles: "Who is the victim? Who is the slayer? Speak!"[40]

A HARSH AND DREADFUL LOVE

Some of the protesters at the makeshift Camp Justice wore Dorothy Day T-shirts. Day was a founder of the Catholic Worker movement whose Las Vegas branch fed the protesters during Shut Down Creech Week. The more I came to know the protesters, the more I realized how much she mattered to them.

I met Dorothy Day by chance in October of 1975 en route to Canada, where I was a foreign student. When I stopped to visit a friend living on the Catholic Workers' farm in Tivoli, New York, Day, a tall and beautiful woman in her seventies, radiating a quiet strength and a "look" her daughter Tamar described as "intense" and "devastating," was living there.[41] In our brief encounter she gave me a gift—a Bible. I'd told her of my ten years in seminaries and convents where I had sought sanctity before, at age twenty-one, I'd lost religious faith. Day's Catholic religiosity was conservative but rooted in radical commitment to social and political action. Her intensity, combined with comforting closeness, made her memory, like the Bible she gave me, a treasure. When I told the antidrone protesters how I had met Dorothy, I felt their immediate warmth and acceptance.

Day's friend Eugene O'Neill would tell her they must "face the tragedy of life."[42] In the early 1920s, they'd go all night drinking in East Side bars and walk the waterfront and he'd recite "The Hound of Heaven." These were the years she spent among socialists, anarchists, and communists, while writing for the socialist *Daily Call*. It was also her bohemian period, which included an abortion that left her traumatized, two suicide attempts by overdose, and a marriage of convenience at age twenty-two that lasted one year. She had hit rock bottom; it was either sink or rise. Day wrote a novel, *The Eleventh Virgin*, about her past; from its sales and movie rights she bought a house on Staten Island, where she met and fell in love with an English scientist, Foster Batterham, and had a child with him in 1926. This was also the moment of Day's "conversion" to Catholicism. When she insisted on baptism and marriage, tensions between the couple grew and Foster left.

"A conversion is a lonely experience," she wrote, never sure if her faith was real or if she simply wanted to believe. Faith "is so much an act of will," she said,[43] and she was on the brink of losing it because of the church's disregard for the poor.[44] When in 1932 she met Peter Maurin, a French-born peasant and vagabond philosopher twenty years her senior, who proposed they start a movement of radical social change inspired by the gospels, they launched the weekly the *Catholic Worker*. Within two years, its distribution grew to 150,000. Maurin proposed Houses of Hospitality to the Catholic bishops, and soon homeless men and women began arriving at Day's apartment. She rented one apartment, then another, until they had their own building on Charles Street with coffee and a pot of soup always ready. By 1936, hundreds of people each day were lining up for a meal.

A traditionalist in her religious life, Day nourished her spiritual life with sacramentality and prayer, giving up sex outside marriage because "the best thing to do with the best things in life is to give them up."[45] But ideologically she was a leftist, writing and picketing against Franco's fascists in Spain despite the Catholic Church's support for Franco. She joined anti-Hitler protests and spoke out for the Jews in Germany. In her radical pacifism, she even opposed World War II, which brought her much criticism, even inside the Catholic Worker movement.

"Everything is sacramental," she'd say.[46] And since her first vocation was *writing*—being a journalist, editing the *Catholic Worker*—one could add that writing was her first sacramental act to show that "the world will be saved by beauty," words that she borrowed from Dostoyevsky and never tired of repeating, and that her granddaughter, Kate Hennessy, chose for the title of her remarkable biography of Day. Writing was her way "to relate everything to the infinite."[47] It was linked also to God and love, for "Those who do not believe in God—they believe in love," a belief she needed when, years later, her daughter, Tamar, gave up religious belief.[48]

Day's pacifist stance during World War II split the movement, and *Catholic Worker* readership significantly diminished. The dominant trend in the Catholic Church accepted the legitimacy of war. There was an ideological fissure between radicals who, on a whole range of issues such as class conflicts, unions, democracy, or nationalism, saw America as deeply flawed in light of the gospel and others who believed problems would be resolved through reformist measures, individual action, and American values.[49] In 1940, the Association of Catholic Trade Unionists began to see the utopian rhetoric of the Catholic Worker movement as "crackpot." When the ACTU supported the expansion of weapons production, the Catholic Worker broke with them. Anticommunism was another point of contention. For the Catholic Worker movement communism was evidence of the failure of historical Christianity.[50] When in the 1940s the McCarthyist Un-American Activities Committee began accusing citizens of being suspected communists, Day wrote an editorial entitled "We Are Un-American; We Are Catholics."

It was that movement created by Day decades earlier that was now energizing the resistance to drone warfare at Creech. It is hard to overstate how profoundly radical it was: the combination of Day's sacramentalism with Maurin's anarchist attack on mass production and technological abundance. Together it amounted to a nonviolent revolution against capitalism. What their ACTU critics looked for were the virtues of the American liberal tradition with "its emphasis on individual liberty, equal opportunity, practical accommodation to change, distrust of fanaticism and closed ideologies, and faith in human nature and the future of liberal society."[51] There was no way to reconcile Day's radicalism with American liberalism. Her movement represented a novel phenomenon within American pacifism in that it broke with the tradition of "just war." Her pacifism required being a fool for Christ's sake, "for the cause of justice, tilting at windmills like any Don Quixote."[52]

The *Catholic Worker*'s militant pacifism inhabited an "intellectual front" as well, considered as relevant to the cause of peace as its political activism. It wasn't enough to act: action had to be thought out as well to engage religious ideals with harsh political facts. The *Catholic Worker* argued against both limited nuclear war and just-war theorists, claiming that their notions were "from the same 'happy if imaginary land' where there were also 'clean bombs' and 'contained radioactivity.'"[53] In addition to Catholic intellectuals like Thomas Merton and Jacques Maritain, Day's movement found admirers from people with various religious and political backgrounds, including, among others, James Farrell, Dwight Macdonald, T. S. Eliot, Hanna Arendt, Lewis Mumford, James Wallis, Claude McKay, and W. H. Auden.[54]

In June of 1955, Day, the associate editor of Day's *Catholic Worker* Ammon Hennacy, and a group of twenty-eight others disobeyed the government-imposed drill by which people were ordered to enter air raid shelters as a rehearsal for a potential nuclear attack. They were jailed for five days. Their disobedience and arrest were reenacted yearly; the protest drew thousands to City Hall until, in 1962, the drills were canceled, evidence of the power of ritualized action. Day insisted that "the ordinary is subversive" and that "we live in the shelter of each other."[55] In September 1965, at the conclusion of the Second Vatican Council, Day traveled to Rome to fast for ten days and support the Council Fathers in their deliberations on war and peace and push for the Council's approval of the pastoral constitution "Gaudium et Spes," which included the words: "Any act of war aimed indiscriminately at the destruction of entire cities or of extensive areas along with their population is a crime against God and man himself. It merits unequivocal and unhesitating condemnation."[56]

Catholic Worker activists were prominent in organizing the first major anti-Vietnam demonstrations, during which Day spoke over counter-demonstrator chants of "Moscow Mary," saying: "I speak today as one who is old, and who must endorse the courage of the young who themselves are willing to give up their freedom. I speak as one whose whole lifetime has seen the cruelty and hysteria of war in the last half century."[57] In 1972, Day refused to pay taxes that fund the war, risking jail for doing so. A year later, at age seventy-five, she was arrested for picketing with the United Farm Workers. In 1975, she joined the Koinonia Community in Americus, Georgia, in defiance of segregation. In a speech on August 6, 1976, at the

Eucharistic Congress in Philadelphia, she reminded the audience of Hiroshima, *the* sin of her country in the twentieth century, on the anniversary that too many had forgotten.[58]

Among the activists who visited Day was Daniel Ellsberg, the antinuclear activist and expert on the Doomsday Machine whose ideas we discussed in the previous chapter.[59] His son Robert joined Day's movement at age nineteen and worked with her during the last five years of her life, becoming the managing editor of *Catholic Worker* for two years and later the editor of Orbis Books. He published Day's diaries and letters. He knew from his father's experience the reality of nuclear madness. "Much as we want to, we do not really know ourselves," Dorothy Day had written. "Could we bear it [self-knowledge], weak as we are? . . . . We do not really know how much pride and self-love we have."[60] What other alternative was there but Day's "harsh and dreadful" love, the new vision she sketched while serving on the soup line?

Late in her life she confessed, "I feel like an utter failure," yet it was, she believed, a failure intrinsic to her Christian vocation, "since Christ was the world's greatest failure."[61] She never wavered in her belief that "we must do that seemingly utterly impossible thing—love your enemy."[62] Like William Blake who spoke against the British Empire, Day confronted America's imperial ambitions of the twentieth century: "In the face of Empire, the Way of Love," she wrote in 1972.[63] Like Paul and Lenin, Day knew that truth (in her case the truth against nuclear armaments) is *partisan* and demands a *militant* position on the subject. "I am dogmatic," she protested, with regard to her belief in Christ as redeemer and in his resurrection.[64] As Michael Harrington, who was with the *Catholic Worker* in the early fifties, put it: "We appeared as a small band of nuts. Catholic puritans. Totally marginal radicals."[65]

"Love in practice is a harsh and dreadful thing compared with love in dreams."[66] Day often quoted Dostoevsky's Father Zossima. Dostoevsky examines how our secret thoughts and desires can make us murderers in our intentionality. For Day systematic planning for the nuclear holocaust fell into a similar murderous purpose, a crime that is committed *now* under the name of deterrence, regardless of when the bombs will explode. There is no better insight into the spirituality of Day and her followers protesting at the NTS and Creech than Dostoevsky's paradoxical theodicy, summed up thus by one of Day's favorite thinkers, Nikolai Berdyaev: "The existence of evil is a proof of the existence of God. If the world consisted wholly and uniquely of goodness and righteousness there would be no need for God, for the world itself would be god. God is, because evil is. And that means that God is because freedom is."[67] For the men and women inspired by Day and protesting in the Nevada desert, the nuclear buildup for the end of humanity—the epitome of Evil calling for a redeeming God—makes that place at once apocalyptic and sacred.

DOWN BY THE RIVERSIDE

On Sunday, October 9, 2016, some 150 Catholic Workers are gathered in a semicircle on makeshift pews for mass, at the entrance to the Nevada Test Site. We walked there under intense sun, with a brass band playing as we sang the Negro spiritual "Down by the Riverside":

> We're gonna lay down our sword and shield down by the riverside,
> down by the riverside, down by the riverside . . .
> We're gonna lay down our sword and shield down by the riverside,
> I ain't gonna study war no more.

Days earlier, I had called the Las Vegas Catholic Worker to introduce myself and my interest in the organization's history in Nevada. A woman named Julia answered and soon invited me to join them that weekend, as representatives of the various Catholic Worker houses were to arrive in Las Vegas for their annual meeting. I drove down from Reno with my wife for their gathering. An hour of liturgy and peace witnessing in front of the Nevada Test Site gate was part of the scheduled events. With the band still playing "Down by the Riverside" in the background, the rest of us were silent, earnest with purpose. We were there to perform a symbolic act that was for us far more than mere ritual—it was symbolism turned into action to show who we are as Catholics, Jews, or atheists and to demand with our presence that America "lay down our sword."

Father Steve Kelly, a Jesuit and close friend to Daniel Berrigan, who had been one of the Creech 14 arrested and tried in 2009 for their antidrones protest, stood at the center of the semicircle. He evoked the presence of

Jerry Zawada, a pacifist Franciscan who was also a member of the Creech 14 and who had spent years in prison for his many arrests but whose health no longer allowed him to come to the site. People called out his name: "Presente!" For these men religion had been anything but pious consolation; it had wounded and electrified them, forced them into a destitute life of illegal action and jail time.

Someone began on guitar the Christian hymn "Gather Us In," and congregants joined in, accompanied by drums and a flute in the background, our voices diffusing into the desert vastness: "Here in this place, new light is streaming / now is the darkness vanished away . . . Give us to drink the wine of compassion / give us to eat the bread that is you / nourish us well and teach us to fashion / lives that are holy and hearts that are true."

A rabbi with his flute added a phrase.

Then the Jesuit continued:

> We come to this wilderness this morning, we come for transformation, but more importantly we know that there are many before us who came for transformation to the wilderness, a place for renunciation, a place of survival. . . . We join the lives of Moses and Jesus and Mohammed and many others who came to the wilderness not just to change themselves but to change the world. Moses was yet to enter the wilderness when he was in the far side of the Red Sea and Egyptians were coming behind him and what was the man to do? There was supposedly a man who was coming in the back of the line and stepped into the water up to his ankle and he said: Here I am, God. And the waters didn't split. And he stepped to his knee. Here I am, God. His waist. His shoulders. And the waters didn't split. Not until the water was up to his chin, and he said, Here I am, God, and took one more step in till the water went up over his head. Only then did the Red Sea part. Only then did God step in. Only with that blessing may we have strength and the courage and the faith to take the steps necessary to transform the world.

The rabbi's soft flute, again.

Father Kelly pulled red pants and a red vest over his yellow shirt: "I don't wish to distract you, I am not into gimmicks, but we are vesting today with the vests of prisoners, and we think of our jailed friends, and we also think of Guantánamo, a perennial problem, even for this administration that wanted to release them but couldn't. So without being a distraction I am vested as Christ would among those who are at the margins.

We are hearing from Luke's Gospel today about outcasts." The mass followed with its prayers and penitential rites, a first reading from Kings, a psalm, a second reading from 2 Timothy, the song "Alleluia," plus a third reading from the Gospel of Luke on how the ten lepers were cured by Jesus but only the Samaritan—foreigner and enemy of the Jews—came back to thank him.

It was now time for the sermon, and, in the heat of the desert, Father Kelly reminded us of the disintegration of nature and corruption of social institutions. "We don't have the luxury to despair and publish an existential book about it," he said. He brought the example of Dorothy Day who chose "The Duty of Delight" as the title for her book of diaries. With her chores and the drudgery of her work she expressed her joy. And Father Kelly returned to the gospel, to the untouchable lepers of that time, like the AIDs patients of the eighties, and the current millions of prisoners, *les misérables* of today, he said.

Father Kelly called us to pray for the church and those in power, and for the marginal people and the American Indians on whose land we were standing. Then he blessed the bread and the wine and recited the canonical words: "This is my body which is given for you. Do this in memory of me." "This is my blood that will be shed for everyone. Do this in memory of me." The song followed: "Christ is dead, Christ is risen."

One didn't need to be a believer to be taken by the force of that communal bread and wine in front of the NTS gate. You knew that the reality of that meal wasn't a matter of belief in some theological system but a matter of faith in the power of life over death, in the truth of our antinuclear stance, in keeping a pact with each other. We were bound, not by some religious fiction, but by the horror of the nuclear test site before us and the Creech Air Base nearby. There was no other God but the man on the cross, the *ecce homo* shown to a mob about to lynch him who, before he was crucified, forsaken, said, "Do this in memory of me" during his last supper. It was quite hot under the desert sun, and Father Kelly mentioned the end of nature, in reference to climate change. Brian Terrell took the mike and told us that just three days earlier two B-2 bombers had dropped two seven-hundred-pound faux nuclear bombs right there in the desert—tests in preparation for World War III, he added. At the NTS you can sense the urgency that the world is about to end.

As we walked to the test site gate the band started up again: "We're gonna stick our swords in the golden sand, down by the riverside, down by the riverside." Then it went on to "Brother Can You Spare a Dime" and "We Shall Overcome," the song, after the death of Martin Luther King, about which Day had written, "Always, I think, I will weep when I hear [it]."[68] We were ordered to disband. About twenty people refused the order and were arrested, while the band continued "Gonna walk with the source of peace, down by the riverside, down by the riverside." Then the band intoned *No nos moverán* ("We won't be moved").

Months earlier Steve Kelly had spoken at the funeral of Daniel Berrigan, the Jesuit who had articulated the opposition to war in his writings. Berrigan's central biblical axiom was simple: "Do not kill." Kelly had been one of the eight hundred people who, on a rainy morning in May, had gathered in New York to pay Berrigan homage by marching for peace from Maryhouse (a house founded by Day) in Manhattan to the Church of St. Francis Xavier on West Sixteenth Street, singing "Down by the Riverside." Kelly, a participant himself in Plowshares actions and antidrone protests at Creech and a veteran of years in federal prisons, led the homily for his longtime friend. Berrigan's life experience, Kelly said, had been a "total commitment, not a partial desire," nourished by the "sacrament of resistance." Kelly humorously advised the FBI that Berrigan's file could be closed at last. Resurrection was the focus of Kelly's homily—the notion on which Christian spirituality hinges and on whose experience, Christian or not, one's understanding and commitment depends.

Berrigan had written about "an ethic of resurrection" that in essential ways echoes Paul's doctrine. For Berrigan, "The 'No' to the state, uttered by the unarmed Christ, is vindicated in the resurrection," and the glory of the true Christians is that "we are witnesses of the resurrection. We practice resurrection. We risk resurrection."[69] The figure of broken people breaking bread is not mere metaphor for Berrigan's radical Christians, for the ethics of resurrection is "the ethics of the body given, of the blood outpoured! The act led straight to the scaffold and to that 'beyond' we name for want of a better word, resurrection."[70] This resurrection is what "we want to taste" and can be translated as "the hope that hopes on." But there is a "blasphemy against this hope [which] is named deterrence, or Trident submarine, or Star Wars, or preemptive strike, or simply any nuclear weapon."[71] While challenging the ethics of nuclear weapons with the ethics of resurrection, we knew at the NTS gathering that we might seem simple-minded and foolish. And yet nothing was trivial about that congregation in the Nevada desert.

In 1968 during the Vietnam War the Berrigan brothers and another seven activists burned draft files with home-made napalm at Catonsville, Maryland. Berrigan wrote then about "the Pentecostal fire of Catonsville": "State violence ... is commonly considered bearable, a matter of toleration. . . . Almost any level of official violence is sanctioned. . . . The seven (or nine, or twelve) rules of justification of war lurch forth, for all the world like the classic figures of a steeple clock. The law, the law! It will tell the hour right! Only let someone contradict the clock, dare cry 'Murder!'"[72] As Berrigan said in his trial, "One could not indefinitely obey the law" because "the bombings [of Vietnam] were a massive crime against humanity."[73] And his words of exorcism to the trial judge: "We have chosen to say with the gift of liberty / if necessary our lives: / the violence stops here / the death stops here / the suppression of truth stops here / this war stops here."[74]

Berrigan had taken advantage of the floodgates opened by the general of the Jesuits Pedro Arrupe for the expression of a theology of the poor and the oppressed. Arrupe was living four miles from Hiroshima when the bomb was dropped and became a vocal witness to the holocaust. Berrigan, who would be visited by Arrupe when he was staying at Danbury Prison, followed his antinuclear stance. Like Arrupe, who saw the clock stop in Hiroshima at 8:10 a.m. ("That clock, silent and immobile, has been for me a symbol. . . . Hiroshima has no relation to time: it belongs to eternity," Arrupe wrote),[75] and in the tradition of Loyola's new "seeing" in Manresa after his conversion experience, Berrigan wrote of a "second sight" by which he could "see / washed ashore / the last hour of the world— / the murdered clock of Hiroshima."[76] But this new sight was not without consequences, for, as he put in his poem "Prophecy," "The way I see the world is strictly illegal / To wit, through my eyes / Is illegal, yes . . . / This is not permitted / that I look on the world / and worse, insist that I see / what I see /—a conundrum, a fury, a burning bush."[77]

In Bilbao I had met some of these radicalized men and women while I was writing an ethnography of the Basque city. I called them "Christian atheists" since they opposed the traditional use of religious sacraments and church practices as being part of the oppression of the poor.[78] These Jesuits were Arrupe's followers and had been friends with the Jesuits murdered in El Salvador (by the Atlacatl Battalion, trained and equipped by the United States) and with Bishop Romero, as was Berrigan, who visited them in Nicaragua and wrote about them.[79] Their position regarding the "death of God" was that it "paradoxically opens up the space for the new postmetaphysical religion, a kenotic Christianity focused on Agape."[80]

As for my own participation at the ceremony in the Nevada desert, surrounded by militant Catholic Workers, I felt anchored to the idea of resurrection from the perspective of an atheistic Christianity—as articulated for instance in Alain Badiou's provocative essay on Saint Paul. Paul's proclamation of Christ's resurrection, upheld by the subject as the real Event, establishes for atheist Badiou a universal logic. What matters for him is the founding power of this subjective gesture, a truth that goes beyond any national or communitarian allegiance. This was also what impressed me about the radical Catholics and Jews and feminists protesting in front of the NTS and Creech—their antiwar truth was based solely on their subjective conviction. It was not based on any complex theology or expert knowledge but was the bare preference for life over death summed up in the commandment "Don't' kill." It was a truth that did not allow legal categories to define the duty of a Christian.[81]

In Badiou's Event-based reading,

> The Resurrection . . . is not, in Paul's own eyes, of the order of fact, falsifiable or demonstrable. It is pure event, opening an epoch, transformation of the relations between the possible and the impossible. . . . Its genuine meaning is that it testifies to the possible victory over death, a death that Paul envisages . . . not in terms of facticity, but in terms of subjective disposition. Whence the necessity of constantly linking resurrection to *our* resurrection, of proceeding from singularity to universality and vice versa. . . . It is in this sense that it is grace, and not history.[82]

But for Badiou, and for those celebrating mass in front of NTS, this grace was not a spiritualist escape confined to religion; it was rather the immanent materialization of the Event that denies the primacy of death by "a formal, wholly secularized conception of grace." It is by such "materialism of grace" that we can accept "the strong, simple idea that every existence can one day be seized by what happens to it and subsequently devote itself to that which is valid for all,"[83] including the survival of civilization through an end to the nuclear race. In Badiou's reading, Paul's event of the Resurrection is a break that, although placed in a mythological context, "pertains rather to the laws of universality in general."[84] For the protesters of the nuclear bombs and the militarized drones, Christ was not a master; he was strictly "the name of what happens to us universally"[85]—a radical universality that, facing nuclear war, could not allow for even one exception.

At the gate of the NTS, thought turns into apocalypticism. "With the Apocalypse," wrote Gilles Deleuze in his commentary on D. H. Lawrence, "Christianity invents *a completely new image of power*," one in which, "above all, the End must be programmed."[86] This is a new system of judgment in which destiny is deferred and placed *after* death. What matters in this ominous vision is not the immanence of heavens here and now but the establishment of a celestial city, a New Jerusalem, and for that "the Apocalypse needs to destroy the world. . . . [It] calls up the pagan cosmos only in order to finish it off, to bring about its hallucinatory destruction"—the destruction of an anonymous and unspecified enemy ("the Terrorist") now turned into the ultimate act of justice. The Apocalypse's New Jerusalem is for Deleuze "the great military, police, and civil security of the new State" promised by "science fiction" and "the military-industrial plans."[87]

But there is a different perspective on apocalypse, the one articulated by the radical theologian Thomas Altizer: the only valid apocalypse is immanent to the world, and hence "the death of God is the deepest event in modern apocalypticism apart from which there is no possibility whatsoever of a truly new world."[88] The lifelong testimonials by Day, the Berrigan Brothers, King, and so many of their follower militants show the relevancy of this Christian legacy of *kenotic* spirituality.[89] Such experience of subjective revival forces the individual into separating love from law. The congregation singing "Down by the Riverside" in the desert while getting ready to be arrested and jailed revealed the radicalness of that gap.[90]

ON THE SOUP LINE

At 5 a.m. the morning after I joined the Catholic Workers in Las Vegas, in February of 2017, I awoke to the smell of chicken cooking with chile pepper, tomato sauce, onion, garlic, celery, carrots. Julia and Mark were already in the kitchen, presided over by a photograph of Dorothy Day on the wall; they were filling the four large one-meter-tall cook pots for the homeless. Julia was practicing with me what Day had told another writer who had joined one of her houses: "Your work begins at the kitchen sink."[91] Despite the opposition between the worker and the scholar, Julia, like Day, knows people must be both.[92]

Wednesdays through Saturdays, at 6:30 a.m., a dozen or so Catholic Workers, supported by another twenty volunteers from the city, feed approximately two hundred of the homeless in Las Vegas. Wednesdays, Spanish rice; Thursdays, macaroni and cheese; Fridays, Italian pasta; Saturdays, red beans and rice soup. Once a month, the Knights of Columbus make seven/eight hundred pancakes. Some days, Julia brings greens from her garden, a combination of broccoli, collards, Swiss chard, cauliflower, arugula, onions, and garlic. Occasionally she will make dessert; the apple cobbler is a favorite among the homeless. Food preparations begin the afternoon before. In the morning we cut bagfuls of onions, carrots, and celery. In the evenings John boils red beans, fills pots with water. At 6 a.m. we pray. By 6:25 we leave the house at 500 West Van Buren with the food carefully placed in the trailer attached to the car driven by Gary, moving slowly to the vacant lot a mile away at the intersection of G Street and McWilliams to meet and serve the lines of homeless.

While the morning sun rises over the red Las Vegas sky, Julia asks me to serve one of the lines of men and women approaching, one by one, paper plates in hand. I can hardly look at their faces, I can barely say "Good morning" as they extend their plates. Somebody is playing Aaron Neville's "Tell It Like It Is" from a car radio. After weeks serving food with the Catholic Worker, I still can't get used to seeing the rows of hungry veterans, immigrants, sex workers, old and sick people, staying in line with their plates in hand. Occasionally a homeless person touches me on my shoulder to say thank you and there is a lump in my throat. In thirty or forty minutes we are done and I help collect the garbage before we return in silence to 500 Van Buren to wash and dry the pots and prepare for the next day.

The sacrament of food. About serving food to the homeless, Day wrote: "One felt more like taking their hands and saying, 'Forgive us—let us forgive each other! All of us who are more comfortable, who have a place to sleep, three meals a day, work to do—we are responsible for your condition. We are guilty of each other's sins.'"[93] I lived three months in the Catholic Worker house in Las Vegas, helping with everything from kitchen to garden. But there is a radical difference between the Catholic Workers and me. They depend on donations to live, to feed the homeless a morning meal, and to donate food and clothing to the needy. They don't have a university salary. They don't belong to the capitalist economy that includes the Las Vegas industries of tourism and militarism. Their desires don't conform to the academic hierarchies of status and pay. They don't need to intrude anywhere with the pretext of writing a book. The fact that they can live outside the coordinates of capitalist desire affects me, and it's through their filter that I grasp the logic of the surrounding consumerism interlocked with militarism.

The Las Vegas Catholic Worker was founded by Julia Occhiogrosso. Raised by Italian Catholics in Brooklyn, Julia was one of the pilgrims to the NTS who was overtaken by the *tremendum* of the Nevada desert while protesting the nuclear buildup. In 1986, she decided to establish a hospitality house in Las Vegas to tend to the homeless and poor in the spirit of Dorothy Day. Four years later Gary Cavalier, who was working in a homeless shelter in San Luis Obispo, joined the organization and married her. They adopted two boys, two and three years old, whose parents were crack addicts. The boys' damage from their early experience became obvious at adolescence as they became dysfunctional. The boys' trauma became Gary's and Julia's trauma.

From the beginning, Julia was aware of the violence and the lethal radioactivity in the desert surrounding Las Vegas, yet she felt it was also a place imbued with a sense of the sacred: "We're talking about the symbol of the bomb, that is the incredible symbol of death, next to the desert landscape and the enduring hills," Julia said.[94] The legacy Julia and the other activists learned from Day was the sacramentality, including arrest, of everyday experience—"a sacramental vision that transformed the everyday elements of these ordinary lives into something beyond politics, social theory, or formal religion."[95] Even if the topic was labor, the Catholic Worker would discuss it in the language of Christian idealism. The difference between Mother Teresa and Day's Catholic Workers is the insistence that social justice is as important as charity.[96]

I listen to Julia speak to a meditation group at the Catholic Worker. She talks about the works of hospitality as a journey of faith and as a response to injustice. She says there is joy in it as well, and quotes Day: "An experience of the living God is a terrible thing." Utopian ideals meet daily imperfections; and then there is the work of loving your enemy. The works of mercy as opposed to the works of war. Julia told the group that her coming to Las Vegas to create a Catholic Worker house was a combination of boldness and naïveté. She just did it, without asking permission from anyone. Only later did she speak to a bishop, who sent a letter to all the parishes asking them to support her effort. They set up a soup line for six days a week. They collected donations and gave away whatever they received. Their doctrine was simple: one member suffers, everybody suffers. Like the innocent people killed by drone warfare, Julia adds. Every Thursday morning a group of Catholic Workers keeps vigil at the Las Vegas Federal Courthouse to protest militarism and drone warfare, in addition to the vigils they keep at Creech throughout the year. It is Matthew 25:40: "Whatever you did for one of the least of these brothers and sisters of mine, you did for me."

In one of my return visits to the Catholic Worker, Julia welcomes me and takes me to the garden where we had both worked in the spring. I take notes while she shows me the kale, cabbage, fennel, rosemary, beets, collards, chard, sweet peas, radishes, carrots, celery, broccoli, cauliflower, eggplants, peppers, green beans, turnips, garlic, romaine, and arugula—her weapons of mercy. She is basking in glory.

ARREST AS SACRAMENT IN THE NEVADA DESERT

At Easter Week 2017, members of the Catholic Worker and the Shut Down Creech activists took our protest to the Nevada Test Site. The Peace Walk is a sixty-five-mile journey from Las Vegas to the test site and marks decades of resistance. Before that summer of 1957, and coinciding with the anniversary of the August 6, 1945, bombing of Hiroshima, antinuclear militants were already protesting the scheduled explosion of a large hydrogen bomb.[97] Hennacy, who had converted to Catholicism in 1952, picketed the Atomic Energy Commission office in Las Vegas from June 17 through June 28, 1957.[98]

Then, on August 9, a dozen of these pacifists entered the test site and were arrested, faced with the same choice as the monk in Frank Bergon's novel who told his parishioners on the day of the Feast of Transfiguration, also the anniversary of Hiroshima: "You either have faith in the mushroom cloud or in the Cloud of the Unknowing [a mystical text from the Middle Ages]. We reject the energy of death and waste. We choose the vital energy of love."[99]

That same summer on September 7, 1957, two-year-old Terry Tempest Williams was sitting on her pregnant mother's lap in the car her father was driving home to Utah from California. They were driving north, just past Las Vegas, when, an hour or so before dawn, they heard an explosion. "I thought the oil tanker in front of us had blown up," her father recalled later. "We pulled over and suddenly, rising from the desert floor, we saw it, clearly, this golden-stemmed cloud, the mushroom. The sky seemed to vibrate with an eerie pink glow. Within a few minutes, a light ash was raining on the car." Williams was too young to fathom what had happened, but years later, when she was telling her father of a recurring dream, "this flash of light in the night in the desert . . . on the horizon, illuminating buttes and mesas," her father said to her: "You did see it." "Saw what?" "The Bomb. The cloud," and he recounted for her how they had seen it. "I thought you knew that," he said. "It was a common occurrence in the fifties."[100] She realized then that's why she belonged, as she wrote in 1991, to "the clan of one-breasted women"—why her mother and her grandmothers and six aunts had all had mastectomies, why seven of them were dead and the only two survivors had just completed rounds of chemotherapy and radiation, why she herself had had two biopsies for breast cancer and a tumor between her ribs. She and other children had been drinking contaminated milk from contaminated cows, "even from the contaminated breasts of their mothers, my mother."[101]

The government insisted there were no health risks from nuclear fallout. But in May 1984, Judge Bruce S. Jenkins awarded damages to ten of the hundreds of plaintiffs. His ruling was overturned by the US Circuit Court of Appeals, and the Supreme Court refused to review the case. As Williams watched the women of her family die, she knew defending life is more important than patriotism or religion and, in an act of civil disobedience, crossed the line to be arrested at the Nevada Test Site. She said that at night she dreamed of Shoshone grandmothers singing while "women from all over the world circled a blazing fire in the desert,"[102] the desert of the Joshua trees, named by her Mormon ancestors, who likened them to prophets pointing to the Promised Land, the same trees that burned with atomic fire after each nuclear explosion.

The year of 1957, while the first pacifist demonstrations against the Plumbbob atomic tests were taking place at the NTS, a young pilot by the name of Louie Vitale was stationed nearby at Nellis Air Force Base. Born in Southern California in 1932 in a patriotic family, after graduating from college Vitale joined the Air Force. On a routine mission he was ordered to shoot down an approaching aircraft thought to be a Soviet military jet crossing into US airspace. The order was reiterated three times, but at the last moment the crew decided to make a visual inspection, only to discover it was a commercial airliner. Coming so close to a tragedy led him to become a Franciscan, Vitale told me during the summer of 2017 as I visited him in his Oakland retirement center.

Drawing on his own Cold War experience as an Air Force pilot, Vitale interpreted the conversion and religiosity of St. Francis in an unusual manner: "Today we would call this Post Traumatic Stress Disorder."[103] For Vitale, "Although Francis started as a combatant, he became a conscientious objector. He . . . embodied a commitment of disarmament by carrying a cross, not a sword."[104] It was the transformation of war trauma that for Vitale generated Franciscan spirituality.

Because of his lifelong practice of pacifism and his prominent role among the Franciscans, Vitale would become a pivotal figure for the resistance at the Nevada Test Site. His first religious post was in 1968 in Las Vegas, where he founded the Franciscan Center and where he began by helping farmworkers and welfare mothers. Later during the 1970s, he became aware of the NTS's role in the acceleration of the arms race. By the late 1970s, Vitale had been elected provincial of the US Western Province for his Franciscan order. In 1977, Sister Rosemary Lynch joined the Las Vegas Franciscan Center and organized a prayer vigil on the anniversary of Hiroshima. In 1982, Provincial Vitale led his community in a radically new form of liturgy they named "the Lenten Desert Experience," which consisted of "a series of nonviolent vigils over 40 days on the Nevada Test Site culminating in a civil disobedience action in which several dozens . . .

were arrested at the gates of the facility on Good Friday—and a joyful welcoming of the resurrection at the test site on Easter morning."[105] These actions were taking place as the Reagan administration increased nuclear weapons and revived bellicose Cold War rhetoric. Vitale saw militarism as part of consumerist American capitalism.[106]

These Lent days led to the formation of the Franciscan-based organization Nevada Desert Experience in Las Vegas. The organization integrates religious ritual and political action at the gates of the NTS—a combination of witnessing and militancy that has given form to a new type of "desert spirituality." It incorporates antinuclear asceticism into a post-Hiroshima world, nonviolent practices that respect the opponent's views, and a modern adaptation of pilgrimage that journeys to the NTS and Creech as symbolic centers of martial America.[107] As practiced by Vitale and Lynch, the struggle against nuclear arms is not a bipolar narrative of us versus them—in their view we are all responsible for what goes on at the NTS, and all of us belong to the same side. Lynch asked for an interview with General Mahlon Gates, director of the NTS, to request permission to erect a cross by the NTS's gate. Gates provided the permission as well as logistical support for the vigil.

Nellis Air Force Base is at the heart of desert America, a seemingly endless maze with a mirage of the sublime on its horizon in the lights of Las Vegas—"that great whore on the other side of the desert."[108] The emptiness and silence of the desert, where highways are distant vanishing points of speeding and disappearances, an occasional motel or gas station by the road—this is a mineral world of rocks and ash, primitive and ascetic, where Joshua trees hold ground. It is desert America with phantom images of extraterrestrials and airborne mutants—"an appropriate place for fantasies . . . dune buggy maniacs and lone hikers . . . seekers after legendary gold mines . . . explorers of the first atomic devices . . . proponents of advanced missile systems . . . diggers of gigantic earth sculptures . . . In a landscape where nothing officially exists . . . [and] absolutely anything becomes thinkable, and may consequently happen."[109]

How is this place, this Paradise Ranch, this Dreamland of Area 51, real? Thousands of people died from the plutonium fallout of nuclear testing here.[110] Baudrillard wrote about it: "America is neither dream nor reality. It is hyperreality . . . because it is a utopia which has behaved from the very beginning as though it were already achieved. Everything here is real and pragmatic, and yet it is all the stuff of dreams too."[111] The conviction of its supreme power derives from bombs and from "the miraculous premise of a utopia made reality."[112] It is here that writer Bergon placed his monastery at the crossroads of the transfigurations brought by either atomic power or the power of love. It is here that the Nevada Desert Experience anchored its desert spirituality and engineered a powerful antinuclear movement.

Year after year, protests organized by the NDE gathered momentum.[113] Led by Vitale, in October 1984, the "Franciscan Peacemakers" weekend conference was followed by civil disobedience at the gates of the NTS, with twenty-four people arrested. In 1985, 400 people participated in the Lenten Desert Experience and 28 were arrested. During the Hiroshima and Nagasaki anniversaries of the same year, 500 people participated and 121 were arrested. Later that same year, October through November, more protests were organized with 113 people arrested. From May 31 to June 2, 1986, 1,200 people rallied in front of the NTS in an action organized by the American Peace Test; later in September, 139 were arrested. Month by month nonviolent protests grew. On May 5, 1987, two Catholic bishops joined 96 others and were arrested. On May 10, various pacifist groups organized a Mother's Day Action that brought together 3,000 people, and 790 people were arrested, bringing the issue to the attention of the national press. A high point was the march of May 8–16, 1988, at which 8,000 people participated with 2,065 arrests. On April 8–15, 1989, 1,800 people were arrested. During the 1990s, NDE continued organizing vigils, gatherings, and numerous activities.

"We sense that our spirituality is inadequate to the challenges of our time. We need a new vision, or is it an old one?," wrote Vitale.[114] He has been arrested countless times. One of those arrests was a three-month prison term at Nellis AFB Federal Prison near Las Vegas that began in October of 2002. In September of 2007 Vitale and Steve Kelly were arrested in Arizona at the headquarters of the US Army Intelligence. Vitale was sentenced to five months in jail. Vitale has found in prisons, he writes, irredeemable woundedness and the sacred.

In 1990, the NDE inaugurated an annual Holy Week Peace Walk from Las Vegas to the test site; since then, during Easter Week, thousands of people have walked the annual pilgrimage of sixty-five miles from Las Vegas to the test site. There was a large turnout for the tenth anniversary of the first Lenten Desert Experience in 1991; in June 1991, over four hundred women and men came from over 131 religious communities. The relationship between the NDE and the Western Shoshone nation grew closer. In October 1992, in remembrance of the five hundredth anniversary of the arrival of Europeans, the annual "Healing Global Wounds" ceremony was established. After the collapse of the Soviet Union and under relentless pressure from an international movement demanding an end to nuclear testing, President George Bush in 1992 announced a moratorium. In 1996 the Comprehensive Test Ban Treaty was signed by over 150 countries (it is still unratified by the US). The United States continues designing and testing weapons at facilities such as the Livermore National Laboratory and conducting what it terms "subcritical" explosive tests at the NTS.

This history of "arrest as sacrament" in the Nevada desert testifies to the power of resistance to the US military empire of our times.[115] For many of the activists the desert "became a spiritually vibrant terrain that nurtured, taught, and transformed."[116] The desert wilderness was where John the Baptist lived, where Christ was tempted. But earlier in the scriptures the exodus from Egypt marked the paradigmatic Passover experience—the forty years' journey through the desert before reaching the Promised Land. For these Franciscan men and women, as for the Veterans for Peace, Pink Code activists, Catholic Workers, and many other antinuclear and antidrone protesters, the militarized Nevada desert represents the essential apocalyptic site—the battle between life and death.

On Good Fridays some of them get together across from the entrance of the test site to practice the "Stations of the Cross" memorializing Christ's last hours. The *via crucis* had been a daily practice of my religious experience as a seminarian; fifty years later, in 2017, I found myself doing the "Way of the Cross" at the NTS's gate, unsure whether I was ethnographer or once again one of the faithful. When I asked Julia if I could take notes, she said no.

In his "Theses on the Philosophy of History" (1940), Walter Benjamin developed the idea that the past can be understood only from a position of redemption but that each generation has a "weak messianic power, a power to which the past has a claim."[117] The "messianic cessation" revolutionizes the past, for "the past carries with it a temporal index by which it is referred to redemption."[118] Benjamin's famous saying that "there is no document of civilization which is not at the same time a document of barbarism" applies most poignantly to the nuclear predicament.[119] The catastrophe is not the collapse of the system but its continuation; hell is not in the future but already here. Benjamin's depiction of "progress" as a "storm from Paradise" that blows the Angel of History toward a future to which his back is turned while a pile of wreckage at his feet grows ever skyward finds a literal rendering in the storms created by nuclear explosions in the Nevada desert and in the carnage of Hellfire missiles raining over the larger Middle East from Nevada's Paradise Ranch.

Benjamin's "weak messianic force" has been linked to the Pauline maxim that such force gets fulfilled in *weakness*. "We have become, and are still, like the scum of the world, the refuse of all things" (1 Cor. 4:13). What else are those protesting the "progress" brought by nuclear energy and drones at the NTS and Creech but *fools?* And those former pilots traumatized by what they did and saw, what are they but the refuse of the empire's American Dream? Discussing such powerless messianic force, Eric Santner writes, "The crucial difference between the 'old thinking' and the 'new thinking'" is how "in the new thinking the element of the past that is at issue has the structural status of *trauma*, a past that in some sense never fully took place and so continues to insist in the present precisely as drive destiny, the symptomal torsion of one's being in the world."[120]

Cian Westmoreland and Brandon Bryant experienced their past as trauma. Having hit rock bottom, they decided to speak out. As they went public, the security state froze their bank accounts and they were in danger of being sent to jail for espionage. They began writing for the blog *Project Red Hand*. They faced either being paralyzed by trauma and suicide or living through the creativity of writing and resistance; either remaining in self-loathing or turning self-hatred into that harsh and dreadful love for their country. But for such transformation they needed "*a new way of thinking.*"[121] The old Westmoreland's American Dream had turned into the young Westmoreland's American nightmare; the old general's Catch-22s, a "journey to the end of the night" (Céline), had forced the young drone operator into the desperate breakthrough of speaking out for himself and his country.

For Westmoreland, Bryant, and many other former and current drone operators, as well as for the followers of Day, King, or Vitale protesting at Creech and the NTS, and for the scientists who developed the Bomb as well as Cold Warriors such as Kennan, McNamara, Ellsberg, or Perry who brought the world to the brink of Apocalypse, the one redeeming truth is that you must first experience history as trauma in order to transform your thinking and turn your body into resistance. What is happening in their own land under the banner of the American Dream has turned for them into a traumatic symptom archived in their own bodies—it is a past calling to the present for redemption and demanding works of love and a new way of thinking.

EPILOGUE Obama's Troy

KILL ME A SON

Barack Obama was born an American citizen in Hawaii in August 1961. His father, Barack Obama Sr., had moved from Kenya to Honolulu in 1959 to study at the University of Hawaii, where he met Ann Dunham, a seventeen-year-old from Kansas. Shortly after giving birth to her son, Dunham moved with Barack Junior to Seattle. Barack Senior stayed in Hawaii, then transferred to Harvard the following year with a graduate fellowship in economics. In 1964 he and Dunham divorced, and he returned to Kenya, where he worked for the government and for an oil company.

Anwar al-Awlaki was born an American citizen in Las Cruces, New Mexico, in April 1971. His father, Nasser al-Awlaki, a Fulbright scholar, had moved from Yemen (the closest land to the Horn of Africa in the Arabian Peninsula) to the US to earn a master's degree in agricultural economics at New Mexico State University. He completed a PhD at the University of Nebraska and from 1975 to 1977 worked at the University of Minnesota. In 1978, when Anwar was seven, Nasser returned with his family to Yemen, where he served as agriculture minister under President Ali Abdullah Saleh and later became president of Sana University.

After high school, in 1979, Barack Obama Jr. moved from Hawaii to Los Angeles to attend Occidental College. In 1981, he transferred as a junior to Columbia University, where he graduated in 1983, majoring in political science and English literature. Two years later Obama went to Chicago, hired by a church-based organization as a community organizer. In the fall of 1988, he entered Harvard Law School.

After high school, in 1991, Anwar al-Awlaki moved from Yemen to Fort Collins to attend Colorado State University, where he was president of the Muslim Student Association, and in 1994 he completed a BS in civil engineering. He studied but did not complete his degree in education leadership at San Diego University. In 1994 al-Awlaki became a part-time imam of the Denver Islamic Society; from 1996 to 2000, he was imam of a mosque in San Diego, where he had a following of two hundred to three hundred people. After traveling overseas, in January 2001 al-Awlaki settled in the Washington metropolitan area and served as imam in a mosque near Falls Church, Virginia.

9/11 was a watershed event that would shape both Obama and Awlaki. The night of the 9/11 attacks, Awlaki wrote to his brother, "I. . . . think it was horrible. I am very upset about it," as quoted in journalist Scott Shane's thoroughly researched book *Objective Troy: A Terrorist, a President, and the Rise of the Drone*.[1] Within a year of the attacks, Obama was opposing the War on Iraq as a "dumb war." His antiwar position was pivotal in his victory over Hillary Clinton for the Democratic Party nomination and his winning the presidency.

Awlaki's parents, as well as Obama's stepfather and paternal grandparents, were raised Muslim. Obama attended a Muslim school for two years while living in Indonesia; he was never a Muslim, as his political enemies charged, but he was familiar with Muslim religious life. For both Obama and Awlaki the anti-Muslim hysteria on the eve of 9/11 was an affront to the religion they knew and a threat to their careers. Both Obama and Awlaki felt a personal mission to educate the West that the Muslim religion had nothing to do with the heinous crime of 9/11. "We are the bridge between America and 1 billion Muslims worldwide," Awlaki said.[2] He was bothered by the "association between Islam and terrorism, when that's not true at all."[3] Obama would be repeatedly criticized for his unwillingness to link Muslim religion with terrorism. On June 4, 2009, Obama gave his "A New Beginning" speech at Cairo University in Egypt, where he described his personal experiences with Islam and the presence of more than 1,200 mosques in the US; he expressed willingness to "extend a hand" and called for "a new way forward" in the relations between Muslims and the West.

It would not be hyperbolic to state that in their early careers the lives of Obama and Awlaki run partly parallel. It would seem that Obama and Awlaki, both at the intersections of American lifestyles and Muslim tradition, could understand each other and even perhaps become allies. Each was American. Each had ties with family members from Muslim backgrounds. Their fathers had come from Kenya and Yemen to study in American universities, as they did themselves. In their youths they took parallel courses toward politics and religion, both committed to improving the lives of people in poor communities. Yet nothing would be further from an alliance between the two men in what was about to happen.

THE WAR ON TERROR AND THE EDGE

After 9/11, both Obama and Awlaki were caught by the vortex of a political storm that propelled the two men into tragic antagonism. Counterterrorism would inexorably condition and shape each other's fates. Obama was a liberal-to-moderate Democrat; Awlaki, like his father Nasser, was conservative and supported George W. Bush for president. "Tolerance: A Hallmark of Muslim Character" was the title of a speech Awlaki delivered on September 1, 2001, in Chicago, the city where Obama then lived. In sermons caught on camera, Awlaki provided "a paean to conservative social values and American exceptionalism that would not have been out of place at a Republican National Convention."[4] But the War on Terror crosses the Left/Right, Democratic/ Republican divides. Even if Bush stated that Muslim religion was not the enemy, his key statement "Either you are with us or you are with the terrorists" required people not only to condemn 9/11 as a "heinous crime," as Awlaki had done, but to accept a formula pivotal to counterterrorism: the opposition between *them* (Muslim terrorists) and *us* (the rest).The result was a rise in antagonism toward Muslims in general, exemplified by the finding of a 2011 Senate hearing that Muslims made up 1 percent of the population but were victims in 14 percent of religious discrimination cases, even though, as a *New York Times* article on right-wing domestic terrorism remarked, during the thirteen-and-a-half-year period after 9/11, "For every person killed by Muslim extremists, there have been 4,300 homicides from other threats."[5]

One week after 9/11 the FBI began repeated questioning of Awlaki as a suspect collaborator. Unknown to him, three of the suicide bombers had attended his sermons at the San Diego mosque—the same ones who had also spent time in Las Vegas, the city of wars and excess, in the months leading to 9/11. Awlaki insisted at the time on his absolute condemnation of the attacks, and he was not arrested. But the agency opened a formal investigation of him.

In January 2002 Awlaki received an invitation to speak at the Pentagon. Rumsfeld was eager to hear a moderate Muslim, and someone working in the Defense Department had been impressed by a talk he'd heard Awlaki give in nearby Alexandria. In the War on Terror, Awlaki was ready to be one more qualified and willing soldier.

But by then what really mattered to counterterrorism was the hunt for al-Qaeda sleeper cells. FBI agents knocked unannounced on Muslims' doors; more than a dozen Islamic businesses and institutions were targeted in federal raids led by some 150 agents. An angry Awlaki denounced a "campaign . . . against the Muslim community" in his Friday prayers of March 22, 2002, as "an indication of the dangerous route this war on terrorism is taking."[6] He read a long list of organizations that had been raided, asking, "What is next, and who will be safe? . . . This is not now a war on terrorism—we need to all be clear about this. This is a war against Muslims."[7] Days later, Awlaki decided to leave the United States.

But there was more to Awlaki's decision to leave the US. He had discovered that the FBI had a file on him that documented his life in detail. While it had found no evidence of terrorism, there was something else potentially useful to the FBI: Awlaki's visits to prostitutes. The FBI's intent was to use the file "to pressure him to become an informant or, if they decided he was a dangerous influence, to discredit him with a federal criminal case."[8] The evidence of prostitution could be leaked to the media and might well destroy his life.

At the end of March 2002 Awlaki flew to London and participated in the Quran Expo in Birmingham as planned but did not return to the US until six months later. Then, at his father's urging, he decided to finish his doctoral program at George Washington University. At the JFK airport

Awlaki, his wife, and the youngest of their three children were taken aside and held for three hours before being permitted to fly on to Washington. What happened during those hours remains speculation. Shane details the debate inside the FBI between arresting him or letting him free under close surveillance, something that might explain the mysterious encounter between Awlaki and his rival Virginia cleric Ali al-Tamimi.[9] At their meeting, as Tamimi's lawyers later claimed, Awlaki pressed Tamimi to help recruit fighters for jihad but Tamimi suspected Awlaki was working for the FBI and wearing a wire.

Did Awlaki actually become an informant? "On its face," observes Shane, "the notion that Awlaki might have been pressured into helping the FBI has a lot to recommend it."[10] A senior counterterrorism agent told journalist Jeremy Scahill, "My guess is that he pretended to cooperate for a while and then just split."[11] By late December Awlaki left for good. Under the FBI's sword of Damocles, his life had turned into hell.

Awlaki continued lecturing in London and other British cities throughout 2003. His talks on the Book of Jihad began with the disclaimer that "our study of this book is not an exhortation or an invitation to violence or promotion of violence against an individual, or a society or a state—this is purely an academic study."[12] With American troops in Iraq and Awlaki commuting between London and his parents' house in Yemen, his contempt for Islam's enemies was growing. Urged by his father, in the autumn of 2003 Awlaki got in touch with the FBI to inquire about the possibility of a return to the US. A meeting was planned for March 2004, but Awlaki got cold feet and gave up on the meeting. Even though the FBI told him they would not charge him, the prostitution file hung over his head. Circumstantial evidence could be construed into being "material support" to terrorism, as had happened to Ali al-Tamimi. At some point in 2004 he left Britain and settled in Yemen.

He became preoccupied with the political-theological debate as to whether resisting Americans was legitimate jihad. By then everybody knew that the Iraqi invasion was based on groundless facts—an illegal war that had already killed hundreds of thousands of Iraqis. Though Awlaki had been willing to cooperate with the US's War on Terror, supporting the bombing and occupation of Iraq was something else. In 2005 he published a five-hour set of lectures, "Constants on the Path to Jihad," marking a turning point in his thinking. If Muslims had supported the anti-Soviet jihad in Afghanistan, he concluded, the reasons for fighting Americans in Iraq were no less legitimate: "Whenever you see the word *terrorism*, replace it with *jihad*," Awlaki stated.[13] Giving up on jihad was tantamount to defeat. His position was still purely ideological, however, not a call for terrorist attacks.

By then Yemeni officials had questioned Awlaki on several occasions. "I'm not a person who would justify killing or who is in favor of killing—I am a Muslim," he told Mohammed al-Asaadi, editor of the *Yemen Observer*, "But the way they are harassing me, the way they are chasing me, the way they are liaising with the Yemeni authorities to detain me is something annoying, something disturbing." Al-Asaadi adds: "The more pressure he got from the authorities, the more radical he became."[14]

On August 31, 2006, Yemeni authorities, "with their usual eye on American counterterrorism dollars," arrested Awlaki in Sana.[15] He spent eighteen months in prison without being charged with a crime, held in solitary confinement (a form of torture according to human right groups) for more than sixteen months of his eighteen-month incarceration. His prison experience had a profound effect on him. He spent his first nine months in a eight-by-four-foot basement cell with a bare bulb hanging from the ceiling that was on twenty-four hours a day, with nothing to read but the Quran; when he finally had access to Islamic literature, he read Sayyid Qutb, father of modern radical Islamism, who greatly influenced his thinking. By then Awlaki was a hero to millions of Muslims. He was also closer and closer to the edge.

His father Nasser, a former agriculture minister, and his uncle, a wealthy tribal leader, lobbied President Saleh and his intelligence director for Anwar's release; they were told that "Anwar was imprisoned without charges only because of unbearable pressure from the Americans."[16] The Yemenis kept asking the US for evidence of Awlaki's support of terrorism, but "they have not given us anything, not even a single paper," the intelligence director told them.[17] In mid-2007, Nasser convinced his son to talk to two FBI agents, who interrogated him about the 9/11 hijackers. "Certainly at this point there is no evidence that US officials had any basis to charge Awlaki with a crime. He was talking about jihad, but that was not illegal."[18] Six years of harassment had passed since 9/11. Some Bush administration officials, including FBI director Robert Mueller, were uneasy about the indefinite incarceration of an American citizen. Awlaki was released in December 2007.

The debate about America and Iraq strained the relationship between Awlaki and his father. In July 2003 the Congressional Joint Inquiry report on 9/11 mentioned, in reference to Awlaki, the San Diego imam who reportedly had served as "spiritual adviser" to two of the hijackers. In June of 2004, a story in *U.S. News and World Report* mentioned Awlaki's mysterious links to 9/11 and the prostitution records. Nasser, a pro-American man of science and progress, was deeply wounded by these revelations. It was one more step in the cornering of Anwar al-Awlaki.

Out of prison, Awlaki was followed by FBI agents everywhere, so he decided to leave Sana for his family's tribal territory in remote Al Saeed (in Shabwah province), a mud-brick village of a hundred people, where he could live surrounded by relatives. But that was not acceptable to "the Americans," his father and uncle soon learned; they wanted him in Sana, under their surveillance. Anwar's uncle traveled five hours by car to let him know about the Yemeni authorities' request; he offered Anwar his seaside villa in Aden. "Please allow me to live here,"was Awlaki's reply.[19] He stayed for much of 2009 in Al Saeed. In the words of his uncle, "He'd go five times a day to the mosque. At four o'clock in the morning he'd be at the mosque, at sunrise, then maybe he goes home and then again at midday."[20] By then eight years had passed since 9/11, and counterterrorism was increasingly worried about a man living in a tiny isolated hamlet among relatives, going five times a day to pray at a mosque—it was all harmless, except that he had access to the internet and every week or two posted a militant blog on his website.

In the meantime Awlaki's name began to come up in interrogations of all sorts of people arrested in actual or failed terrorism plots; "His name came to be a kind of explanation."[21] Awlaki was "terrorist number one in terms of a threat against us," declared Jane Harman, a Democrat with experience in counterterrorism.[22] Nidal Hasan, the army psychiatrist in Fort Hood who fatally shot thirteen people and injured more than thirty others, was a major reason why Awlaki came into media prominence. Hasan had attended Awlaki's Friday prayers in Falls Church and listened to his CDs. In December 2008 Hasan began writing to Awlaki, asking about what types of violence were religiously sanctioned. His dilemma concerned which loyalty was primary—to the United States, which he had vowed as an army major to defend, or to the Muslim community to which he belonged. Awlaki didn't respond to this or other subsequent questions.[23] Only when Hasan wrote to him that he was organizing a contest, offering an award to the best essay on Awlaki, and added that, if he might remember, they had met briefly when he was an imam at Church Falls, Awlaki replied to say that he did not travel and that he was "too 'embarrassed'" to accept the award. Subsequent notes from Hasan met no reply. In short, "Awlaki offered no encouragement in his personal e-mail messages to Hasan for the idea of killing fellow American soldiers."[24] Still, the media coverage implied Awlaki was behind Hasan's attacks.

He was not guilty of any "material support" to Hasan but was guilty of something else that for counterterrorism might be as dangerous as any concrete act. In July 2009, Awlaki posted a scathing denunciation of Muslim soldiers fighting other Muslims. What Awlaki was doing was, first, to define the wars being waged by the US in religious terms, and second, to establish an antagonism within the *ummah* faith community that replicated Bush's cry of "You are either with us or against us" and made it immoral for Muslims to fight other Muslims.[25] Awlaki, who had ignored Hasan previously, endorsed him after his suicidal attack. This meant Awlaki was openly espousing violence, and by then it was time for him to leave Al Saeed and hide in the mountains of Shabwah. After his blog hailing Nidal Hasan, his website administrator got concerned and ended Awlaki's blog. Awlaki was providing an alternative narrative of defensive religious jihad to the discourse of *terrorism*.[26] He had crossed the line. A most-wanted target for US counterterrorism, he was about to reach his self-fulfilling destination.

THE TRINITY ALTERNATIVE

While Awlaki, hounded by counterterrorism, was moving toward an embrace of al-Qaeda, Obama, having served as Illinois state senator from 1997 to 2004 and then as US senator in Washington, in 2007 embarked on his quest for the presidency of the US. One initial chapter in Obama's story partly runs parallel to but only later veers into opposition to Awlaki's. Just as Awlaki became an imam to help his Muslim community, Obama, a community organizer in Chicago, turned himself into a self-avowed devout Christian.[27] He courted various churches and, in particular, became close to Reverend Jeremiah Wright, the pastor of Trinity Church of Christ, whom he met in 1987 and whose church he joined in 1992 despite the reverend's warning that some "feel like we're too radical."[28] The relationship between Wright and Obama was so close that, as one Chicago woman put it, "Jeremiah Wright was the black male father figure for Barack." Wright would say that Barack was "like a son to me."[29]

After Obama's return from Harvard with a law degree, Wright officiated at the marriage of Barack and Michelle Obama, comparing their marriage to the pillars of Trinity's sanctuary and describing Barack "as a fine pillar of African American manhood."[30] In a television interview following the publication of his first book, Obama called Wright "a wonderful man" who "represents the best of what the black church has to offer."[31] The title of the speech that made Obama nationally known, and of his second book, "The Audacity of Hope," was taken from one of Wright's sermons. But his relationship with Wright would push Obama into a critical tension between the alternative messages of black radical Christianity and mainstream liberal politics. In the end Obama disavowed Wright's radicalism once it became clear that it endangered the candidate's appeal to mainstream white America—the one anchored in the myth of its own exceptionalism. Obama would choose to embrace that myth, rather than be part of the tradition of prophetic resistance that Wright continued to push forward, as in his sermon "God Damn America."[32]

Wright, the father figure and onetime mentor, and the tradition of black Christianity his words called forth, became poison for Obama. He resigned from Wright's church. "I vehemently disagree and strongly condemn" Wright's statements, he replied to an interviewer, and in a specially crafted announcement of his own he declared, "I categorically denounce any statement that disparages our great country."[33] When asked about Obama's disparaging remarks about him, Wright answered that his former parishioner "does what politicians do," which stung Obama.[34] Later, in an appearance on NBC's *Meet the Press* Obama would state, "I never sought his [Wright's] counsel when it came to politics," and to *Newsweek* he would say, "I cannot recall a time where he and I sat down and talked about theology or we had long discussions about my faith."[35]

Words and symbols have a way of repeating themselves and becoming emblematic. "Trinity" was the name of Obama's church in Chicago. But there was another "Trinity" for Obama at the University of Chicago, where he lectured on constitutional law. Enrico Fermi's team of scientists' first self-sustained nuclear reaction in 1942, which preceded the first atomic detonation near Los Alamos, New Mexico, on July 16, 1945, was code-named "Trinity" by Oppenheimer. A 12twelve-foot bronze sculpture by Henry Moore in the form of a mushroom and a human skull was placed at the University of Chicago's old Stagg Field, where the experiment took place, and memorializes the event—a portrait of the Bomb, the ultimate American fetish of the security state. Wright's tradition opposes militarism, and Obama recalls in *Dreams from My Father* Wright preaching about Hiroshima.[36] Baldwin had noted: "We can irrigate deserts and feed the entire earth for the price we are paying to build bombs that we will be able to use, in any event, only once."[37]

Soon after he was elected president, Obama gave a speech in Prague embracing nuclear disarmament, and when he visited Hiroshima at the end of his second term he proclaimed, "We must change our mindset about war itself." But his critics were unsparing about the discrepancies between his words and his actions. Pointing out the proliferation risks of nuclear power programs, they noted that "no president in the last three decades has put more taxpayer dollars behind atom power than Barack Obama."[38] In a gesture of diplomacy Obama had visited Hiroshima, but he had refused to apologize for the massacre. He had called again for an end to nuclear weapons, a major reason why was given a Nobel Peace Prize, but had left his presidency with the commitment of a trillion more dollars "to modernize" nuclear arsenals into the next decade, thus directly pushing for a new arms race.[39] For people in the tradition of radical Christianity, the one espoused by Day and King and Arrupe and Wright, Hiroshima is, after the slavery, the sin of America. When Obama's counterterror guide John Brennan tried to justify drone killings, he brought up Hiroshima, asking, "Did it save a lot of American lives? Yeah, it probably did."[40] If Hiroshima was justified because it saved lives, the unspoken deduction is that so are drone strikes. While claiming for himself the high moral ground, Obama surrounded himself with men like Brennan, Leon Panetta, and Michael Mullen, who posed as devout Christians anxiously fingering their rosary beads while engaged in ruthless extrajudicial killings,[41] men whom Dorothy Day and Elizabeth Anscombe would simply call "murderers." Since you can't have it both ways, Obama faced a "Trinity" alternative between the city's black prophetic church and the university's Trinity nuclear reaction.

"I FACE THE WORLD AS IT IS"

On December 10, 2009, the year Awlaki spent at the hamlet of Al Saeed, President Obama went to Oslo to receive his Nobel Peace Prize. He acknowledged that he stood there because of Martin Luther King, who years earlier had said at that same ceremony that war "solves no social problem: it merely creates new and more complicated ones." Obama then added that he could not be guided only by King and Gandhi's examples, since, he said, "I face the world as it is. . . . For make no mistake: Evil does exist in the world"[42]—meaning, terrorists exist in the world.

Obama used the speech to reframe the War on Terror as a defensive "just war" against al-Qaeda. A week after his Oslo speech, on December 17, alleging signs of impending attacks in Yemen, Obama approved a strike against a suspected AQAP (al-Qaeda in the Arab Peninsula) training camp. US cruise missiles killed an al-Qaeda operative and thirteen militants, plus some forty civilians, including twenty-one children and five pregnant women. The Tomahawk missiles were armed with cluster munitions forbidden by an international convention the United States refuses to sign, and in the following days yellow cluster cylinders the size of soda cans killed another four and injured a dozen or more curious children and adults. Tens of thousands of enraged people rallied against the US and the Yemeni government. Petraeus would come two weeks later to congratulate President Saleh on recent successful operations against AQAP and to increase American aid to $150 million, while Saleh assured him that "we'll continue saying the bombs are ours, not yours."[43] In short, "Collateral damage [was] so extreme that it would permanently poison public opinion. With a single strike, the United States had yielded the moral high ground in Yemen."[44]

During Obama's years in office, a war would break out in Yemen, Saudi-led but fought with US weapons, as well as the gas for the Saudi warplanes and the refueling of the jets paid with American taxpayers' monies.[45] It would claim more than ten thousand lives by 2016—and subsequently create a humanitarian crisis as tens of thousands children were dying from hunger and the majority of the twenty-six million Yemenis were in danger of starvation. If there was little doubt that with Obama America was "complicit in the carnage in Yemen," as a *New York Times* editorial put it, the situation only got worse with the collaboration of the new Trump administration and Saudi Arabia's new brutal leader Mohammed bin Salman.[46]

A week after the December 17 strike on Yemen, on December 24, a second strike with cruise missiles hit a house where a meeting of al-Qaeda was believed to be taking place. According to early false reports, Awlaki and other leaders were among the thirty or so killed. But it was the failed Christmas Day attempt against an airplane over Chicago by Umar Farouk Abdulmutallab, known as the "Underwear Bomber," that turned on all the alerts. He was the son of a wealthy Nigerian father who let the US embassy know that his son was in Yemen and might have joined al-Qaeda, but his name was never added to the no-fly list.

Abdulmutallab confessed to the FBI that he had received instructions from, among others, Awlaki—something Awlaki denied.[47] Nasir al-Wuhayshi, the head of AQAP, had given the order to Abdulmutallab, and it was Ibrahim Hassan Tali al-Asiri who had built the bomb.[48]

Obama became obsessed with getting Awlaki, even though some in the administration doubted the legality of targeting a US citizen without trial. Civil libertarians argued that Awlaki's blogs were mere talk and protected by the First Amendment. Even Harold Koh, the State Department's legal adviser, thought Awlaki's speech was legally protected. But Obama insisted he had the constitutional and legal authority to order Awlaki killed. In February 2010, he added Awlaki to the kill list; "This is an easy one," he said of his decision.[49] It wasn't as easy for law professors such as Kevin Jon Heller, whose post on his international law blog *Opinio Juris* was titled "Let's Call Killing al-Awlaki What It Is—Murder," or for David Barron and Martin Lederman, the two constitutional scholars who both left the government after they had provided the legal reasoning for targeting Awlaki. Obama the constitutional law professor had come to believe that a president could name another American a dangerous terrorist on the basis of secret intelligence and, without trial, order him killed.

On March 16, 2010, the CIA carried out the 202nd Pakistan drone strike of Obama's presidency, "killing upwards of 40 civilians."[50] Its purpose was not to avoid an impending attack: the target was a large gathering of sixty or so elderly men who were holding a *jirga* (a reconciliation meeting) to discuss a local mining dispute. The Pakistani military knew about the meeting, had received a request for the gathering ten days in advance. But the strike went ahead anyway. Upon consultation, US ambassador Cameron Munter tried to halt the plan but was overruled by CIA director Leon Panetta. The CIA's Predator drones struck the village. According to one US official, it was an "act of 'retaliation' for the Davis affair."[51] (Pakistani authorities had arrested a CIA operative, Raymond Davis, and after forty-eight days in custody had charged him on two accounts of murder for having killed two Pakistani youths; within hours a US military plane rushed him out of Pakistan. The drone attack occurred a day after Davis's release.) Similarly, one of Munter's aides told the Associated Press that the attack was "a retaliation for Davis. The CIA was angry."[52] And a former ISI chief told Woods that the *jirga* strike was "clearly a show of [American] anger." The report by the Stanford and NYU law schools found "a troubling correlation between events of political significance and the intensity of drone strikes."[53] Dozens of people with no relation to al-Qaeda died in the *jirga* attack. "I see the world as it is." But did Obama see the severed body parts of those bystanders, strewn hundreds of yards away, being picked up and collected in sacks by their relatives? Panetta, a devout Catholic, joked that he had "said more Hail Marys in the last two years than I have in my whole life."[54] But not only devout counterterrorists, easily forgiven in the confessional given their religious zeal against "Evil in the world," could turn assassination into a joke. At the White House Correspondents' Association dinner in May 2010, forty-five days after the strike, Obama, apparently not much affected by the dozens of families whose members had been murdered by drone missiles he ordered, joked about drones in relation to sex and his daughters. "The Jonas Brothers are here . . . Sasha and Malia are huge fans. But boys, don't get any ideas. I have two words for you, 'predator drones.' You will never see it coming. You think I'm joking."

OBJECTIVE TROY

"Objective Troy" was the Obama administration's code name for the elimination of Awlaki, alluding to the Trojan Horse myth of conquest through deception and betrayal. The excavation of the remains of ancient Troy in the late nineteenth century had a profound impact on the European imagination; the site marked the oldest record of European wars and the earliest case of self-defeating politics. The myths of the Greeks became an inaugural component of modern consciousness, with Troy serving as a symbol of defeat and presaged downfall. Historic episodes of catastrophic defeat, such as the fate of Berlin at the end of World War II, were compared to the fate of Troy.[55]

The story of the Trojan War is the topic of Homer's epic poem the *Iliad*—the most terrifying and greatest of poems, the model for future tragic heroes stubbornly attached to an ideal image of themselves. Its two major heroes are Achilles for the Greeks and Hector for the Trojans. Achilles's military feat was the slaying of Hector at the gates of Troy. Homer condensed the catastrophic conflict of the Trojan War into the archetypal enmity between Achilles and Hector, and the Obama administration's invoking of Troy in the name for its mission of hunting down and eliminating Awlaki prompts an invitation to draft here a parallel narrative by emblematically reducing the War on Terror to another fateful antagonism—the one between Obama and Awlaki. That one can make such a comparison between the *Iliad* and the ongoing War on Terror speaks to the pervasive centrality of war in our own times; it also highlights how little the human condition has changed in three thousand years.

The *Iliad* is the work of a poet.[56] The poet becomes a source of community by framing human passions and errors in the plot of a narrative. He can hardly *explain* war; he can only turn into song or play what appears unsolvable in human experience while trying to affect the imagination and sentiment of the reader or viewer. Homer creates his own "home of the hunters" by bringing animal analogies and hunting scenarios into his poem—lions mauling a running deer, jackals surrounding a wounded stag, hounds circling a lion, lions overpowering a wild boar, hawks chasing after birds, and falcons diving after crows for the kill.[57] Homer took the stories of his times and invented for them a plot, a particular narrative that went beyond the stories themselves; the invention of a plot is, thought Aristotle, the essence of the invention of a poem such as the *Iliad*. Drone warfare, with tragic episodes like "Objective Troy" aimed at Awlaki, requires a kind of ethnography that, like the Homeric poet, "discovers a form in the story, an internal logic," and helps us "recognize the probability or necessity of the sequence."[58] In such crafting of a plot from drone warfare, we could perhaps say of Awlaki, as of Hector, that he "is a hero of illusions; he is finally trapped between a failed illusion and his own incapacity for disillusionment. Hector is surely a figure less grand than Achilles, but it is Hector's story that gives Achilles's story meaning; Hector affirms all that Achilles denies."[59]

As Hector knows of Achilles, Awlaki knows of Obama that he is "far and away a stronger man."[60] "We fight as outlaws,"[61] Hector's Trojans are told, much as Awlaki's followers are today's outlaws. Awlaki's actions kept crying out to Obama, as Hector did, "Bring fire!,"[62] and Obama would reply by raining down on him Hellfire missiles from Creech. Awlaki taunted Obama, as Hector did Achilles: "Don't think for a moment, Achilles, son of Peleus / you can frighten me with words like a child, a fool . . . / Well I know . . . I am far weaker . . . / Weaker I am, but . . . my weapon can cut too."[63]

After the first drone attack on his life, Awlaki could have repeated the words addressed to Hector: "Now, again, you've escaped your death, you dog / but a good close brush with death it was," for "Hector's escaped again, he's risen from the dead!"[64] In the end, Awlaki was, like Hector, the man "shackled fast by his deadly fate" who could identify with Hector's fateful words: "My time has come! / At last the gods have called me down to death. / . . . Athena's tricked me blind. / And now death, grim death is looming beside me, / no longer far away."[65]

But it is the transformation of Achilles, the man of "aristocratic tradition, the man of princely courtesy and innate nobility," suddenly devoured by rage and seized with murderous frenzy over the death of his friend Patroclus, that is most striking about the *Iliad*.[66] Achilles is the greater hero: his "greatness is a greatness of force and negation. He is different from other men by his greater capacity . . . to kill. . . . He is a heroic rather than demonic figure because his negations are founded not on perversity of will but on clarity of intellect," because "Achilles is a hero with exceptional powers of intellect and speech."[67] These words find an echo in Obama the man.

Achilles is the greater hero."But Achilles does not die in the *Iliad*"; instead, "The pathos of the poem is concentrated in the death of Hector," the vanquished hero, remarks James Redfield.[68] In the case of drone warfare and the Hellfire missiles raining from Nevada, nothing is more tragic that the lost lives of the thousands of victims. A true ethnography requires of the writer to ask about his plot, as the Homeric poet does, "What sort of man shall I make my criminal? What sort of man is likely to do such things?"[69] For the writer Hector and Achilles, like the terrorist and the counterterrorist, are not categorically different but belong to the same field. Leaving aside standard reductive counterterrorism discourse, what is required is to see the tragic patterns that unite Awlaki and Obama in order to create intelligibility and, as in the Homeric poem, a cathartic purification of experience.

From beginning to end, from the Bushes to Obama, from the Blind Sheik to Osama bin Laden to the Awlakis, the War on Terror, like the war in Troy between Peleus and Achilles, or between Priam and Hector, is a story of fathers and sons. Mothers and wives and sisters and daughters are missing from the main narratives. They are about *dreams from my father*. Ben Rhodes summed up Obama's and his own biography: "We're both trying to prove something to our fathers and were nurtured and encouraged by our mothers."[70]

When it was made public in early 2010 that Anwar al-Awlaki was on Obama's kill list, a desperate Nasser al-Awlaki began legal action to defend his son.[71] The father had "made several attempts to persuade him [his son] to stop talking about jihad," recalled one of his followers.[72] Anwar displayed much the same attitude as George W. Bush when he responded to the question whether he had consulted with his father before going to war in Iraq: "There is a higher Father that I appeal to."

On May 4, 2011, Predator pilots at Creech thought they had Awlaki in their sights, but by the time they shot the Hellfire missiles he had changed cars. By then Awlaki had accepted his fate; when the appointed time came, he said, paradise would be waiting. As he had quoted from Ibn Taymiyyah in one of his lectures, he was already living in the afterlife. Killing him would only turn him into a martyr. The "self-fulfilling prophecy by both the foreign media and the Obama administration," as skeptics argued regarding Awlaki, was coming to its apotheosis.[73] The ultimate charge against him was that in June 2010 he had started the slick online magazine *Inspire*, a brazen promoter of jihad against the West.[74]

"I want Awlaki," Obama had told his advisers.[75] After bin Laden, there was no one Obama wanted so badly. When during the night of September 30, 2011, operators from Creech in Nevada again spotted their target, this time there was no escape for Awlaki. "It might conceivably have been possible to organize a capture by Yemeni or American commandos," reported Shane. "But a drone strike was politically far less complicated for both countries. . . . It was easier for [the Yemeni president] Saleh to let the Americans take a shot at Awlaki than to send his troops to catch him."[76] It was one more case of "Don't capture, kill."

When a coy but ecstatic Obama gave the news to a gathering of officers and dignitaries on the lawn of the White House, they applauded. Because it was a covert action, the role of the United States could not be publicly acknowledged, but, as in the case of bin Laden, Obama was eager for a personal "declaration of victory."[77] Obama received much praise from commentators, including his archenemy Dick Cheney. Osama bin Laden in May, and now Awlaki in September—Obama the warrior was fighting and seemed unstoppable. But so had Awlaki seemed for his Muslim audience; his legacy of sermons and lectures was "only magnified by his killing, as some Muslim activists had warned."[78]

The greatest triumph in Awlaki's legacy was soon to arrive. In May 2008 Awlaki had made a recording in which he heralded the emergence of the Islamic State of Iraq as a "monumental event." In December 2013 its successor the Islamic State of Iraq and Syria put up a new English-language video on the Internet that showed a portrait of Awlaki and included a passage from his recording to endorse itself.[79] In time the Islamic State would create an "Anwar al-Awlaki Battalion" of English-speaking fighters. Many of the Westerners who headed for Syria's jihad would be Awlaki followers. Three years after his death, in January 2015, the murderers of a dozen people working at *Charlie Hebdo* claimed Awlaki as their guide. Eighteen people indicted in the US on terrorism chargesafter Awlaki's death, including Dzhokhar Tsarnaev, who with his brother planted the bombs at the Boston Marathon in 2013, killing three people and injuring more than 260, cited his influence in their radicalization.[80] By then there were eighty thousand YouTube videos for "Awlaki." "Martyrdom, courtesy of a CIA Hellfire missile, had only given Awlaki a more exalted pedestal."[81] The actions of Obama, the president who dreamed he could eliminate Awlaki and could contain terrorism with drone warfare, only caused Muslim extremists to control large areas of Iraq and Syria during his second term. The trillions spent in the War on Terror by the US only added to the terrorists' unprecedented success.

Awlaki's downfall begins with his initial error of not paying attention to his father's advice. The father wished Anwar to become an engineer, not an imam, but what the father really objected to was that he should read in religious terms the antagonism between the US and the Muslims and call his followers to jihad. In an echo of Homeric societies, where war is central to human activity and "the most powerful type of affection . . . is that felt by a father for his grown son," both Awlaki and Obama's relationship to their fathers is at the core of who they are.[82] Awlaki respected his father but defied him because of what he believed to be his obligation to Muslims worldwide; his error of falling into jihad was the error of a believer who felt compelled to act.

Nasser hated what Anwar was doing but understood his son and tried to save his life once he discovered that Obama had placed him on the kill list. Once Awlaki became operationally involved with AQAP, it was the consummation of a great error, and there was now no possible retreat for him. The hero's failure is internal to himself, to his lack of self-knowledge. Awlaki was led by religious desire to political violence—altruism transformed into egotism. Like Hector, he "has long acted blindly, but at the end he can see his fate coming toward him and resolves to go to meet it."[83] By taking refuge in ideology he had promised himself and his followers that future victory was inevitable.

Homer's heroic stories are fiction for Aristotle, yet they show "what sort of thing is possible, probable, or necessary" in human experience.[84] While the historian uses causal chains to reconstruct an event and point out the motives of a crime, a "teller of tales" begins with the event, the crime, and asks what sort of a man commits such an action—killer and victim are not categorically different but belong to the same human domain. Probability and necessity create a *plot* that reveals the internal logic of a chain of events. The same story can engender various plots depending on how it is framed. The battle between Obama and Awlaki has multiple plots with heroic, tragic, and ironic results. The wisdom of the tragic poet derives from showing us a conception unified by probability and necessity that can lead to the combination of emotion and learning, or, in Aristotelian terms, *catharsis*. For Aristotle, the *Iliad's* heroic world was full of absurdity, but the imitative art of the poets who tell our stories, like the ethnographer's subjective premise, compels them to look at action from the point of view of the actor or the native.

A tragic narrative tests the limits of a culture. In Aristotle's words, "A fine [tragic] plot must . . . move . . . from good fortune to ill fortune, not through crime but through a great error."[85] The tragic error "is really an error, yet it is the sort of error a good man would make. It is thus an act both free and conditioned."[86] Could we say of Awlaki, a religious person who dedicated his life to the Muslim community, that he was also a good man who fell into error, and that his drama, like the defeated hero's, "lay in his relation to others," as "the consequence of his special place within the action, as the leader of a hopeless war"?[87] If we see the internal logic by which a Muslim like Awlaki, in the US and during the War on Terror, is year after year inexorably pushed to the edge, feeling that he, honor bound, must defend his community and family, we learn something important about the limits of Muslim and American cultures, and also ourselves.

What matters to the epic poet, as it matters to us, is the interpretation of what sort of error the hero makes. "The hero's error," Redfield summarizes, ". . . . is not forced upon him, but he makes it under conditions so adverse that we watch him with compassion. . . . Hector's freedom can be understood only in relation to the imperfections of his power and knowledge; these define his acts."[88] Such meditation is the writer's task in order to produce a cathartic effect on the readers and viewers of the play. For the counterterrorist, Awlaki is nothing if not Evil leading to terrorism—but in a poem like the *Iliad* he would turn into a tragic character. And so would his nemesis, Obama.

THE ANTIFUNERAL: OBAMA AS A TRAGIC CHARACTER

Combat is a negation of community, but there is something worse: "The perfected negation of community . . . inheres not in killing the enemy but in denying him a funeral," for "so long as the warriors promise each other a funeral . . . they respect each other's communities."[89] Conflict produces chaos and terror because of its threat of impurity; "the emblem of this chaos within the *Iliad* is the antifuneral,"[90] and the terror of such impurity takes quintessential form in the dead warrior left unrecovered and unburied, like a dead animal to be eaten by vultures and dogs. This was Achilles's initial intent when he dragged Hector's dead body across the bloodied battlefield. In the perspective of the *Iliad*, Obama's antifuneral stance—his allowing a policy of bombing mourners at funerals—reveals most glaringly his error.[91]

Nothing is more telling about drone warfare's disregard for the rules of war than its antiburial policy. "Hector's story begins, as it ends, with his funeral";[92] Awlaki's story, like bin Laden's, ends with the *nonfuneral.* Achilles's words after killing a Trojan warrior and throwing him into a river describe bin Laden's end as well when his remains were reportedly thrown to the sea: "There— / lie there! Make your bed with the fishes now, / they'll dress your wound and lick it clean of blood— / so much for your last rites!"[93] As in ancient Homeric societies, in Awlaki's and Obama's Muslim traditions, respect for the funeral practices of the dead is central—as it is also for American and European societies that devote whatever resources are needed to recover the remains of their fallen soldiers.[94]

But drones frequently obliterate and disintegrate the identity of the bodies of enemy targets. A typical situation is described by Awlaki's uncle when, on December 17, 2009, a week after Obama's Nobel Peace Prize acceptance, he reached the scene of the drone attack that had killed four-teen militants and forty-one civilians. Seeing body parts everywhere, he said in an interview, "We don't know if it belongs to dogs, goats, or human beings. So we buried it all together."[95]

The killings of Osama bin Laden and Anwar al-Awlaki, claimed as the two foremost victories in the War on Terror, illustrate the US antiburial policy. After bin Laden's killing, Obama said in his address that the SEALs "took custody of his body." When everyone expected that his body would be produced, reporters were told that bin Laden's body had been flown to the USS supercarrier *Carl Vinson* and buried at sea. Under questioning by the press, John Brennan replied that they thought the "burial at sea" would be "the best way to ensure that his body was given an appropriate

Islamic burial"—this after "appropriate specialists and experts" were consulted.[96] But there were no photographs of the burial process, or any indication as to who washed and wrapped the body, or who the Arabic speaker was who conducted the funeral.

Like so much else in the coverage of terrorism news, bin Laden's burial was shown to be mostly a fabrication by Seymour Hersh's careful reconstruction of the facts. Item by item, Hersh reveals how Obama and his administration lied to the public about every aspect of the killing of bin Laden, beginning with claims that it was an all-American affair of which Pakistan's army and intelligence services knew nothing. Two longtime consultants to Special Operations Command with access to intelligence told Hersh that the funeral aboard *Carl Vinson* never took place.

A particular complication went to the heart of what happened: "Some members of the SEAL team had bragged to colleagues and others that they had torn bin Laden's body to pieces with rifle fire. The remains . . . were thrown into a body bag and, during the helicopter flight back to Jalalabad, some body parts were tossed out over the Hindu Kush mountains."[97] The cover story was going to be that bin Laden had been killed in a drone strike. According to the initial plan, news of the killing would not be released for seven days; afterwards Obama would announce that DNA analysis confirmed that it was bin Laden who had been killed. The fact that six of the most experienced SEALs faced an unarmed elderly man belies the White House claim that the killing was in self-defense. Brennan insisted on the fairy tale that "he was engaged in a firefight . . . hiding behind women who were put in front of him as a shield. . . . [It] just speaks to I think the nature of the individual he was,"[98] embellishing the fiction that, if possible, the SEALs were to take bin Laden alive. As a former SEAL commander told Hersh: "We are not going to keep bin Laden alive. . . . By law, we know what we're doing inside Pakistan is a homicide. . . . [We] say to ourselves, 'Let's face it. We're going to commit a murder.'"[99]

In its 2011 annual report Amnesty International described the killing as "unlawful."[100] The White House gave the impression that bin Laden was still in charge of al-Qaeda. As to the alleged intelligence troves captured in bin Laden's raid, a retired intelligence officer told Hersh that "every single thing they have created turns out not to be true. It's a great hoax."[101] To avoid the true story coming out, the White House silenced the SEALs by promising civil penalties and a lawsuit against anyone who spoke privately or in public about the mission. In the meantime, stories of how "gutsy" the president had been and photos of Obama's inner circle hunkered down at the White House with anguished faces were released. One of the SEALs who took part in the raid said: "The killing of bin Laden was political theatre designed to burnish Obama's military credentials. . . . Bin Laden became a working asset."[102] Obama's approval ratings went up 11 percent.[103]

As to Awlaki's funeral, when the local sheikh went to the spot where a drone had vaporized him, "there were just craters and the burned frames of trucks."[104] Since there was no body, no burial was needed.

Journalist Woods was able to confirm ten incidents in which first responders to a drone strike were deliberately targeted, the so-called double taps.[105] The Bureau of Investigative Journalism identified fifteen instances of double taps and eighteen instances of funerals targeted by CIA's drones. The Stanford and NYU law schools identified more cases.[106]

United Nations special rapporteur Christopher Heyns wrote that targeting the wounded and medical personnel "constitutes a war crime."[107] The report by the law schools of Stanford and NYU noted that "the 'double tap' pattern of strikes on first responders raises crucial moral and legal concerns" and that "as international law experts have noted, intentional strikes on first responders may constitute war crimes."[108] They concluded that "traditional burial practices are rendered impossible."[109] The domain of religious or political sacrifice, primordial to any society, did not apply to those targeted. The fictional film *Easy Kill* shows a critical moment in which the drone pilot's alienation from his job reaches a point of no return. A drone strike has killed a group of alleged terrorists, and the survivors gather to bury the dead; the pilots can't believe they are receiving orders from Langley that they should strike against those burying the dead as well—they are *bare life* to be killed with no rights to burial, and the survivors are equally outside of society.

When Achilles killed the father of Hector's wife Andromache, he gave his enemy proper burial—the funeral was a recognition of the enemy's community. Injury and death are expected components of combat and thus sufferable, even ennobling. But it is the impurity of combat unmediated by cultural forms—epitomized by the denial of funeral ceremonies to your enemy—that is the source of ultimate chaos and terror. Such "ultimate impurity" of the dead warrior's body left unburied is a sort of cannibalism and "is the quintessential terror of the *Iliad*."[110] When in battle, Achilles was unrelenting, for the combatants were beast-like enemies to each other to be hunted and killed. But when Achilles fatally wounded him, Hector begged his slayer to return his body to Troy for burial: "I beg you, beg you by your life, your parents—don't let the dogs devour me by the Argive ships!" In his wrath Achilles replied: "Beg no more, you fawning dog— begging me by my parents! . . . The dogs and birds will rend you—blood and bone!"[111] Hector told Achilles he had "iron inside your chest" and warned him: "Beware, or my curse will draw god's wrath / upon your head."[112] In response, Achilles tied Hector's body to his chariot and "dragged him back and forth."[113]

But Achilles was to undergo a change of heart. Since killing evokes more killing and, in the end, brings no victory, the *Iliad* faces the problem of artistic closure—how to end the war and the poem. So Homer makes Achilles hear the Olympian gods telling him, "The hearts of the great . . . can always change."[114] Zeus orders Achilles to give Hector's body back, sending Achilles's mother Thetis to tell him, "The gods are angry with you now," to which Achilles replies in obedience: "So be it."[115] Priam, Hector's aged father, and Achilles the young warrior meet in the Greek camp. Priam "goes [to Achilles] as father to son" and kisses Achilles's hand, the hand that killed his own boy.[116] Priam talks to Achilles about his own father, Peleus, and Achilles weeps. Through the primordial relation between Priam and Peleus, both fathers and old men, besieged by mortality, a basis for reconciliation is created as Achilles sees the tragedy from Priam's point of view. Achilles allows Priam to take Hector's body, allows for a funeral. Achilles even calls Priam "old friend"[117]—deadly enemies have turned into friends, a miracle has occurred. The *Iliad* produces artistic unity by showing that the two heroes are mirror opposites of each other, products of each other in a larger unifying pattern. The last verse of the *Iliad* is the burial: "And the Trojans buried Hector breaker of horses."[118] Burying the victims allows for an ending. Nasser al-Awlaki would never experience such an ending.

"Whereas Hector can do nothing but die, Achilles can do nothing but kill."[119] A similar relation, we might say, obtained between Awlaki and

Obama. Both Hector and Achilles were for Homer good men who fell into error. Awlaki's errors of fanaticism at the end of his life were glaring. But so were Obama's errors: he was an extraordinarily graceful and intelligent man, who tried hard to extricate the US from its permanent war in the Middle East but turned into a commander who disregarded the ethics of war.

"Achilles wept . . . for his father" as he saw Priam weeping for Hector.[120] Obama says he went to his Kenyan father's grave and wept: "When my tears were finally spent, I felt a calmness wash over me. I felt the circle finally close."[121] Obama the poet succeeded in turning his African heritage and family into powerful aesthetic objects while "they joyed as they looked upon each other." Obama understood with compassion the tragic side of his own father's follies. But he wasn't able to see the fatherly tragedy of Nasser al-Awlaki. Achilles in the end controlled his wrath and felt pity for Priam. Obama could find no pity for Awlaki and others he helped kill, could not see in them anything but "terrorists" undeserving of a trial and the rule of law, *homo sacer* to be killed with impunity, whose deaths were neither political fate nor patriotic sacrifice and thus were due no pity or ritual. Such blindness presents Obama as a tragic figure. His brand of universality is based on the exclusion of the alleged "terrorist"—a biopolitical exclusion that in the end makes us all potential terrorists. This despite the fact that the living man he came to admire the most, Nelson Mandela, had also been considered a *terrorist*.

HIGHWAY 61 REVISITED: "KILL ME A SON"

"Oh, God said to Abraham, 'Kill me a son,'" Bob Dylan sings in "Highway 61 Revisited." It wasn't enough for Obama to obliterate Anwar al-Awlaki. Two weeks later Awlaki's sixteen-year-old American son, Abdulrahman, was also killed by drones while camping with his friends. The decision to kill Nasser's son Anwar, Obama said, had been "an easy one." But killing Anwar's son, Abdulrahman, was, he said, a "fuck-up."[122] No other act contributed more to alienate ordinary Yemenis, wrote London *Times* reporter Iona Craig; angry protesters burning American flags in the streets chanted, "If he's Al-Qaeda we're all Al-Qaeda."[123]

But killing Abdulrahman al-Awlaki had not been exactly an unforeseen "fuck-up." He was paying for his father's sins if you listen to Obama's press secretary, Robert Gibbs, when he was asked why Abdulrahman was killed even though he was "an American citizen . . . targeted without due process of law, without trial. And he's underage. He's a minor." Gibbs replied: "I would suggest that you should have a far more responsible father if they are truly concerned about the well-being of their children. I don't think becoming an al-Qaeda jihadist terrorist is the best way to go about doing your business."[124] The same happened to bin Laden: the father wasn't enough, the son also was killed in the attack.

The killing of the son was the last straw for Cian Westmoreland: "[It] outraged me," he said in his Las Vegas presentation, ". . . the killing of Abdulrahman al-Awlaki. They explained it that he just had the wrong dad. That doesn't sit well with me. I was raised as a Christian and I was taught that killing is not sanctioned by God."

Numerous news outlets reported that Abdulrahman was twenty-one, and anonymous US officials added that he was "military-age." Other reports stated that he was an al-Qaeda supporter. It was said that he had been in the company of Ibrahim al-Banna, an Egyptian AQAP coordinator, though this was later disclaimed by AQAP. The United States released a statement feigning ignorance about the strike. Some senior US officials added that he had been an "unintended casualty" and that it was "an outrageous mistake" but never revealed the intended target.

Meanwhile, his family began to wonder whether Abdulrahman was the actual target of the strike. When asked about the killings of the Awlakis, senator and majority leader Harry Reid, who had reviewed the intelligence on the strike, left little doubt: "I do know this, the American citizens who have been killed overseas . . . are terrorists, and, frankly, if anyone in the world deserves to be killed, those three deserved to be killed."[125] Similarly, another member of the Intelligence Committee, Representative Peter King, with access to the classified information, said about Abdulrahman's death: "I'm convinced . . . that every attack that's been carried out in Yemen and Afghanistan . . . I believe that the United States had reason to carry them out and I support them." Asked whether that included Abdulrahman's case more specifically, he again left little doubt: "Yeah, that would be a logical deduction."[126] It was Abdulrahman's predicament from birth to be killed because of his father. Nasser al-Awlaki kept asking why his son and grandson had been assassinated. The US government invoked the state secrets privilege to deny answers.

There was someone in the United States who could understand what it was like to be born in the United States, the grandson and son of African Muslim men himself, and who could grasp the saga of the al-Awlakis, Nasser, Anwar, and Abdulrahman, as well as the anguish of teenager Abdulrahman in search for his lost father. That man's memoir describes the difficult process of becoming a man in the United States, the process of reconciling with the ghosts of the Old Man from Africa—"something unknown ... volatile and vaguely threatening."[127] His father, like Abdulrahman's grandfather and father, "had boarded the plane to America, the land of dreams," to attend US universities and return to his homeland a man of influence. One could say of them, that each returned "a divided man, his plans, his dreams, soon turned to dust."[128] The writer's initial problem with his father, like Abdulrahman's, was the realization that "my father was missing."[129] Surely this writer could understand Abdulrahman's need when he himself confessed, "It was into my father's image, the black man, son of Africa, that I'd packed all the attributes I sought in myself. . . . My father's voice had remained untainted, inspiring. . . . You must help in your people's struggle. Wake up, black man!"[130] It was this American writer and constitutional scholar who truly knew of his Old Man, as Abdulrahman knew of his father, that "I couldn't escape him,"[131] to the point that "I would find myself . . . feeling as if I was living out a preordained script, as if I were following him in error, a captive to his tragedy."[132] He did in fact say that Trayvon Martin could have been himself some thirty-five years earlier; couldn't he also have been Abdulrahman al-Awlaki?

In a pilgrimage to his African roots, the author wrote that he was overwhelmed by what he found about the Old Man. "I feel my father's presence. . . . I see him in the schoolboys. . . . I hear him in the laughter. . . . I smell him in the cigarette smoke. . . . The Old Man is here. . . . He's here, asking me to understand."[133] The American writer could have been the much-needed proxy father for the teenager Abdulrahman who left his grandparents' home to search for his real father.

Maybe his father Anwar would explain things to Abdulrahman in a way that he could understand. Why, for example, against his parents' wishes, had Anwar become a religious imam? Why had he prayed at the Pentagon after 9/11? Had he been an FBI informant?[134] Why had he, who had preached a religion of peace for decades, ended up a militant of AQAP? The American writer's memoir might have helped young Abdulrahman free himself from his own dead father's ghost and come to the realization that "the fantasy of my father had at least kept me from despair. Now he was dead, truly. He could no longer tell me how to live."[135] This American writer turned politician could have taught Abdulrahman what he knew about his own father, that upon returning to his homeland "he forgot what holds everything together here" and that essentially "he was lost."[136] Yes, someone had to tell Abdulrahman that his Old Man "was lost." Still, the writer could add that it had been okay for Abdulrahman to experience "the need to live up to his [father's] expectations" but that now it was his time "to make up for all his mistakes."[137] He would have asked for time for Abdulrahman, listening to "the voices of my father," to come out of his dream.[138] The American author had written, "The pain I felt was my father's pain."[139] Yes, Abdulrahman would agree.

This American author is of course Barack Obama. The story of "personal fall" followed by "subsequent redemption," writes Obama in his memoir, was one that impressed him regarding the black ministers he met in Chicago, men who confessed to him that at some point they had hit bottom and their pride had been shattered.[140] This shattering of pride wasn't the story Obama would attribute to himself. His life model was rather the *self-invention* plot he attributes to his grandfather ("He will have to reinvent himself in this arid, solitary place. Through force of will, he will create a life out of the scraps of an unknown world") and father ("He, too, will have to invent himself").[141] American writer Obama could have told Abdulrahman that, much like himself, Abdulrahman should reinvent himself through narrative by learning from his father's mistakes—"Sins of the father, you know. I've learned to accept that."[142] What Abdulrahman needed was perhaps time. And, perhaps, like the American writer, all he needed was to go to his father's grave and weep. Perhaps Abdulrahman could join Obama in Chicago, where he couldn't live "pretending that these children are somehow not our own."[143] Because, Obama had added, "We're all part of one tribe . . . The human tribe."[144]

Obama didn't help Abdulrahman free himself of the "dreams from my father." What he did instead was perform the mandate given to the believer Abraham: if you truly love me, if you truly care for national security, kill me a son. As president he answered that Call—not once, but twice. Nasser's son Anwar was after all a terrorist, a *homo sacer* who in his impurity could not be sacrificed to the gods. Gods prefer innocent victims that in their immaculate child-like purity leave no doubt that their immolation is not an act of revenge or justice but only the offering of ritual sacrifice. Like Isaac for Abraham—the beloved, most precious only son. Anwar's teenage son Abdulrahman was the perfect offering. So Obama answered the Call and sacrificed Abdulrahman with a Hellfire missile sent from Creech.

But not even this was enough for the bloodthirsty God. On January 29, 2017, al-Awlaki's eight-year-old daughter, Nawar al-Awlaki, was killed as well in a US commando attack in Yemen, ordered by President Trump, which also killed at least eight other women and seven children. At close range, "she was hit with a bullet in her neck and suffered for two hours" before dying unattended, Nasser said. "Why kill children?" Nasser asked.[145] Why revisit Highway 61?

IT WAS EARLY IN THE MORNING

It was early in the morning, just past 6 a.m., when Abdulrahman al-Awlaki arose in his grandparents' spacious house in Sana and wrote them a note saying—"I will be back in a few days."[146] Abdulrahman had not seen his father for two years. He was an American citizen, born in Denver, and had lived in the US until he was seven. He had long hair, he loved hip-hop music and Facebook, he liked hanging out with his friends, goofing off. They took pictures of themselves posing as rappers. He was tall and slim, wore glasses, was a well-liked and gentle boy. He knew his father had been targeted, and he was deeply concerned.

His unannounced departure was not like him, so his grandparents Nasser and Saleha were alarmed; they feared he might become the bait to capture his father. Their fear was not unwarranted: as his grandfather

Nasser called Abdulrahman's friends, he was told that a teacher had become close to him recently, that they used to go eat pizza together; when Nasser tried to find the teacher, he had vanished.[147]

When Abdulrahman set out to find his father, one might imagine a repetition of Soren Kierkegaard's script about Abraham and Isaac, a story written in the book of Genesis some two to three centuries after the *Iliad*:

"It was in the early morning, Abraham arose betimes, he had the asses saddled, left his tent, and Isaac with him, but Sarah looked out of the window after them until they had passed down the valley and she could see them no more. They rode in silence for three days. . . . And Abraham's face was fatherliness. . . . But Isaac was unable to understand him. . . . He embraced Abraham's knees, he fell at his feet imploringly, he begged for his young life. . . . Isaac trembled and cried out in his terror. "Oh God in heaven, have compassion upon me. God of Abraham, have compassion upon me. If I have no father now upon earth, be Thou my father!"[148]

Kierkegaard appears overwhelmed by what he has just written and begins again: "It was in the early morning. Abraham arose betimes, he kissed Sarah, the young mother, and Sarah kissed Isaac, her joy, her delight for all times . . . and he rode to Mount Moriah. There he cast himself down on his face and prayed to God to forgive him his sin in that he had been about to sacrifice his son Isaac, and in that the father had forgotten his duty toward his son. . . . He could not grasp that it was a sin that he had wanted to sacrifice to God his most precious possession, him for whom he would most gladly have died many times. But, if it was a sin . . . what sin was more terrible?"

But nothing Kierkegaard writes can comprehend the abyss he is contemplating. So he begins again: "It was in the early morning, Abraham arose betimes, he embraced Sarah, the bride of his old age, and Sarah kissed Isaac . . . who was her pride, her hope for all time. . . . Silently he laid the wood in order, he bound Isaac, in silence he drew the knife—then he saw the ram which God had prepared. Then he offered that and returned home. . . . From that time on Abraham became old, he could not forget that God had required this of him. Isaac throve as before, but Abraham's eyes were darkened, and he knew joy no more."[149]

Kierkegaard tries one more time: "It was early in the morning, Abraham arose betimes, he kissed Sarah, the young mother, and Sarah kissed Isaac, her delight, her joy at all times. . . . He climbed Mount Moriah, he drew the knife. . . . He prayed God to forgive him his sin, that he had been willing to offer Isaac, that the father had forgotten his duty toward the son."[150]

But nothing he writes seems to capture the abyss, so Kierkegaard tries a final time: "It was early in the morning, everything was prepared for the journey in Abraham's house. He bade Sarah farewell. . . . They rode together in harmony, Abraham and Isaac, until they came to Mount Moriah. But Abraham prepared everything for the sacrifice, calmly and quietly; but when he turned and drew the knife, Isaac saw that his left hand was clenched in despair, that a tremor passed through his body—but Abraham drew the knife.

Then they returned again home, and Sarah hastened to meet them, but Isaac had lost his faith."[151]

Isaac had lost his faith! This was the horrifying consequence of Abraham's idolatry in the biblical parable reimagined by Kierkegaard. Afraid that his son might misinterpret what had happened at Mount Moriah, Abraham tells his son that the sacrificial killing he was about to commit was not in fact divine will but his own willful idolatry: "I am an idolater. Dost thou suppose that this is God's bidding? No, it is my desire."[152] Abraham wants Isaac to conclude that the monster is Abraham himself, not God. The father is idolatrous in his mad obedience to God's order of "Kill me your son," his willingness to override the ethical for a higher teleology and to see the ethical as "a temptation" not to fulfill God's will. "Abraham is therefore at no instant a tragic hero," Kierkegaard concluded, "but something quite different, either a murderer or a believer."[153]

Isaac's story has never lost its relevance. It is what happened to Sergeant Leonard Shelton, who, after killing in the rage of battle, said "I stopped praying; I grew up in a Christian environment, but I didn't believe it anymore. Human flesh melting on steel?"[154] The same happened to Cian Westmoreland and Brandon Bryant: they had been forced to witness the calls coming from on High ordering the killing of innocent people with drones. And to Hans, Frank's son—"If there was a God, He wouldn't have let me see all that fucked up shit in Iraq."[155] They had gone into the army as patriotic Americans and left in disbelief and traumatized from what they had been forced to do. The president who was ordering it all could only be "a believer or a murderer."

It was Sunday, September 4, 2011, when Abdulrahman woke early in the morning before the others. He took the equivalent of forty dollars from his mother's purse. "I am sorry for leaving in this kind of way," he wrote on a piece of notepaper. "I miss my father and want to see if I can go and talk to him. I will be back in a few days. Please forgive me. Love, Abdulrahman."[156] He had turned sixteen nine days earlier. It was shortly after 6 a.m.

By the end of the month Abdulrahman would hear the fatal news: on September 30 his father had been killed with a drone. He stayed in Shabwah province mourning. According to sources, he met AQAP militants and was willing to join them, something that in the tribal culture of the Awlakis was almost mandatory.[157] He talked to his grandmother Saleha and promised he would soon return to Sana. The family members comforted him on the phone and told him to get out with his cousins. The evening of October 14 he joined his cousins and other friends for an outdoor barbecue, not far from Al Saeed, the Awlakis' ancestral village where his father had lived. At 9 p.m. drones killed them all.

There was only one recognizable remnant of Abdulrahman: a fragment of the back of his head with hair attached. The other body parts could not be identified or separated. They put the remains of the seven boys in a cement bag, as Nasser later told visitors. A former minister of the Yemeni government and former president of Sana University, Nasser released an audio message asking Americans for justice and adding that, for his family, Obama was nothing more than a child killer. Nasser tried a second lawsuit but would get no answer from the justice system he had idealized in the past. Obama had no apology to offer his family,[158] no explanation to give the world, nothing to counter those who thought the killing was the deliberate murder of a teenager. His killing "represented a watershed moment in modern US history."[159]

HERE TROY WAS

Art Sotloff, the father of the American-Israeli journalist Steve Sotloff who was kidnapped by ISIS in August 2013 and decapitated a year later in September 2014, asked Obama: "How did you feel when my son was being held up by his neck and they were saying that this message is for you, President Obama. Steven's life depends on your next decision. How do you feel about that?"[160] Obama looked down, speechless.

The Sotloffs had received an audio message from the FBI that ISIS had created to pressure the US government. It was the voice of their son: "Mom, please don't let Obama kill me, Mom you can still save my life just like the families of my previous cellmates." Soon the boy was beheaded. Art Sotloff's question had shocked Obama, and Sotloff would later say to Lesley Stahl in the *60 Minutes* interview, "It shocked me that I even asked him that." Obama was speechless. It was Abraham's silence in his readiness to sacrifice Isaac.

Stahl asked Obama's chief counterterrorism adviser, Lisa Monaco, how she felt about the beheadings. "I feel like in many respects we did not do right by these families. That we failed them." Other European governments had negotiated the release of their kidnapped prisoners with ransom money.

In his anger, for days Achilles had dragged Hector's dead body around and around the gates of Troy from his racing chariot until the gods ordered Thetis to tell her son that he must stop and relinquish the body to his father Priam in exchange for ransom. The gods also sent a messenger to Priam, urging him to supplicate himself before Achilles to redeem the body of his son. When the old man made his way across the battlefield carrying chests of embroidered raiment, bars of gold, and a golden cap, Achilles, remembering his own father, wept, Priam wept with him, and the declared enemies, Priam and Achilles, for a time met as man to man and ate and drank together.

At the beginning of World War II, Simone Weil wrote the essay "The *Iliad* or the Poem of Force."[161] In it she argues that *force*—that which turns anybody subjected to it into a *thing*, even a corpse—is the true subject of the poem, "as pitiless to the man who possesses it, or thinks he does, as it is to the victims; the second it crushes, the first it intoxicates. The truth is, nobody really possesses it."[162] Neither the strong nor the weak are aware of the limits of their power or weakness: "They have in common a refusal to believe that they both belong to the same species."[163] They can know in moments, however, as Priam and Achilles knew.

Force is penalized by the cycle of retribution it generates—its name is Nemesis. The *Iliad* tells its audience about the transience of victory: "The auditors of the *Iliad* knew that the death of Hector would be but a brief joy to Achilles, and the death of Achilles but a brief joy to the Trojans, and the destruction of Troy but a brief joy to the Achaeans."[164] Hence emerges the idea of destiny imagined as an external force that overpowers the executioner and the victim, both "condemned men," with equal measure of innocence and guilt. Initially the terrible necessity of war may inspire promises of honor and glory, "the illusion that war is a game," a *hunt*, but as fear and defeat and the death of comrades become real, war's reality "is hard, much too hard to be borne, for it enfolds death"[165]—when the soldier realizes that death is the future awaiting him.

War's terrible secret is, Weil observes, how it transforms its brave warriors into beasts; it is "always a mystery," the "petrifactive quality of force," which the warrior will not escape "except by a miracle."[166] What could be the miracle to reverse those beastly transformations? Weil's answer: the friendship between comrades. But there is something even more essential: "the purest triumph of love, the crowning grace of war, is the friendship that floods the hearts of mortal enemies. . . . Before it . . . the distance between benefactor and suppliant, between victor and vanquished, shrinks to nothing."[167]

Counterterrorists labeled the operation against Awlaki "Objective Troy," but the War on Terror is no *Iliad*, they'd argue. Terrorists are unable to learn or change or be human, they'd say. Homeric society consists of people on both sides ready to die and kill for their community, but in drone warfare robots lead and only the *other* should die. In the Homeric world a community's borders are a potential battlefield, but in drone warfare the overwhelming technological advantage make borders dissolve. In the Homeric view, the central ethical problem is that the hero must act while aware of the limits of his knowledge; counterterrorism suffers no such ethical dilemmas and sees no such limits to its self-assurance. It was Obama's embrace of the counterterrorist worldview that pushed him in the direction of a tragic character—a good man turned president falls into self-deception by his own intoxication with force that allows for no *Iliad* reconciliation with the vanquished.

An essential characteristic of the Aristotelian tragic hero, the moment of *recognition* when the hero discovers his error, is missing in Obama. Such lack of admission of an error makes Obama closer to the figure of Abraham who is simply following orders, no matter how horrified he is about his own readiness to kill his son—the Abraham who, in Kierkegaard's words, "is . . . at no instant a tragic hero, but something quite different, either a murderer or a believer." Placed between such harsh alternatives, Obama had to choose where he stood.

"Amazing grace! How sweet the sound / that saved a wretch like me"— Obama led the song at Charleston's Emanuel Church after the eulogy for the nine people killed in a racist gun attack. "I once was lost, but now am found / was blind, but now I see." Obama spoke movingly about the power of grace, not as something earned, but as a gift. Obama had disavowed Wright's prophetic Trinity Church in Chicago, and he is essentially a secular man, but the power of that hymn penned by a white slave trader as he realized he must renounce his ways electrified a standing congregation of black people at Emanuel Church and cast Obama as a man of faith and in possession of healing power. Abraham's fate: either a murderer or a believer. Obama had to choose. In Charleston Obama was a believer, admitting that "we are all sinners," that the place of crime is also the place of forgiveness, singing, and praying for grace.

But it is precisely when we look at this inspiring Obama through his system of beliefs that he appears as the most tragic figure. For if we look at his presidential campaign promises and his discomfort with some of the laws he signed, he appears *not to really believe in* those exceptional laws he implemented for the sake of the War on Terror, or to share counterterrorism's anti-Muslim worldview. This echoes the ambivalence of his religious belief: he declared himself a "devout Christian," yet he also said, "I was a heretic. Or worse," someone who "could no longer distinguish between faith and mere folly."[168] Despite the politician's claims to Christian devotion, Obama lives in a modern world where belief in God is no longer an ethical requirement and where our lives depend not on Fate but on willful self-creation. He couldn't blame, as in "classic" tragedy, some tyrannical power forcing him to act the way he did in a desubjectivized manner.

Obama's is the thoroughly modern tragedy in which he has the power of choice, a tragedy in which "the subject is asked to assume with enjoy-

ment the very injustice that he finds horrifying."[169] Bush and Cheney
believed that Hussein was a monster and were ready to kill hundreds of
thousands to prove it. Obama didn't believe in the links between Muslims
and terrorists and was horrified by what counterterrorism had done in the
name of fighting terror, yet he embraced it and killed thousands of people
as if his political survival depended on it. Obama did not believe in the
need for Hiroshima's massacre either ("There's something about the way
we did it," he observed to Rhodes) and yet, while enjoying one of the largest crowds of his presidency during his visit there, he was unable to condemn it either, saying he didn't want to "second-guess Truman's decision."[170] Only in modernity might we get the idea that an ethics of
responsibility regarding the security state could demand *giving up* the
very ethical reasons for which one got into politics.

"What if we were wrong?" Obama confided in Rhodes after Clinton's
loss to Trump. Surprised by the question, Rhodes adds: "The one thing
I never lost faith in was the confidence that I was a part of something
that was *right*."[171] But the question kept returning: "What if we were
wrong? . . . Maybe we pushed too far." *What if.* One imagines Obama
thinking, What if we were wrong when we killed hundreds of children and
innocent bystanders in our White House manhunts? What if I pushed too
far when I signed those laws, like the one allowing indefinite detention of
US citizens, laws I didn't agree with?[172] Yes, "There is Evil in the world," to
repeat Obama's favorite axiom. But what if Evil is primarily the corruption
of the Good—for instance, the defeat of the hope that Obama's promise
brought to the nation and the world—the defeat of those of us who rooted
for him? Cian Westmoreland and Brandon Bryant are relentless in their
self-recrimination—by having followed presidential orders, they consider
themselves serial murderers and war criminals. What if Obama and
Rhodes could break through their screening fantasies and accept that they
are no less guilty than the drone pilots who operated under their orders?
What if. In May of 2013 Obama's speech on the future of drone warfare
was interrupted by Medea Benjamin, who challenged him to say why he
was killing children with drones. As she was being carried out by the security service, Obama observed: "The voice of that woman is worth paying
attention to." Later he added: "Those deaths will haunt us as long as we
live."[173]

"Here Troy was," exclaimed a defeated Don Quixote in reference to that Greek city of pride, betrayal, and ruin as he was leaving Barcelona, having lost a duel, having been deprived of his honor, and having realized that it's not enough to dream yourself a hero: "Here Fortune made me a victim of her caprices; here the luster of my achievements was dimmed."[174] Here was Awlaki's Troy. Here was Obama's Troy.

Acknowledgments

First and foremost I owe a very special debt of gratitude to Elisa Adler for her thorough and creative editing of every line of this book; she helped me clarify my thought and greatly improved the text by rewriting many of its passages. I am also once again most grateful to Goretti Etxaniz for her careful reading and editing of the entire book, as well as her daily support of my work. Richard Siegel and Garazi Zulaika read parts of the manuscript and challenged me to clarify many concepts. I first heard about drones from a paper delivered by Jeff Sluka; his criticisms have substantially improved chapter 4. Mark LeVine and two anonymous reviewers produced most insightful comments that I have done my best to incorporate. Sociologist Robert Futrell, who codirected the Nevada Test Site Oral Project, and historian Michael Green, both from the University of Nevada, Las Vegas, guided me in the study of Las Vegas's history. I have learned the most about Las Vegas's arts from my friends the late Kirk Robertson and Valerie Sherpa; Cheryll Glotfelty and Michael Branch introduced me to literary Nevada. Justin Race's encouragement during the initial stages of the manuscript kept me going. Debora Boehm was instrumental in the completion and publication of the manuscript. During my fieldwork I missed dearly my late colleague Penny Schwartz, who contributed so much to my career and who used to host me in Las Vegas. Joannes Zulaika, as always, helped me keep my feet on the ground. I am much indebted to them all. I also thank the faculty, staff, librarians, and graduate students of the William Douglass Center for Basque Studies at the University of Nevada, Reno, for the feedback and support they have long provided me. I am most thankful to Naomi Schneider at the University of California Press for her advice and careful attention to the manuscript and to copyeditor Elisabeth Magnus who made significant changes.

I owe a great debt to Nico Colombant and Kari Barber, who introduced me to the Las Vegas antidrone movement and to the members of Code Pink, who twice a year organize the protests at Creech Air Force Base. I am thankful in particular to Toby Blomé, Eleanor Levine, Maggie Huntington, Cecile Pineda, Fred Bialy, Ann Wright, and many others from Code Pink who shared their life experiences with me. To Shoshone chief Jonnie Bobb I am grateful for the predawn prayers at Creech. Among the Veterans for Peace whom I met and interviewed are Don Kimball, John Amadon, Michael Kerr, Gary Mesker, Jacqueline F. Casey, and Frank Pauc. While in Las Vegas I also interviewed veteran peace activists Brian Terrell, George Killingsworth, Christian Stalberg, Steve Kelly, JoAnn Lingle, Linda Sator, and Marcus Collonge. In his Oakland retirement Center Louie Vitale shared with me episodes of his life. Retired Colonel Vern Frye spoke to me about being a combat fighter pilot in Vietnam. I also conducted phone interviews with Kathy Kelly, Karl Meyer, and David Swanson. Frank Bergon, in whose Nevada novels I found a literary universe parallel to my own ethnography, spoke to me about Yucca Mountain and the antinuclear resistance. I am deeply indebted to them all for graciously sharing with me their experiences of militant pacifism. I hope this book meets their courage.

Julia Occhiogrosso and Gary Cavalier hosted me at the Las Vegas Catholic Worker for three months while I interviewed members of the community, resisters, and academics. I joined them and the people at the Nevada Desert Experience in their daily tasks of feeding the homeless and keeping vigils for peace at the Las Vegas Federal Courthouse and Creech Air Force Base. I was much helped there by Robert Majors, John LaLone, Mark Kelso, Henry Freeman, Eric Hernandez, Ming Lai, and Laura-Marie Taylor. Their lives became for me a counterpoint to capitalist desire; their impact will be long lasting.

In Las Vegas I was fortunate to meet former drone operators Cian Westmoreland and Brandon Bryant, young men traumatized by their serial killing, yet uniquely alive and courageous in speaking out against imperial America's military fantasies. I dedicate this book to them—and to the many former and current drone pilots who are experiencing similar traumas.

Notes

PROLOGUE

1. See Badiou (2015: 72).

2. In 2013, according to the Pew Research Center (2015), 23 percent disapproved of drone strikes; in 2015, 35 percent did. With the exception of Israel and Kenya, in no other country does a majority of the population favor drone strikes.

3. Kennebeck (2016).

4. Woods (2015: 171).

5. *New York Times* (2017).

6. Thompson (1998: 164–65).

7. Thompson (1998: 123). Emphasis in original.

8. Thompson (1998: 191). Emphasis in original.

9. Coates (2017: 115).

10. For a review of the growing inequality between the rich and the poor in the US, see Putnam (2015).

11. Geertz (1984: 275).

CHAPTER 1. THE REAL

1. Martin (2010: 37, 81).

2. Martin (2010: 236).

3. Martin (2010: 46).

4. Martin (2010: 252).

5. Martin (2010: 19, 221).

6. Zulaika (1990: 109–10); Martin (2010: 53).

7. Cockburn (2015: 14).

8. Cockburn (2015: 24); Gusterson (2016: 9).

9. Singer (2009: 56).

10. Chamayou (2013: 13).

11. Quoted in Chamayou (2013: 31–32).

12. Arkin (2015: 216).

13. Gusterson (2016: 25); Chamayou (2013: 31).

14. For the full official transcripts of this air strike on February 21, 2010, see Cloud (2011).

15. Jaffer (2016: 12).

16. Becker and Shane (2012: A1).

17. Quotes in Becker and Shane (2012: A10).

18. Quotes in Becker and Shane (2012: A10).

19. Rhodes (2018: 195).

20. Becker and Shane (2012: A1).

21. M. Benjamin (2013: 69).

22. Ahmad (2011).

23. Quoted in Sluka (2011: 73).

24. See Queally (2014).

25. See Press (2018).

26. See the Bureau of Investigative Journalism website home page, https://www.thebureauinvestigates.com/projects/drone-war, for their continuously updated current statistics.

27. See Ahmad (2011).

28. Bergen and Braun (2012).

29. Stanford Law School and NYU School of Law (2012: vii).

30. Bergen and Rowland (2015: 15). Similarly, the Stanford and NYU report mentions the work of a Reuters journalist who in 2010 concluded "that of the 500 'militants' the CIA believed it had killed since 2008, only 14 were 'top-tier militant targets' and 25 were 'mid-to-high-level' organizers of Al Qaeda, the Taliban, or other hostile groups" (Stanford Law School and NYU School of Law (2012: 31). According to Bergen and Rowland (2015: 15), fewer than 13 percent of drone strikes carried out under Obama killed a "militant leader," whereas under President Bush about a third did. The report warns that it is difficult to obtain data on strike casualties "because of US efforts to shield the drone program from democratic accountability" (Stanford Law School and NYU School of Law 2012: vi).

31. Arkin's (2015: 191).

32. Stanford Law School and NYU School of Law (2012: 12–13).

33. Cockburn (2015: 233).

34. Quoted in Woods (2015: 259).

35. Becker and Shane (2012: A10).

36. Calhoun (2016: 84). Emphasis in original.

37. Ahmad (2011).

38. Becker and Shane (2012: A12).

39. Scahill and Greenwald (2016: 97).

40. Calhoun (2016: 43, 75–76, 51 [emphasis in original]).

41. Agamben (1998: 8).

42. For an extended application of the notion of taboo to terrorism, see Zulaika and Douglass (1996).

43. Quoted in Agamben (1998: 3).

44. Agamben (1998: 4).

45. Mbembé (2003: 11).

46. See Zulaika (1990).

47. Sperber (1975).

48. Quoted in Cockburn (2015: 139).

49. Reciprocally, people under drone surveillance are forced to disregard the voyeuristic gaze of those watching them from the sky as if it were the "innocent" gaze of animals in whose presence one need not be ashamed.

50. Becker and Shane (2012: A11).

51. Scahill (2016b: 4–5).

52. Currier (2016: 56).

53. Shane (2013: A1).

54. Shane (2015b: 211).

55. Quoted in Woods 2015: 220).

56. Arkin (2015: 250).

57. Mazzetti (2013: 121).

58. Quoted in Mazzetti (2013: 219).

59. Davies (2010).

60. Woods (2015: 220).

61. Klaidman (2012: 124).

62. Quoted in Mazzetti (2013: 247).

63. Quoted in Klaidman (2012: 125).

64. Klaidman (2012: 126).

65. Quoted in Klaidman (2012: 257).

66. Quoted in Klaidman (2012: 9–11).

67. Scahill (2013: 17–18).

68. Quoted in Mazzetti (2013: 98).

69. Arkin (2015: 75).

70. Quoted in Arkin (2015: 75).

71. Mazzetti (2013: 122).

72. Since killing with bare hands is rather difficult, the guide recommended a contrived accident, such as "a fall of 75 feet or more onto a hard surface" (quoted in Cockburn (2015: 83). The CIA's plots to kill Fidel Castro, at the urging of the Kennedy brothers, are legendary. The CIA's Phoenix Program in Vietnam boasted of having killed 20,587 people by 1971.

73. Quoted in Cockburn (2015: 84).

74. Quoted in Klaidman (2012: 50).

75. Mazzetti (2013: 242–43). In the words of Emira Woods, director of Foreign Policy in Focus, "Somalia is an example of the US military policy gone completely amok. It helped destabilize Somalia and strengthen Al Shabab, which barely existed before the US heavy-handed response to the ICU [Islamic Court Union]." Quoted in M. Benjamin (2013: 205).

76. Schmitt and Savage (2019).

77. Mbembé (2003: 19).

78. Madley (2016).

79. Madley (2016: 356).

80. Quoted in Zinn (1999: 132).

81. Quoted in Madley (2016: 3).

82. Madley (2016: 3).

83. Madley (2016: 12, 351).

84. Madley (2016: 13).

85. Madley (2016: 178).

86. Quoted in Madley (2016: 186); Madley (2016: 186).

87. Madley (2016: 10, 151).

88. Madley (2016: 190, 191).

89. Quoted in Madley (2016: 192).

90. A correspondent quoted in Madley (2016: 192).

91. Madley (2016: 195).

92. Quoted in Madley (2016: 197).

93. Augustus W. Knapp quoted in Madley (2016: 207).

94. Madley (2016: 206, 345).

95. Madley (2016: 355).

96. Mbembé (2003: 24).

97. Baldwin (1998: 804).

98. See Grossman (1995: 134–37).

99. Ben Shalit quoted in Grossman (1995: 136).

100. Quoted in Grossman (1995: 136).

101. Quotes in Nadelson (2005: 124).

102. See the case of Mohamedou Ould Slahi in chapter 2.

103. Zulaika (1989).

104. See Lotchin (1984).

105. Nickel (2005: 1).

106. Nickel (2005: 15).

107. Parker, Munier, and Reynolds (2011: 29).

108. Moehring (2000: 13).

109. Moehring and Green (2005: 91).

110. Patton (1998: 72).

111. Nickel (2005: 6).

112. Florence Lee Jones quoted in Moehring and Green (2005: 107).

113. Gerald D. Nash quoted in Nickel (2005: 2).

114. Nickel (2005: 7).

115. Moehring and Green (2005: 115).

116. Davis (1998: 59).

117. Davis (1998: 68).

118. Moehring and Green (2005: 197).

119. Moehring and Green (2005: 132).

120. Nickel (2005: 25).

121. Titus (1986: 93).

122. Nickel (2005: 27).

123. See Denton and Morris (2001).

124. Enloe (2014: 157).

125. Enloe (1993: 145). See also Stewart (2014).

126. Martin (2010: 43). Emphasis added.

127. The comparison of falconry to war is an old one. The names of top US fighter jets recall the metaphoric association: "Nighthawk," "Fighting Falcon," "Strike Eagle," "Raptor." Macdonald (2014: 190–91) draws the links between romantic medievalism and the technology of modern war.

128. See Zulaika (1995).

129. This theory of metaphoric appropriations and ritual transformations in hunting scenarios that I developed in Zulaika (1990) owes much to the work of James W. Fernandez (1986).

130. Macdonald (2014: 43).

131. Macdonald (2014: 80).

132. Macdonald (2014: 95).

133. Macdonald (2014: 186).

134. Macdonald (2014: 176).

135. Macdonald (2014: 83). Emphasis in original.

136. Macdonald (2014: 129). Emphasis in original.

137. Klaidman (2012: 39).

138. Cockburn (2015: 225).

139. Cockburn (2015: 225).

140. Klaidman (2012: 40).

141. Woods (2015: 155).

142. Brooks (2009).

143. Quoted in Rhodes (2018: 76).

144. See Cohn (2015b: 13–25).

145. Scahill (2013: 253); Tutu (2015: 12).

146. Quoted in Scahill (2013: 520).

147. Quoted in Stanford Law School and NYU School of Law (2012: 122).

148. Woods (2015: 65).

149. Woods (2015: 104).

150. Stanford Law School and NYU School of Law (2012: 123).

151. Quoted in Caryl (2011: 56).

152. Fuller (2017: 16).

153. Priest and Arkin (2011: 35).

154. Jaffer (2016: 2–3).

155. Jaffer (2016: 7).

156. Scahill (2016b: 2).

157. Greenwald (2016: 182).

158. Press (2018).

159. Stanford Law School and NYU School of Law (2012: 106, 103).

160. Bennis (2015: 61).

161. Woods (2015: 155).

162. Jaffer (2016: 12).

163. Becker and Shane (2012: A11).

164. Klaidman (2012: 122).

165. Quoted in Mazzetti (2013: 228).

166. Mayer (2015: 74).

167. Devereaux (2016: 164).

168. Devereaux (2016: 164).

169. Woods (2015: 157).

170. Woods (2015: 161).

171. Quoted in Stanford Law School and NYU School of Law (2012: 115).

172. Amnesty International (2013: 28–31); Stanford Law School and NYU School of Law (2012: 74–76).

173. Obama considered the Taliban "a domestic political actor inside Afghanistan" that "wasn't necessary to destroy" to accomplish the goals of the War on Terror (Rhodes 2018: 73–74).

174. Calhoun (2016: 51, 75–76).

175. Mayer (2015: 68).

176. Greenwald (2016: 185).

177. Calhoun (2016: 92).

178. Baker (2012: 8).

179. N. Johnson (2014).

180. Quoted in Klaidman (2012: 42).

181. Quoted in Cockburn (2015: 226).

182. Klaidman (2012: 42),

183. Quoted in Klaidman (2012: 271).

184. Rhodes (2018: 51).

185. Priest and Arkin (2011: 72).

186. Jameson (2016).

187. Needham (1980: 65).

188. Frazer (1963: 1).

189. Needham 1980: 70).

190. Zulaika (1988: xxiii–xx).

191. Arkin (2015: (207).

192. Arkin (2015: 215).

193. Martin (2010: 2).

194. Martin (2010: 33, 85).

195. Martin (2010: 40).

196. Martin (2010: 214).

197. Martin (2010: 47).

198. Priest and Arkin (2011: 52).

199. "Washington's corridors of power stretch in a nearly straight line from the Supreme Court to the Capitol to the White House. Keep going west, across the Potomac River, and the unofficial seats of power—the private, corporate ones—become visible. There, in Virginia suburbs, are the flags of Top Secret America: the Northrop Grumman, SAIC, General Dynamics logos that define the skyline at night" (Priest and Arkin 2011: 176).

200. See Priest and Arkin (2011, 35).

201. See Savage (2015: 14).

202. Munter was US ambassador to Pakistan during the years 2010–12.

203. Mazzetti (2013: 292–93).

204. Mazzetti (2013: 223).

205. Obama quoted in Mazzetti (2013: 228).

206. Mazzetti (2013: 300–302).

207. Quoted in Cockburn (2015: 214–15).

208. Woods (2015: 220).

209. Quoted in Greenwald (2016: 182).

210. *New York Times* (2010).

211. Klaidman (2012: 5)

212. Klaidman (2012: 27).

213. J. Schwartz (2009).

214. Holder quoted in Klaidman (2012: 89).

215. Bruck (2016).

216. Quoted in Klaidman (2012: 116).

217. Obama (2006: 86).

218. Obama (2006: 321).

219. Quoted in Klaidman (2012: 134).

220. Quoted in Žižek (1989: 30).

221. Žižek (1989: 30).

222. Agamben (1998: 57).

223. Badiou (2002: 61, 77, 91). Emphasis in original.

224. Arkin (2015: 209). Eric Schlosser (2013: 466) writes that "One of the most important secrets of the Cold War was considered so secret that the president of the United States wasn't allowed to know it."

225. Second to Creech, the most important high-tech satellite relay station of the US drone program is in Ramstein, Germany; legal experts interviewed by *Der Spiegel* "claimed that U.S. personnel could be charged as war criminals by German prosecutors" (quoted in Scahill 2016c: 71). It should be no surprise that some experts in International Criminal Court have been investigating the potential criminal liability of US leaders (see Mirer 2015: 154).

226. Arkin (2015: 216, 81).

227. Arkin (2015: 84).

228. Arkin (2015: 168).

229. Arkin (2015: 167).

230. McKelvey (2015: 187).

231. General Cartwright quoted in McKelvey (2015: 187).

232. Quoted in Klaidman (2012: 202).

233. Quoted in Klaidman (2012: 206).

234. Klaidman (2012: 210).

235. Quoted in Klaidman (2012: 210).

236. Leach (1977: 36).

237. Harold Koh quoted in Becker and Shane (2012: A10).

238. See M. Schwartz (2018).

239. See Mayer (2009).

240. Becker and Shane (2012: A11).

241. M. Schwartz (2018).

242. Becker and Shane (2012: A12).

243. Becker and Shane (2012: A12).

244. Needham (1980: 69).

245. Fuller (2017: 133).

246. Press (2018).

247. M. Schwartz (2018).

CHAPTER 2. FANTASY AND THE ART OF DRONE ASSASSINATION

1. These quotes come from a talk in Las Vegas that accompanied the screening of *National Bird* on April 25, 2017.

2. The judgment against Eichmann is quoted in Arendt (1963: 246–47). Emphasis in original.

3. Arendt (1963: 276).

4. Butler (1990: 108). Emphasis in original.

5. Butler (1990: 106).

6. Butler (1990: 107).

7. Nader (2012: 113).

8. Martin (2010: 3).

9. Martin (2010; 26).

10. Martin (2010: 31). Emphasis in original.

11. Martin (2010: 46).

12. Martin (2010: 108).

13. Martin (2010: 70).

14. Amos Oz quoted in Margalit (1994: 10).

15. Leach (1977: 36).

16. White (1978: 154). Emphasis in original.

17. Baldwin (2017: 23). Emphasis added.

18. Baldwin (2017: 22).

19. Baldwin (2017: 39).

20. Baldwin (2017: 58).

21. Baldwin (2017: 60).

22. Baldwin (2017: 69).

23. Baldwin (2017: 103).

24. Baldwin (2017: 109).

25. Nadelson (2005: 144).

26. Moehring and Green (2005: 205).

27. McGowan (2016: 39).

28. Quoted in McGowan (2016: 47–48).

29. N. Brown (1959: xviii).

30. Rodman (2016: 102, 103).

31. Brents, Jackson, and Hausbeck (2010: 219).

32. Rodman (2016: 261).

33. Rodman (2016: 248).

34. Rodman (2016: 61). Emphasis in original.

35. Rodman (2016: 63, 70).

36. McGowan (2016: 179–80).

37. McGowan (2016: 185).

38. Fitzgerald (1925: 95).

39. Trump quoted in Parker, Munier, and Reynolds (2011: 150).

40. Corrigan (2014: 149).

41. Corrigan (2014: 147).

42. Quoted in Corrigan (2014: 169).

43. Corrigan (2014: 175).

44. Fitzgerald (1925: 180).

45. Whippman (2016: 80).

46. Whippman (2016: 81, 74).

47. See Whippman (2016).

48. Paradise was founded in 1950 to keep local taxes to a minimum.

49. Whippman (2016: 89).

50. Parker, Munier, and Reynolds (2011: 140).

51. Hsieh quoted in Whippman (2016: 71).

52. Patton (1998: (206).

53. Patton (1998: 217).

54. Bob Lazar became well known for his claims that he reverse-engineered UFO technology and that the government possessed documents showing that extraterrestrial visits to Earth had taken place for thousands of years. He brought the existence of Area 51, regularly visited by aliens according to him, to the attention of the general public.

55. Stalin had felt betrayed at the July 1945 Postdam Conference when Truman informed him of the first atomic test in the New Mexico desert. Inside the crashed disc at Roswell was Russian writing in Cyrillic. The Soviets, as well as the Americans, worked with German engineers at the end of the World War II to create new technologies. This flying disc was far more advanced than any drone technology the US had at the time. This advanced technology created legitimate alarm that the Soviets could deliver a devastating attack. The disc's Soviet connection remained top secret to avoid mass hysteria in the US.

56. By 1952 the air force had recorded as many as 1,900 sightings, resulting in about seventy-four thousand pages of evidence.

57. Quoted in Jacobsen (2011: 72).

58. Jacobsen (2011: 329).

59. Singer (2009: 138).

60. Quoted in Singer (2009: 154).

61. Singer (2009: 160).

62. Singer (2009: 161).

63. See chapter 3's section "The Body's Betrayal and the Myth of Invulnerability."

64. Greg Heines, head of the Dragon Runner project, quoted in Singer (2009: 68).

65. Patton (1998: 56).

66. Patton (1998: 6). Since its inception with the passing of the Atomic Energy Act of 1946, the system of secret keeping that took hold in Area 51 was unprecedented. The civilians working in Area 51 swore an oath of secrecy. Not even their wives knew where they worked. Indeed, the system was so secret that not even the president "needed to know"; the agency was run by civilians who would maintain secrets to which the notion of "born classified" was applied and over which not even the president had control. Such terrifying power, by which secrets were professionally classified as pertaining to *unanswerable authority*, is for Jacobsen (2011: xviii) the "cold, hard, and ultimately devastating truth" of Area 51's history.

67. Carl Jung quoted in Patton (1998: 213).

68. Patton (1998: 97).

69. Patton (1998: 111).

70. Patton (1998: 247).

71. In February 1954, during a low point in his acting career, Reagan performed a song-and-dance review at Las Vegas' Last Frontier nightclub; later, when he and his wife, Nancy, were leaving the city, which he described as the place where he'd "hit rock bottom," he told her, "Never again I will sell myself so short" (Denton and Morris (2001: 175, 176). But when he was running for president, like most other candidates in the modern era, Reagan cultivated and was beholden to Las Vegas money and influence.

72. Patton (1998: 209–10).

73. Masco (2014: 5).

74. Masco (2014: 16).

75. Masco (2006: 17).

76. Žižek (2012: 688).

77. Titus (1986: 93).

78. Welsome (1999: 489).

79. Dr. Richard D. Klausner, director of the National Cancer Institute, quoted in Welsome (1999: 489).

80. See Titus (1986: 114–30).

81. The case was *Allen v. United States*. Later, by March 2015, 18,087 downwinders, 3,578 test site workers, and nearly 8,000 miners had been awarded $2 billion in compensation for the nuclear testing program (Johns 2017: 183–84).

82. Žižek (2005: 17).

83. Žižek (2005: 17).

84. Zulaika (2012: 51).

85. Jackson (2015: 44). Emphasis in original.

86. See Priest and Arkin (2011).

87. Priest and Arkin (2011: 77).

88. Priest and Arkin (2011: 270).

89. The "Underwear Bomber" tried to blow up a Northwest Airlines Flight 253 over Detroit on Christmas 2009.

90. C. Johnson (2007: 209).

91. Priest and Arkin (2011: 24).

92. Kilcullen (2009: 293).

93. Zulaika (2009: 186–94).

94. Mazzetti (2007).

95. National Commission (2004).

96. Johnston and Schmitt (2004).

97. See Copjec (1994: 169–79).

98. Kilcullen (2009: 263, 264, 38).

99. Kilcullen (2009: 25, 274).

100. Kilcullen (2009: 114).

101. Kilcullen (2009: 268).

102. Kilcullen and Exum (2009).

103. Michael Frank (2017: 51); Stampnitzky (2013: 20).

104. Ahmed (2013: 317).

105. Ahmed (2013: 317).

106. Ahmed (2013: 326).

107. Žižek (1989: 151–16).

108. Powell (2003).

109. Masco (2014: 144).

110. Vidal-Naquet (1991: 328).

111. For an insightful analysis of the cultural imaginary of terrorism, see M. Frank (2017).

112. Castle (1991: 30). *Adventure* was written by Charlotte Moberly and Eleanor Jourdain, two well-educated and proper women who recounted in great detail how they, while visiting Versailles as tourists, saw a lady who was none other than Marie Antoinette.

113. Freud quoted in Castle (1991: 12).

114. Žižek (1989: 128).

115. Žižek (1989: 128).

116. Slahi (2015: 292).

117. For a more extensive treatment of this case, see Zulaika (2018).

118. Slahi had been first arrested and interrogated in January 2000 when he returned to his home country Mauritania from Canada, where he felt watched by the US intelligence services. Two months after 9/11, Slahi turned himself in to the Mauritanian authorities for questioning; he was arrested and rendered for eight months to a "black site" in Jordan, then taken to the infamous Bagram Base, and from there to Guantánamo in August of 2002.

119. Ginzburg (1991: 321). Emphasis added.

120. Slahi (2015: 214).

121. Slahi (2015: 244).

122. Slahi (2015: 232).

123. Slahi (2015: 275).

124. Slahi (2015: 275).

125. Slahi (2015: 278).

126. Slahi (2015: 278).

127. Slahi (2015: 278).

128. Wilkerson (2010).

129. Slahi (2015: 280).

130. Slahi (2015: 280).

131. Slahi (2015: 288).

132. Slahi (2015: 282).

133. Slahi (2015: 291, 292).

134. Žižek (1997: 8).

135. Slahi (2015: 229).

136. Slahi (2015: 276).

137. Slahi (2015: 230).

138. The writer Edurne Portela, in her *El eco de los disparos* (2003), mentions how a Basque photographer was censored for a photograph he took of a woman crying over the corpse of her ETA brother.

139. On the back cover of the book.

140. Azmi quoted in Kurnaz (2007, 240). Emphasis added.

141. Kurnaz (2007: 144).

142. Kurnaz (2007: 175).

143. Kurnaz (2007: 248).

144. Kurnaz (2007: 234).

145. Maltby quoted in Žižek (2007: 83).

146. Žižek (2007: 83).

147. Becker and Shane (2012).

148. Veyne (1988: 27, 84).

149. Žižek (2007: 84).

150. See Zulaika and Douglass (1996).

151. See Shane (2013). "'Assassination' is banned by executive order, but for decades that has been interpreted . . . as prohibiting the killing of political figures, not suspected terrorists. Certainly most of those killed are not political figures. . . . Were we to use 'assassination' routinely about drone shots, it would suggest that the administration is deliberately violating the executive order, which is not the case" (Shane quoted in Sullivan 2013). But Shane does not provide the arguments why it "is not the case" that the administration is violating the executive order

against assassinations, which is precisely the point made by the United Nations rapporteurs and international jurists.

152. Sanger (2012: 253, 255).

153. See, for example, M. Schwartz (2018).

154. Quoted in N. West (2017: 307).

155. Quoted in Chamayou (2013: 31–32).

156. M. Benjamin (2013: 98).

157. Shane (2015b: 206).

158. Cockburn (2015: 237).

159. Cockburn (2015: 229). Emphasis added.

160. Cockburn (2015: 223).

161. Mazzetti (2013: 100).

162. Cockburn (2015: 116).

163. Mazzetti (2013: 14–15).

164. See Scahill and Greenwald (2014); Wemple (2014).

165. Rice quoted in Rhodes (2018: 115).

166. De Quincey (1890: 60, 13, 12). Emphasis in original.

167. Wilson (2016: 223).

168. Martin (2010: 2, 33).

169. Martin (2010: 11). Emphasis added.

170. Martin (2010: 77).

171. Martin (2010: 121).

172. Martin (2010: 47).

173. Martin (2010: 62, 111).

174. Martin (2010: 46).

175. Klaidman (2012: 122).

176. Woods (2015: 286).

177. Obama quoted in Cockburn (2015: 242); Shane (2015b: 306); Scahill and Greenwald (2016: 106).

178. Savage (2015: 237).

179. Quoted in W. Benjamin (1968: 241).

180. Quoted in Maier (1976: 103–4).

181. W. Benjamin (1968: 241).

182. W. Benjamin (1968: 242).

183. The reality might be something different, as we know from former drone pilots' testimonies in *National Bird*. Or as Marc Garlasco put it, the Predator was "unable to discriminate the highly distinctive outline of two Marines (with full battle equipment) from the irregular enemy" (quoted in Holewinski 2015: 57).

184. De Quincey (1890: 46–47).

185. De Quincey (1890: 54).

186. Arkin (2015: 98).

CHAPTER 3. DRONE WARS RETURNING FROM THE
FUTURE

1. Merton (1968: 477).
2. Lacan quoted in Žižek (1989: 57).
3. Lacan quoted in Žižek (1989: 58).
4. Lacan quoted in Žižek (1989: 60).
5. Caryl (2011: 58).
6. Becker and Shane (2012: A11).
7. Stanford Law School and NYU School of Law (2012: 125).
8. Stanford Law School and NYU School of Law (2012: 134).
9. Quoted in Stanford Law School and NYU School of Law. (2012: 132).
10. Bacevich (2008: 66).
11. Bacevich (2008: 112).
12. Bacevich (2008: 9).
13. Bacevich (2008: 10–11, 42).
14. Army Lieutenant Colonel Paul Yingling quoted in Bacevich (2008: 88).
15. Bacevich (2008: 132, 131, 130). In the words of Carl von Clausewitz, "War is the realm of chance" (quoted in Bacevich 2008: 156).
16. Bacevich (2008: 164).
17. Arendt (1958: 385).
18. Bacevich (2016: 311).
19. Bacevich (2016: 311).
20. Quoted in Bacevich (2016: 312).
21. Linschoten and Kuehn (2012: 327) conclude that "Al-Qaeda and the Afghan Taliban remain two distinct entities, with different memberships, ideologies and objectives." The authors also warn against labeling the Haqqani network "terrorists" because of "the dangers of self-fulfilling prophecies" (333).
22. Quoted in Woods (2015: 285).
23. Quoted in Woods (2015: 149).
24. Rhodes (2018: 116, 118).
25. Bacevich (2016: 343).
26. Bacevich (2016: 344).
27. Cockburn (2015: 149).
28. Cockburn (2015: 150).
29. Quoted in Woods (2015: 83).
30. Rex Rivolo, veteran pilot of several wars, studied records of two hundred cases where high-value targets had been killed and found that hitting the high-value targets *increased* attacks on Americans by 40 percent within a three-kilometer radius over the following thirty days (Cockburn 2015: 157–66).
31. Quoted in Cockburn (2015: 204).
32. Imtiaz (2015: 89–90, 103).

33. Quoted in Braun (2015: 275).

34. True (2015: 293).

35. Quoted in Woods (2015: 160).

36. Mothana (2012).

37. Quoted in Ahmed (2013: 82).

38. Scahill (2013: 518).

39. Scahill (2013: 521).

40. Arkin (2015: 265).

41. An army colonel quoted in Singer (2009: 64).

42. Singer (2009: 123).

43. Caryl (2011: 55).

44. Caryl (2011: 58).

45. Kaag and Kreps (2014: 134).

46. Shachtman quoted in Singer (2009: 124).

47. Singer (2009: 126, 127).

48. Singer (2009: 127).

49. Singer (2009: 128).

50. Singer (2009: 128).

51. Caryl (2011: 56).

52. Sluka (2011: 72).

53. Sluka (2011: 72).

54. Quoted in Shane (2015b: 233).

55. Quoted in Hari (2010).

56. Quoted in Stanford Law School and NYU School of Law (2012: 136).

57. Quoted in Stanford Law School and NYU School of Law (2012: 135).

58. Quoted in Calhoun (2016: 74).

59. Quoted in Jaffer (2016: 18).

60. Quoted in Cockburn (2015: 259).

61. Blair (2011).

62. Quoted in Stanford Law School and NYU School of Law (2012: 143).

63. Banks (2015: 155).

64. Jones et al. (2018).

65. Aaronson (2011: 30).

66. Quoted in Aaronson (2013: 72).

67. Aaronson (2013: 73). Emphasis added.

68. Aaronson (2013: 75).

69. Quoted in Aaronson (2013: 85).

70. Aaronson (2011: 30).

71. Vitello and Semple (2009: A1).

72. Quoted in Aaronson (2013: 86).

73. Aaronson (2013: 87).

74. Quoted in Aaronson (2013: 150).

75. Aaronson (2013: 207).

76. Aaronson (2013: 226, 236, 234).

77. See Zuckerman, Bucci, and Carafano (2013).

78. Travis (2014).

79. Aaronson (2013: 15).

80. The three exceptions were Najibulla Zazi, who attempted to bomb the New York City subway in September 2009; Hesham Nohamed Hadayet, who fired a gun at the Los Angeles airport's El-Al ticket counter; and Times Square failed bomber Faisal Shahzad.

81. Aaronson (2013: 15).

82. Quoted in Aaronson (2011: 33).

83. Aaronson (2013: 24).

84. Quoted in Aaronson (2013: 33).

85. For a longer discussion of these events, see Zulaika (2009: chap. 8).

86. MacFarquhar (1995: A9). Emphasis added.

87. *New York Times* (1995: A14).

88. J. Miller and Stone (2002: 74).

89. J. Miller and Stone (2002: 74).

90. J. Miller and Stone (2002: 88).

91. Friedman (1995: 46).

92. Bergen (2006: 204).

93. Worth (2018: 69); Associated Press (2018a).

94. Frazer (1963: 1).

95. See Zulaika and Murua (2017).

96. For a discussion of this theme, see Zulaika and Douglass (1996: 151–52).

97. Douglas (1966: 94).

98. Lincoln (1989: 166).

99. Gusterson (2016: 131).

100. Gusterson (2016: 137).

101. Gusterson (2016: 143).

102. Fanon (1991: 39).

103. Fuller (2017: 248–49).

104. Quoted in Gusterson (2016: 148).

105. Jaffer (2016: 40).

106. Bateson (1972: 184).

107. "The Unabomber" was the play name given to Ted Kaczynski, former Berkeley mathematician turned terrorist trickster who, in June of 1995, brought California's airports to a standstill with a letter to the *San Francisco Chronicle* claiming that within a week he would down an airliner, while simultaneously sending another to the *New York Times* declaring the threat a "prank." The Unabomber was front-page news for weeks.

108. See Swanson's *War Is a Lie* (2016).

109. Aretxaga (2005: 223).

110. Aretxaga (2005: 224).

111. Merton (1968: 475).

112. Stampnitzky (2013: 168). Emphasis in original.

113. Mueller (2006: 1).

114. English (2009).

115. Feldman (1991: 14).

116. White (1978: 2). Emphasis in original.

117. Palmerton (1988:107).

118. Young (2017: 102–3).

119. See the Epilogue.

120. Young (2017: 314).

121. Young (2017: 336).

122. Young (2017: 96).

123. Samuels (2016a).

124. Quoted in Samuels (2016a).

125. Loizeau quoted in Garrow (2017: 532).

126. Quoted in Garrow (2017: 531).

127. Garrow (2017: 531). Emphasis in original.

128. Young (2017: 288, 307).

129. Frankfurt (2005: 60).

130. Young (2017: 308).

131. Young (2017: 444).

132. Quoted in Young (2017: 338).

133. Tanya Somanader, director of digital response at Obama's White House, quoted in Samuels (2016a).

134. Samuels (2016b).

135. Shachtman (2009).

136. Martin (2010: 31).

137. John Nagl quoted in Bacevich (2016: 316).

138. Shah (2015: 160).

139. Hersh (2016: 9). Emphasis added.

140. Cockburn (2015: 147–48).

141. Quoted in Cockburn (2015: 223).

142. Martin (2010: 263).

143. Cockburn (2015: 116–17). Emphasis added.

144. Cockburn (2015: 138).

145. See Priest and Arkin (2011).

146. Crawford (2016); Masco (2006: 336).

147. See Masco (2006: 336).

148. Singer (2009: 271).

149. Singer (2009: 35).

150. Bacevich (2016: 354, 268–69).
151. Zulaika (2009).
152. Zupančič (2003: 19).

CHAPTER 4. TRAUMA

1. Harvey (1989).
2. For a wide-ranging analysis of the pathologies created by double binds, see Bateson (1972).
3. Singer (2012: 5).
4. Priest and Arkin (2011: 220).
5. See Zulaika and Douglass (1996: 158–59).
6. Mazzetti (2013: 89).
7. Mazzetti (2013: 125).
8. Priest and Arkin (2011: 211).
9. Grossman (1995: 120).
10. Grossman (1995: 121).
11. Grossman (1995: 123).
12. Nadelson (2005: 50).
13. Addams ([1915] 2003: 78).
14. Grossman (1995: 122).
15. Grossman (1995: 128).
16. Martin (2010: 43–44). Emphasis in original.
17. Martin (2010: 72).
18. Martin (2010: 119). Emphasis in original.
19. Martin (2010: 271).
20. S. A. Stouffer quoted in Grossman (1995: 162).
21. Martin (2010: 31).
22. Chamayou (2013: 117).
23. M. Benjamin (2013: 97).
24. Martin (2010: 54).
25. Martin (2010: 212).
26. Martin (2010: 55).
27. Martin (2010: 213).
28. Martin (2010: 21).
29. Martin (2010: 23). Emphasis in original.
30. Martin (2010: 121).
31. Martin (2010: 162).
32. Martin (2010: 297).
33. Martin (2010: 45).
34. Woods (2015: 176).

35. Abé (2012).

36. Abé (2012).

37. Bryant quoted in Woods (2015: 119–20).

38. Bryant quoted in Abé (2012).

39. Drone Pilot (2015: 116).

40. Calhoun (2016: 158).

41. Woods (2015: 171).

42. Bryant quoted in Calhoun (2016: 158).

43. Grossman (1995: 191–92).

44. Woods (2015: 188).

45. Abé (2012).

46. Abé (2012).

47. Press (2018).

48. The documentary film *Drone* (Schei 2014) was directed and produced by Tonje Hessen Schei. It features among others the experiences of the former drone pilot Brandon Bryant.

49. Arkin (2015: 125).

50. Woods (2015: 11).

51. Major General Jim Poss quoted in Woods (2015: 12).

52. Quoted in Cockburn (2015: 143).

53. Kilcullen quoted in Woods (2015: 86).

54. Woods (2015: 87).

55. M. Benjamin (2013: 158).

56. Nadelson (2005: 125).

57. Press (2018).

58. Press (2018).

59. Žižek (2007: 24).

60. See Margalit (1994).

61. Grossman (1995: 210).

62. Žižek (1989: 133).

63. Richard Boothby quoted in Žižek (2012: 689).

64. Rosaldo (1989).

65. Nadelson (2005: 58).

66. Rosaldo (1989: 18).

67. Gray quoted in Grossman (1995: 193).

68. Grossman (1995: 87).

69. Quote from Chamayou (2013: 199). See the case of the *miliciano* who "forgave the life" of Rafael Sánchez Mazas during the Spanish Civil War (Zulaika 2014: 242–46).

70. Chamayou (2013: 147).

71. The robotic researcher Bart Everett quoted in Singer (2009: 147).

72. On self-immolation, see, for example, Mia Bloom (2005), Robert Pape (2005), and Yoram Schwitzer (2006).

73. Chamayou (2013: 73)

74. Ignatief (2000: 214–15).

75. For the technical vulnerabilities of drones, see Chamayou (2013: 75–76).

76. During the Clinton administration, the US Army operated with the premise that military casualties should be avoided at all costs, even if such avoidance implied, as proved to be the case during NATO's intervention in Kosovo, greater vulnerability for civilians. The claim that saving the life of your own soldiers is more important than saving the lives of however many foreign civilians is an aberration for the theorists of just warfare.

77. Suskind (2006).

78. Kilcullen (2009: 274). Emphasis in original.

79. Quoted in Buck-Morss (1992: 38).

80. See Foster (1991).

81. Ernst quoted in Foster (1991: 73).

82. Foster (1991: 75).

83. Enchanted weapons that turn men into invulnerable heroes have been a staple in stories, films, comic books, and video games (see Tlusty 2015).

84. Quoted in Singer (2009: 165).

85. Buck-Morss (1992: 4).

86. Buck-Morss (1992: 5).

87. Pauc (2015: 6).

88. Pauc (2015: 9).

89. Pauc (2015: 11).

90. Pauc (2015: 9–10).

91. Pauc (2015: 12).

92. Pauc (2015: 13).

93. Pauc (2015: 62).

94. Pauc (2015: 17).

95. Pauc (2015: 52).

96. Pauc (2015: 131).

97. Pauc (2015: 76).

98. Pauc (2015: 80).

99. Pauc (2015: 83).

100. Pauc (2015: 88). Frank writes regularly in his frankisemptiness.blog.

101. Sites (2013: xx).

102. Quoted in Rhodes (2018: 122).

103. Corporal William Wold quoted in Sites (2013: 35).

104. Wold quoted in Sites (2013: 36).

105. Quoted in Sites (2013: 177).

106. Quoted in Sites (2013: 132).

107. Quoted in Sites (2013: 166).

108. Quoted in Sites (2013: 168).

109. Grossman (1995: 158).

110. Grossman (1995: 93).

111. Sites (2013: 107).

112. Shay (2002: 54).

113. Sites (2013: 127).

114. Junger (2016: 81–82).

115. After conducting research among World War II veterans, Army Brigadier Marshall (1947) concluded that an average of only 15 to 25 percent fired their weapons against the enemy in the battlefront. For a criticism of Marshall's and Grossman's findings, see for example Engen (2008).

116. Nadelson (2005: 47).

117. Nadelson (2005: 55).

118. Nadelson (2005: 58).

119. Nadelson (2005: 90, 100).

120. Grossman (1995: 88).

121. Quoted in Grossman (1995: 116).

122. Quoted in Grossman (1995: 116).

123. Quoted in Grossman (1995: 116–17).

124. British scientist James Tuck quoted in Monk (2012: 418).

125. Monk (2012: 445).

126. Quoted in Isaacson (2007: 483).

127. Quoted in Isaacson (2007: 483).

128. Quoted in Isaacson (2007: 485).

129. Quoted in Isaacson (2007: 485).

130. Isaacson (2007: 488).

131. Isaacson (2007: 490).

132. Quoted in Isaacson (2007: 494).

133. Quoted in Isaacson (2007: 491). Emphasis added.

134. Quoted in Leahy (1950: 441).

135. Quoted in R. Ellsberg (2008: 95).

136. Anscombe (1981: 64). Anscombe was a student of Wittgenstein and an authority on his work; on Wittgenstein's death, Anscombe became one of his three literary executors.

137. Anscombe (1981: 66).

138. Anscombe (1981: 69).

139. Quoted in R. Ellsberg (2008: 167–68).

140. Monk (2012: 442).

141. Quoted in Monk (2012: 455).

142. Quoted in Monk (2012: 456).

143. Monk (2012: 467).

144. Monk (2012: 468).

145. Oppenheimer's secretary Anne Wilson quoted in Monk (2012: 461).

146. Monk (2012: 449).

147. Physicists quoted in Monk (2012: 579).

148. Quoted in Monk (2012: 474).

149. Monk (2012: 579).

150. Conant (2017: 315).

151. Physicist Abraham Pais quoted in Monk (2012: 516).

152. "What are we to make of a civilization which has always regarded ethics as an essential part of human life . . . [but] which has not been able to talk about killing almost everybody except in prudential and game-theoretical terms?" (quoted in Monk 2012: 671).

153. Robert Bacher, head of weapons physics at Los Alamos, quoted in Schwartz (2017: 248); D. Schwartz (2017: 249).

154. D. Schwartz (2017: 198).

155. See D. Schwartz (2017: 260–64, 354).

156. Quoted in D. Schwartz (2017: 313).

157. D. Schwartz (2017: xviii).

158. Oppenheimer quoted in Monk (2012: 446). The experiments included injecting plutonium into patients who didn't know they were being used as guinea pigs, causing their deaths or most serious harm (see Welsome 1999).

159. Monk (2012: 463).

160. Quoted in Monk (2012: 492).

161. Quoted in Monk (2012: 494); Monk (2012: 449).

162. Quoted in Monk (2012: 503).

163. Quoted in D. Ellsberg (2017: 2).

164. Quoted in Sorley (2012: 94).

165. McNamara (1995: 194).

166. Stone and Kuznik (2012: 340, 36–64, 386, 387, 393).

167. Morris (2004).

168. McNamara (1995: 322).

169. Quoted in Gaddis (2011: 620–21). Emphasis in original.

170. Quoted in Gaddis (2011: 648).

171. Gaddis (2011: 434–35). Emphasis added.

172. Quoted in Gaddis (2011: 645–46).

173. Quoted in Gaddis (2011: 666, 668).

174. Gaddis (2011: 668).

175. D. Ellsberg (2017: 313).

176. D. Ellsberg (2017: 11).

177. D. Ellsberg (2017: 338)

178. D. Ellsberg (2017: 339).

179. D. Ellsberg (2017: 341).

180. See J. Brown (2016).

181. Perry (2015).

182. Perry (2015: 5).

183. Perry (2015: 48–49). Emphasis added.

184. Perry (2015: 50).

185. Perry (2015: 55) writes bluntly: "I see a historically all-too-familiar irrational, impassioned thinking, a thinking that has led to wars throughout human history, and a thinking in the nuclear era more dangerous than ever . . . [that] brought us to the brink of blundering into a nuclear war. It was a colossal failure of imagination not to see where this was leading. Even before the nuclear arms buildups of the 1970s and 1980s, our nuclear forces were more than enough to blow up the world. Our deterrent forces were fearsome enough to deter any rational leader. Yet we obsessively claimed inadequacies in our nuclear forces. We fantasized about a 'window of vulnerability.' Both governments—ours and that of the Soviet Union—spread fear among our peoples."

186. Perry (2015: 156).

187. Perry (2015: 179). Emphasis added.

188. Perry (2015: 196).

189. See Sorley (2012).

190. Quoted in Sorley (2012: 52).

191. McMaster (1997: 333).

192. McMaster (1997: 326, 334).

193. McNamara (1995: 321–22).

194. These data and transmissions are "between radar operators, battlespace managers, Tactical Air Control Parties, Joint Tactical Air Controllers, UAVs, satellites, imagery analysts, pilots (both UAV and manned), sensor operators, troops in contact, the Battlefield Airborne Communications Node, the Air Support Operations Center, and various individuals located at the Combined Air Operations Center in Al Udeid" (Westmoreland 2015).

195. Arkin (2015: 215).'

196. Quoted in Sorley (2012: 97). Emphasis in original.

197. Historian Stephen Ambrose and the Peers Report quoted in Sorley (2012: 214–15).

198. Westmoreland (2015).

199. "Simply put, these strikes have saved lives," quoted in Rogers (2017).

200. Westmoreland (2016).

201. Journalist Peter Braestrup quoted in Sorley (2012: 265).

202. Quoted in Sorley (2012: 98).

203. Quoted in Sorley (2012: 262).

204. Westmoreland (2014).

205. Quoted in Sorley (2012: 263).

206. Quoted in Sorley (2012: 266).
207. Westmoreland (2014).
208. Quoted in Westmoreland (2014).
209. Westmoreland (2014).
210. Westmoreland (2014).
211. Westmoreland (2014).

CHAPTER 5. RESISTANCE

1. For a legal history of these relations, see Mander (1991).
2. Solnit (1994: 30).
3. For a description of the Las Vegas jail experience, see Terrell (2016).
4. Quoted in De Quincey (1890: 11).
5. Wright (2008).
6. Wright (2008: xii).
7. Wright (2008: 1).
8. See Schlosser (2013: 365–67).
9. Sartor (2014: 5).
10. Sartor (2014: 99, 4.
11. Quoted in Kelly (2005: 6).
12. Kelly (2005: 152).
13. St. Clair and Cockburn (2005: 168).
14. Quoted in Berrigan (2009: 177).
15. Baldwin (1998: 799).
16. Kelly (2018).
17. Associated Press (2018b).
18. García Lorca (2007).
19. Marcelle Auclair quoted in Josephs and Caballero (2016: 80).
20. Capote (1994: 319).
21. Shay (1994: 193).
22. Cabana (1996: 172).
23. Cabana (1996: 176).
24. Cabana (1996: 177).
25. Cabana (1996: 181).
26. Cabana (1996: 177).
27. Cabana (1996: 187).
28. Cabana (1996: 15–16).
29. Cabana (1996: 187).
30. Solotaroff (2001: 203).
31. Solotaroff (2001: 198).
32. Cabana (1996: 190).

33. Cabana (1996: 183).

34. García Lorca (2007: 146).

35. Quoted in Solotaroff (2001: 17).

36. Quoted in Inge (1987: 67).

37. Solotaroff (2001: 25).

38. Quoted in Solotaroff (2001: 198).

39. Shay (1994: 51).

40. Quoted in Solotaroff (2001: 197).

41. Quoted in Hennessy (2017: 343).

42. Hennessy (2017: 15).

43. Hennessy (2017: 50).

44. Hennessy (2017: 65).

45. Father Hugo quoted in Hennessy (2017: 126).

46. Quoted in Riegle (2003: 78).

47. Nina Polcyn Moore quoted in Riegle (2003: 139).

48. Quoted in Hennessy (2017: 213). The Dorothy/Tamar religious drama echoed the Abraham/Isaac paradox by which, in Kierkegaard's reading, the parent's religious idolatry provoked the child's loss of faith.

49. See Piehl (1982: 150–59).

50. See W. Miller (1973: 16).

51. Piehl (1982: 166).

52. Quoted in R. Ellsberg (2008: 17).

53. Edward Morin, editor of the *Catholic Worker*, quoted in Piehl (1982: 220).

54. See Piehl (1982: 247).

55. Butigan (2003: 39, 40).

56. Quoted in R. Ellsberg (2008: 214).

57. Quoted in Piehl (1982: 232).

58. Quoted in R. Ellsberg (2008: 562).

59. See R. Ellsberg (2008: 575, 591).

60. Quoted in D. Ellsberg (2017: 4).

61. Quoted in Hennessy (2017: 344).

62. Hennessy (2017: 258).

63. Quoted in R. Ellsberg (2008: 314).

64. Quoted in R. Ellsberg (2008: 530–31).

65. Quoted in Riegle (2003: 58). Harrington's highly influential *The Other America* (1962), a book thoroughly imbued with his Catholic Worker experience, would instigate one of the major social innovations of the Kennedy-Johnson administration (see Piehl 1982: 172–80).

66. Day (1983: 264).

67. Berdyaev (1957: 87).

68. Quoted in R. Ellsberg (2008: 417).

69. Berrigan (2009: 279).

70. Berrigan (2009: 280–81).

71. Berrigan (2009: 281).

72. Berrigan (2009: 123).

73. Berrigan (2009: 124, 133).

74. Berrigan (2004).

75. Arrupe quoted in La Bella (2007: 18).

76. Berrigan (2009: 28).

77. Berrigan (2009: 136–37).

78. See Zulaika (2014: 228–37).

79. On the Atlacatl Battalion, see Chomsky (2010: 30).

80. Žižek (2009: 255).

81. Badiou dwells on a world ruled by Saint Paul's axiom: "For you are not under law, but under grace" (Rom. 6:14). Under such rule the very axis of life and death gets altered in a manner similar to the Resurrection for Paul—a resurrection, writes Badiou (2003: 62), "on the basis of which life's center of gravity resides in life, whereas previously, being situated in the Law, it organized life's subsumption by death." In St. Paul's writings death has a key name: "Law." There is, however, an apparent contradiction in Paul's thought about Christ being the end of law and love being the fulfillment of law. It does not mean that the born-again Christian subject is lawless, for, as Paul writes to the Romans, "The law is holy, and the commandment is holy and just and good" (Rom. 7:12), and he even asserts that "the law is spiritual" (Rom. 7:14). This leads to the "extraordinarily difficult question concerning *the existence of a transliteral law, a law of the spirit*" (87; emphasis in original). In the contradiction between the Christian abolition and fulfillment of law, Badiou's thesis is that "under the condition of faith, of a declared conviction, love names a nonliteral law, one that gives to the faithful subject his consistency, and effectuates the postevental truth in the world" (87). Paul calls "love" (agape) this universal address of pure subjectivation by faith.

82. Badiou (2003: 45). Emphasis in original.

83. Badiou (2003: 66).

84. Badiou (2003: 108).

85. Badiou (2003: 60).

86. Deleuze (2013: 383, 385). Emphasis in original.

87. Deleuze (2013: 388).

88. Altizer (1977: 14).

89. Since the fourth century in traditional Christian spirituality, the desert represented "kenotic nothingness" or divinity's "emptying." Theologian Javier Vitoria (2008: 63, 65) wrote that "kenosis" means God's "impotence in the world" and that "God's kenosis on the cross leads to an authentic revolution in the image we have of God," leading to a Jewish mystical theme: "the one of God's *self-limitation* to give space to the existence and autonomy of the world."

90. It is the gap between politics and unconditional ethics. Or, for the philosopher, the gap between the history of Being and the historicity of the Event, which is a sort of miracle. Or, according to psychoanalysis, the fundamental gap inside the fullness of fantasy, the structural impossibility that is the very condition of desire.

91. Day quoted in Riegle (2003: 15).

92. See Riegle (2003: 171).

93. Quoted in R. Ellsberg (2008: 80).

94. Occhiogrosso quoted in Butigan (2003: 152).

95. Brandon-Falcone (1988: 314).

96. "Dorothy helped the people and also attacked the system." Joe Zarrella quoted in Riegle (2003: 191).

97. Between 1951 and 1956 forty-nine nuclear bombs were exploded in southern Nevada. Area 51 was in place for the 1957 Operation Plumbbob, a series of thirty nuclear explosions. Plumbbob tests dropped fallout from Oregon to New England. One-millionth of a gram of plutonium is enough to kill a person. As part of the Operation Plumbbob, on July 5, 1957, the "Hood bomb" was tested; its flash, seen from Canada to Mexico and eight hundred miles out to sea, lighted and shook the predawn darkness. It took twenty-five minutes for the nuclear wave to travel 350 miles west to Los Angeles, where the headline at the *Los Angeles Times* announced: "LA Awakened. Flash Seen. Shock Felt Here. Calls Flood Police Switch Board" (quoted in Jacobsen 2011: 121). The army conducted various other tests during the explosion. Above-ground testing continued until July of 1962.

98. Butigan (2003: 40).

99. Bergon (1993: 191).

100. Tempest Williams (1991: 282–83).

101. Tempest Williams (1991: 283).

102. Tempest Williams (1991: 287).

103. Vitale (2015: 13).

104. Vitale (2015: 25).

105. Vitale (2015: 15).

106. A critical text for Vitale was Jesuit John F. Kavanaugh's *Following Christ in a Consumer Society* (1981).

107. See Butigan (2003: xi–xii).

108. Baudrillard (2010: 3).

109. Banham (1982: 44).

110. See Welsome (1999: 489).

111. Baudrillard (2010: 28).

112. Baudrillard (2010: 83).

113. These numbers are taken from Butigan (2003: 73–75).

114. Vitale (2015: 37).

115. See Schmidt (1994).

116. Butigan (2003: 92).

117. W. Benjamin (1968: 254).

118. W. Benjamin (1968: 254).

119. W. Benjamin (1968: 256).

120. Santner (2005: 126). Emphasis in original.

121. Westmoreland (2015). Emphasis added.

EPILOGUE

1. Shane (2015b: 82).

2. Quoted in Shane (2015b: 86–87).

3. Quoted in Shane (2015b: 89).

4. Shane (2015a).

5. *New York Times* (2011); Kurzman and Schanzer (2015).

6. Quoted in Shane (2015b: 103).

7. Quoted in Shane (2015b: 103–4).

8. Shane (2015b: 109).

9. Al-Tamimi was the imam who had recommended Awlaki's appointment at Falls Church in 2000, and whom he later may have tried to ensnare in an FBI trap. Tamimi had been charged with supporting terrorism, and, while expecting indictment, he and Awlaki had made joint appearances in Britain. To the shock of many civil libertarians, Tamimi was condemned to life in prison.

10. Shane (2015b: 125).

11. Scahill (2013: 71).

12. Quoted in Shane (2015b: 145).

13. Quoted in Shane (2015b: 161).

14. Quoted in Shane (2015b: 163).

15. Shane (2015b: 163). The initial aid package for the corrupt dictator Saleh to allow the drone program was $400 million (Calhoun 2016: 7).

16. Shane (2015b: 169).

17. Quoted in Shane (2015b: 170).

18. Shane (2015b: 170).

19. Quoted in Shane (2015b: 175).

20. Quoted in Shane (2015b: 237).

21. Shane (2015b: 178–79).

22. Quoted in Shane (2015b: 190).

23. Hasan wrote back offering money for his trip, adding a postscript asking help in finding a compatible woman. Awlaki replied with a friendly note. Hasan then sent him his biography, hoping it would help in a search for a companion. But that and subsequent notes met no reply.

24. Shane (2015b: 192).

25. See Shane (2015b: 193).

26. For the constitutive nature of terrorism discourse, see Zulaika and Douglass (1996).

27. "I am a Christian and I am a devout Christian. I believe in the redemptive death and resurrection of Jesus Christ. I believe that that faith gives me a path to be cleansed of sin and have eternal life" (Pulliam and Olsen 2008).

28. Obama (1995: 283).

29. A Chicago woman and Wright quoted in Garrow (2017: 324).

30. Garrow (2017: 479).

31. Quoted in Garrow (2017: 534).

32. This sermon, and his remark after 9/11 that "America's chickens are coming home to roost," were in the black American tradition that goes back to Frederick Douglass's "I have no love for America"—the America whose much-heralded democracy was predicated upon "the enslavement of Africans [which were] over 20 percent of the population" (C. West 1993: 156). W. E. B. Du Bois and James Baldwin and Malcolm X were in that tradition, as well as the Martin Luther King who, during the war in Vietnam, called America "the greatest purveyor of violence in the world today" (Quoted in Coates 2017: 136).

33. Quoted in Garrow (2017: 1042). Wright, who was offered by Eric Whitaker, a close friend of Obama, $150,000 "not to preach at all," would return to the public stage in an interview with Bill Moyers. In it Wright complained that the media had painted him "as some sort of fanatic," which was unfair and untrue, and "un-American," when "I served six years in the military." He also condemned the support for "state terrorism against the Palestinians."

34. Quotes in Garrow (2017: 1045).

35. Quotes in Garrow (2017: 1047).

36. Obama (1995: 293).

37. Baldwin (1998: 807). In that same page Baldwin wrote about "blacks called upon to represent the Republic are, very often . . . prohibited from representing blacks" and "the myth and menace of global war are nothing more than nothing less than a coward's means of distracting attention from the real crimes and concerns of this Republic."

38. J. Frank and St. Clair (2012b: 87).

39. Feffer (2012).

40. Quoted in M. Schwartz (2018).

41. "Mullen fingered his rosary beads" during the operation to capture bin Laden (Rhodes 2018: 134).

42. Obama (2009).

43. Quoted in Shane (2015b: 207).

44. Shane (2015b: 209).

45. See Schmitt (2018: A9).

46. *New York Times* (2016).

47. Savage (2015: 253).

48. Ahmed (2013: 120–21).

49. Quoted in Shane (2015b: 224).

50. Woods (2015: 231).

51. Quoted in Woods (2015: 231).

52. Quoted in Woods (2015: 233).

53. Stanford Law School and NYU School of Law (2012: 116).

54. Quoted in Mazzetti (2013: 228).

55. See Tuchman (1984).

56. There is a long academic debate, known as "The Homeric Question," regarding who Homer was, the authorial singularity or multiplicity of both the *Iliad* and the *Odyssey,* and the oral and written nature of the poems.

57. *Iliad* 11.132–33, 339–41, 557–59; 12.50–51; 16.959; 17.846–48 (Homer 1990).

58. Redfield (1975: 58).

59. Redfield (1975: 28).

60. *Iliad* 7.132 (Homer 1990).

61. *Iliad* 7.404 (Homer 1990).

62. *Iliad* 15.832 (Homer 1990).

63. *Iliad* 20.489–94 (Homer 1990).

64. *Iliad* 11.425–26; 15.340 (Homer 1990).

65. *Iliad* 22.6, 350–55 (Homer 1990).

66. Knox (1990: 57).

67. Redfield (1975: 27, 17).

68. Redfield (1975: 29).

69. Redfield (1975: 57).

70. Rhodes (2018: 47).

71. Nasser joined forces with the ACLU and the Center for Constitutional Rights and filed suit in August against Barack Obama, the CIA director Leon Panetta, and the defense secretary Robert Gates. It was a matter of fundamental rights, his lawyers alleged, that the government could not kill an American citizen without a criminal charge, without a trial, with evidence kept secret. Besides, Nasser added, there were other means to neutralize him; capture was feasible.

72. Shane (2015b: 229).

73. Shane (2015b: 250).

74. The magazine was in English and was being published in a country where just over 1 percent of the population had access to the internet and where the gross annual domestic product was less than what Walmart earned in one month (Shane 2015b: 253).

75. Klaidman (2012: 220).

76. Shane (2013: A1).

77. Shane (2015b: 293).
78. Shane (2015b: 302).
79. Quoted in Shane (2015b: 317).
80. Shane (2015b: 318).
81. Shane (2015b: 305).
82. Redfield (1975: 111).
83. Redfield (1975: 158).
84. Redfield (1975: 56).
85. Quoted in Redfield (1975: 89).
86. Redfield (1975: 128).
87. Redfield (1975: 153, 159, 202).
88. Redfield (1975: 128).
89. Redfield (1975: 183).
90. Redfield (1975: 183).
91. In Sophocles's *Antigone,* the tragic struggle between the heroine and the ruler Creon is also about his nonburial order against Polyneices.
92. Redfield (1975: 127).
93. *Iliad* 21.138–41 (Homer 1990).
94. In Laos, for instance, the remains of 273 Americans had been recovered as of 2018, as "extraordinary efforts were put into finding even the most minimal traces of life" (Rhodes 2018: 336); currently in Spain hundreds of mass graves of people killed in the 1936–39 civil war are being exhumed after decades of neglect were unable to erase the ultimate abomination of their nonfuneral (see Ferrándiz and Robben 2017).
95. Quoted in Shane (2015b: 208).
96. Hersh (2016: 44).
97. Hersh (2016: 47).
98. Quoted in Hersh (2016: 35).
99. Quoted in Hersh (2016: 27).
100. Quoted in Scahill (2013: 452).
101. Quoted in Hersh (2016: 39).
102. Quoted in Hersh (2016: 47).
103. Shane (2015b: 281).
104. Shane (2015b: 291).
105. Woods (2015: 161).
106. Jaffer (2016: 12).
107. Quoted in Woods (2015: 161).
108. Stanford Law School and NYU School of Law (2012: 76).
109. Stanford Law School and NYU School of Law (2012: 94).
110. Redfield (1975: 183).
111. *Iliad* 22.399–400, 407–17 (Homer 1990).
112. *Iliad* 22.421–23 (Homer 1990).

113. *Iliad* 23.216 (Homer 1990).

114. *Iliad* 15.243 (Homer 1990).

115. *Iliad* 24.95, 163, 168 (Homer 1990).

116. Redfield (1975: 214).

117. *Iliad* 24.764 (Homer 1990).

118. *Iliad* 24.944 (Homer 1990).

119. Redfield (1975: 222).

120. *Iliad* 24.597–98 (Homer 1990).

121. Obama (1995: 429–30).

122. Shane (2015b: 296).

123. Quoted in Woods (2015: 141).

124. Scahill (2013: 510).

125. Quoted in Scahill (2013: 510).

126. Quoted in Scahill (2013: 510).

127. Obama (1995: 63).

128. Obama (1995: 277).

129. Obama (1995: 26).

130. Obama (1995: 220).

131. Obama (1995: 265).

132. Obama (1995: 227).

133. Obama (1995: 323).

134. Scahill (2013: 71).

135. Obama (1995: 221).

136. Obama (1995: 322).

137. Obama (1995: 227).

138. Obama (1995: 389).

139. Obama (1995: 430).

140. Obama (1995: 280).

141. Obama (1995: 427–28).

142. Obama (1995: 355).

143. Obama (1995: 438).

144. Obama (1995: 349).

145. Ghobari and Stewart (2017).

146. Scahill (2013: 431).

147. Scahill (2013: 497).

148. Kierkegaard (1941: 27).

149. Kierkegaard (1941: 28).

150. Kierkegaard (1941: 28–29).

151. Kierkegaard (1941: 29).

152. Kierkegaard (1941: 27).

153. Kierkegaard (1941: 67).

154. Quoted in Sites (2013: 132).

155. Pauc (2015: 17).

156. Quoted in Scahill (2013: 496).

157. Shane (2015b: 296).

158. Obama apologized only when two white men held hostage by al-Qaeda, an American and Italian, were killed by a drone.

159. Scahill (2013: 511).

160. He had been held with twenty-two other hostages; the four Americans and two British prisoners were killed, sacrificed for their government's policies of not negotiating with terrorists; the other sixteen Europeans secretly paid the ransom and were released. When the Sotloff parents tried to raise money to meet the kidnappers' request, they were told it was illegal and they would be prosecuted for doing so. James Foley's decapitation preceded Sotloff's.

161. Weil (1986: 162–95).

162. Weil (1986: 171).

163. Weil (1986: 173).

164. Weil (1986: 178).

165. Weil (1986: 180, 181).

166. Weil (1986: 185).

167. Weil (1986: 187).

168. Obama (1995: 163, 286).

169. Lacan quoted in Župančič (2000: 213), in a commentary on Claudel's figure of Sygne de Coufontaine.

170. Rhodes (2018: 376, 375).

171. Rhodes (2018: xvi–xvii). Emphasis in original.

172. Quoted in Klaidman (2012: 271).

173. Obama (2013).

174. *Don Quixote*, pt. 2, bk. 66 (Cervantes 2016).

Bibliography

Aaronson, Trevor. 2011. "The Informants." *Mother Jones*, October, 30–43.

Aaronson, Trevor. 2013. *The Terror Factory: Inside the FBI's Manufactured War on Terrorism*. Brooklyn, NY: Ig.

Abé, Nicola. 2012. "Dreams in Infrared: The Woes of an American Drone Operator." *Spiegel Online*, December 14. https://www.sott.net/article/254875-Dreams-in-infrared-The-woes-of-an-American-drone-operator.

Addams, Jane. {1915] 2003. "The Revolt against War." In *Women at The Hague*, edited by Jane Addams, Emily G. Balch, and Alice Hamilton, 27–38. New York: Humanity Books.

Agamben, Giorgio. 1998. *Homo Sacer: Sovereign Power and Bare Life*. Stanford, CA: Stanford University Press.

Ahmad, Muhammad Idrees. 2011. "The Magical Count of Body Counts." *Al Jazeera*, June 13, 2.

Ahmed, Akbar. 2013. *The Thistle and the Drone: How America's War on Terror Became a Global War on Tribal Islam*. Washington, DC: Brookings Institution Press.

Altizer, Thomas J. J. 1977. *The Contemporary Jesus*. Albany: State University of New York Press.

Amnesty International. 2013. *"Will I Be Next?" US Drone Strikes in Pakistan*. London: Amnesty International. https://www.amnestyusa.org/files/asa330132013en.pdf.

Anscombe, G. E. M. 1981. "Mr. Truman's Degree." In *Ethics, Religion and Politics*, vol. 3 of *The Collected Philosophical Papers of G. E. M. Anscombe*, 62–71. Oxford: Blackwell.

Arendt, Hannah. 1958. *The Origins of Totalitarianism*. Cleveland, OH: World.

Arendt, Hannah. 1963. *Eichmann in Jerusalem: A Report on the Banality of Evil*. New York: Viking Press.

Aretxaga, Begoña. 2005. "Playing Terrorist: Ghastly Plots and the Ghostly State." In *States of Terror: Begoña Aretxaga's Essays*, edited by Joseba Zulaika, 215–29. Reno, NV: Center for Basque Studies.

Arkin, William W. 2015. *Unmanned: Drones, Data, and the Illusion of Perfect Warfare*. New York: Little, Brown.

Associated Press. 2018a. "Saudi-UAE Coalition 'Cut Deals' with al-Qaeda in Yemen." August 6. https://hiiraan.com/news4/2018/Aug/159414/report_saudi_uae_coalition_cut_deals_with_al_qaeda_in_yemen.aspx.

Associated Press. 2018b. "Yemen: Strike Kills at Least 20 at Wedding, Officials Say." *Guardian*, April 22.

Bacevich, Andrew J. 2008. *The Limits of Power: The End of American Exceptionalism*. New York: Metropolitan Books.

Bacevich, Andrew J. 2016. *America's War for the Greater Middle East: A Military History*. New York: Random House.

Badiou, Alain. 2002. *Ethics: An Essay on the Understanding of Evil*. Translated by Peter Hallward. London: Verso.

Badiou, Alain. 2003. *Saint Paul: The Foundations of Universalism*. Translated by Ray Brassier. Stanford, CA: Stanford University Press.

Badiou, Alain. 2015. *Plato's "Republic": A Dialogue in 16 Chapters*. Translated by Susan Spitzer. Introduction by Kenneth Reinhard. New York: Columbia University Press.

Baker, Nicholson. 2012. "Nicholson Baker: By the Book." *New York Times, Sunday Book Review*, September 13.

Baldwin, James. 1998. *James Baldwin: Collected Essays*. Edited by Toni Morrison. New York: Library of America.

Baldwin, James. 2017. *I Am Not Your Negro*. Compiled and edited by Raoul Peck. New York: Vintage International.

Banham, Peter Reyner. 1982. *Scenes in America Deserta*. Salt Lake City, UT: Peregrine Smith Book.

Banks, William C. 2015. "Regulating Drones: Are Targeted Killings by Drones outside Traditional Battlefields Legal?" In Bergen and Rothenberg 2015: 129–59.

Bateson, Gregory. 1972. *Steps to an Ecology of Mind*. Chicago: University of Chicago Press.

Baudrillard, Jean. 2010. *America*. With an introduction by Geoff Dyer. London: Verso.

Becker, Jo, and Scott Shane. 2012. "Secret 'Kill List' Proves a Test of Obama's Principles and Will." *New York Times,* May 29.

Benjamin, Medea. 2013. *Drone Warfare: Killing by Remote Control.* London: Verso.

Benjamin, Walter. 1968. "Theses on the Philosophy of History." In *Illuminations,* translated by Harry Zohned, edited with an introduction by Hanna Arendt, 253–64. New York: Schocken Books.

Bennis, Phyllis. 2015. "Drones and Assassination in the US's Permanent War." In Cohn 2015a: 13–25.

Berdyaev, Nicholas. 1957. *Dostoevsky.* New York: Meridian Books.

Bergen, Peter L. 2006. *The Osama bin Laden I Know: An Oral History of al Qaeda's Leader.* New York: Free Press.

Bergen, Peter L., and Megan Braun. 2012. "Drone Is Obama's Weapon of Choice." CNN, September 6. https://www.cnn.com/2012/09/05/opinion/bergen-obama-drone/index.html.

Bergen, Peter L., and Daniel Rothenberg, eds. 2015. *Drone Wars: Transforming Conflict, Law, and Policy.* Cambridge: Cambridge University Press.

Bergen, Peter L., and Jennifer Rowland. 2015. "Decade of the Drone: Analyzing CIA Drone Attacks, Casualties, and Policy." In Bergen and Rothenberg 2015: 12–41.

Bergon, Frank. 1993. *The Temptations of St. Ed and Brother S.* Reno: University of Nevada Press.

Berrigan, Daniel. 2004. *The Trial of the Catonsville Nine.* New York: Fordham University Press.

Berrigan, Daniel. 2009. *Essential Writings.* Selected with an introduction by John Dear. Maryknoll, NY: Orbis Books.

Blair, Dennis C. 2011. "Drones Alone Are Not the Answer." *New York Times,* August 14.

Bloom, Mia. 2005. *Dying to Kill: The Allure of Suicide Terror.* New York: Columbia University Press.

Brandon-Falcone, Janice. 1988. "Experiments in Truth: An Oral History of the St. Louis Catholic Worker, 1935–1942." In *Revolution of the Heart: Essays on the Catholic Worker,* edited by Patrick G. Coy, 313–36. Philadelphia: Temple University Press.

Braun, Megan. 2015. "Predator Effect: A Phenomenon Unique to the War on Terror." In Bergen and Rothenberg 2015: 253–84.

Brents, Barbara G., Crystal A. Jackson, and Kathryn Hausbeck. 2010. *The State of Sex.* New York: Routledge, 2010.

Brooks, David. 2009. "The Tenacity Question." *New York Times,* October 29.

Brown, Jerry. 2016. "A Stark Nuclear Warning." *New York Review of Books,* July 14, 11–13. https://www.nybooks.com/articles/2016/07/14/a-stark-nuclear-warning/.

Brown, Norman O. 1959. *Life against Death: The Psychoanalytical Meaning of History*. Middletown, CT: Wesleyan University Press.

Bruck, Connie. 2016. "Why Obama Has Failed to Close Guantánamo." *New Yorker*, August 1. https://www.newyorker.com/magazine/2016/08/01/why-obama-has-failed-to-close-guantanamo.

Buck-Morss, Susan. 1992. "Aesthetics and Anaesthetics: Walter Benjamin's Artwork Essay Reconsidered." *October* 62:1–25.

Butigan, Ken. 2003. *Pilgrimage through a Burning World: Spiritual Practice and Nonviolent Protest at the Nevada Test Site*. New York: State University of New York Press.

Butler, Judith. 1990. "The Force of Fantasy: Feminism, Mapplethorpe, and Discursive Excess." *Difference: A Journal of Feminist Cultural Studies* 2 (2): 105–25.

Cabana, Donald A. 1996. *Death at Midnight: The Confession of an Executioner*. Boston: Northeastern University Press.

Calhoun, Laurie. 2016. *We Kill Because We Can: From Soldiering to Assassination in the Drone Age*. London: Zed Books.

Capote, Truman. 1994. *In Cold Blood*. New York: Vintage.

Caryl, Christian. 2011. "Predators and Robots at War." *New York Review of Books*, September 29, 55–57. https://www.nybooks.com/articles/2011/09/29/predators-and-robots-war/.

Castle, Terry. 1991. "Contagious Folly: *An Adventure* and Its Skeptics." In *Questions of Evidence: Proof, Practice, and Persuasion across the Disciplines*, edited by James Chandler, Arnold I. Davidson, and Harry Harootunian, 11–42. Chicago: University of Chicago Press.

Cervantes, Miguel de. 2016. *Don Quixote*. Translated by John Ormsby. Edited by Anthony Uyl. Woodstock, Ontario: Devoted Publishing.

Chamayou, Grégoire. 2013. *A Theory of the Drone*. Translated by Janet Lloyd. New York: New Press.

Chomsky, Noam. 2010. *How the World Works*. Berkeley, CA: Soft Skull Press.

Cloud, David S. 2011. "Transcripts of U.S. Drone Attack." *Los Angeles Times*, April 8. http://documents.latimes.com/transcript-of-drone-attack/.

Coates, Ta-Nehisi. 2017. *We Were Eight Years in Power: An American Tragedy*. New York: One World.

Cockburn, Andrew. 2015. *Kill Chain: The Rise of High-Tech Assassins*. New York: Picador.

Cohn, Marjorie, ed. 2015a. *Drones and Targeted Killing: Legal, Moral, and Geopolitical Issues*. Northampton, MA: Olive Branch Press.

Cohn, Marjorie. 2015b. "Introduction: A Frightening New Way of War." In Cohn 2015a: 13–25.

Conant, Jennet. 2017. *Man of the Hour: James B. Conant, Warrior Scientist*. New York: Simon and Schuster.

Copjec, Joan. 1994. *Read My Desire: Lacan against the Historicists*. Cambridge, MA: MIT Press.

Corrigan, Maureen. 2014. *So We Read On: How The Great Gatsby Came to Be and Why It Endures*. New York: Little, Brown.

Crawford, Neta C. 2016. "US Budgetary Costs of Wars through 2016: $4.79 Trillion and Counting: Summary of Costs of the US Wars in Iraq, Syria, Afghanistan and Pakistan and Homeland Security." Watson Institute of International and Public Affairs, Brown University, September. https://voxpopulisphere.com/2016/09/16/dr-neta-c-crawford-costs-of-wars-through-2016-4-79-trillion-and-counting/.

Currier, Cora. 2016. "The Kill Chain." In Scahill 2016a: 54–67.

Davies, Nick. 2010. "Afghanistan War Logs: Task Force 373—Special Forces Hunting Top Taliban." *Guardian*, July 25.

Davis, Mike. 1998. "Las Vegas versus Nature." In *Reopening the American West*, edited by Hal K. Rothman, 53–73. Tucson: University of Arizona Press.

Day, Dorothy. 1983. *Dorothy Day: Selected Writings*. Edited and with an introduction by Robert Ellsberg. Maryknoll, NY: Orbis Books.

Deleuze, Gilles. 2013. "Nietzsche and Saint Paul, Lawrence and John of Patmos." In *Paul and the Philosophers*, edited by Ward Blanton and Hent de Vries, 383–85. New York: Fordham University Press.

Denton, Sally, and Roger Morris. 2001. *The Money and the Power: The Making of Las Vegas and Its Hold on America, 1947–2000*. New York: Alfred A. Knopf.

De Quincey, Thomas. 1890. *The Collected Writings of Thomas De Quincey*. Vol. 13. Edited by David Messon. Edinburgh: Adam and Charles Black.

Devereaux, Ryan. 2016. "Manhunting in the Hindu Kush." In Scahill 2016a: 152–76.

Douglas, Mary. 1966. *Purity and Danger*. London: Routledge and Kegan Paul.

Drone Pilot. 2015. "It Is War at a Very Intimate Level." In Bergen and Rothenberg 2015: 113–17.

Ellsberg, Daniel. 2017. *The Doomsday Machine: Confessions of a Nuclear War Planner*. New York: Bloomsbury.

Ellsberg, Robert. 2008. *The Duty of Delight: The Diaries of Dorothy Day*. Milwaukee, WI: Marquette University Press.

Engen, Robert. 2008. "Killing for Their Country: A New Look at 'Killology.'" *Canadian Military Journal* 9 (2): 120–28.

English, Richard. 2009. *Terrorism: How to Respond*. New York: Oxford University Press.

Enloe, Cynthia. 1993. *The Morning After: Sexual Politics at the End of the Cold War*. Berkeley: University of California Press.

Enloe, Cynthia. 2014. *Bananas, Beaches and Bases: Making Feminist Sense of International Politics*. 2nd ed. Berkeley: University of California Press.

Fanon, Franz. 1991. *The Wretched of the Earth*. Translated by C. Farrington. New York: Grove Weidenfeld.

Feffer, John. 2016. "Obama's Nuclear Paradox." *Foreign Policy in Focus*, June 1. https://fpif.org/obamas-nuclear-paradox/.

Feldman, Allen. 1991. *Formations of the Body: The Narrative of the Body and Political Terror in Northern Ireland*. Chicago: University of Chicago Press.

Fernandez, James. 1986. *Persuasions and Performances: The Play of Tropes in Culture*. Bloomington: Indiana University Press.

Ferrándiz, Francisco, and Antonius Robben, eds. 2017. *Necropolitics: Mass Graves and Exhumations in the Age of Human Rights*. Philadelphia: University of Pennsylvania Press.

Fitzgerald, F. Scott. 1925. *The Great Gatsby*. New York: Scribner.

Foster, Hal. 1991. "Armor Fou." *October* 57:65–97.

Frank, Joshua, and Jeffrey St. Clair. 2012. "Obama and Nuclear Power: Resurrecting a Failed Industry." In *Hopeless: Barack Obama and the Politics of Illusion*, edited by Joshua Frank and Jeffrey St. Clair, 87–89. Oakland, CA: AK Press.

Frank, Michael. 2017. *The Cultural Imaginary of Terrorism in Public Discourse, Literature, and Film*. New York: Routledge.

Frankfurt, Harry G. 2005. *On Bullshit*. Princeton, NJ: Princeton University Press.

Frazer, J. G. 1963. *The Golden Bough: A Study in Magic and Religion*. New York: Macmillan.

Friedman, Robert. 1995. "The CIA's *Jihad*." *New Yorker*, March 27, 40–49.

Fuller, Christopher J. 2017. *See It/Shoot It: The Secret History of the CIA's Lethal Drone Program*. New Haven, CT: Yale University Press.

Gaddis, John Lewis. 2011. *George F. Kennan: An American Life*. New York: Penguin Books.

García Lorca, Federico. 2007. *Blood Wedding*. Translated by A. S. Kline. Poetry in Translation website. https://www.poetryintranslation.com/PITBR/Spanish/BloodWeddingActI.php.

Garrow, David J. 2017. *Rising Star: The Making of Barack Obama*. New York: HarperCollins.

Geertz, Clifford. 1984. "Anti Anti-relativism." *American Anthropologist* 86:263–78.

Ghobari, Mohammed, and Phil Stewart. 2017. "Commando Dies in U.S. Raid in Yemen, First Military Op OK'd by Trump." Reuters, January 28. https://www.reuters.com/article/us-usa-yemen-qaeda-idUSKBN15D08J.

Ginzburg, Carlo. 1991. "A Rejoinder to Arnold I. Davidson." In *Questions of Evidence: Proof, Practice, and Persuasion across the Disciplines*, edited by James Chandler, Arnold I. Davidson, and Harry Harootunian, 321–24. Chicago: University of Chicago Press.

Greenwald, Glenn. 2016. "Afterword: War without End." In Scahill 2016a: 179–86.

Grossman, Dave. 1995. *On Killing: The Psychological Cost of Learning to Kill in War and Society.* Boston: Little, Brown.

Gusterson, Hugh. 2016. *Drone: Remote Control Warfare.* Cambridge, MA: MIT Press.

Hari, Johann. 2010. "Obama's Escalating Robot War in Pakistan Is Making a Terror Attack More Likely." *Huffington Post,* October 15. www.commomdreams.org/print/61390.

Harrington, Michael. 1962. *The Other America: Poverty in the United States.* New York: Macmillan.

Harvey, David. 1989. *The Condition of Postmodernity.* Cambridge, MA: Blackwell.

Hennessy, Kate. 2017. *Dorothy Day: The World Will Be Saved by Beauty.* New York: Scribner.

Hersh, Seymour M. 2016. *The Killing of Osama bin Laden.* London: Verso.

Holewinski, Sara. 2015. "Just Trust Us: The Need to Know More about the Civilian Impact of US Drone Strikes." In Bergen and Rothenberg 2015: 42–70.

Homer. 1990. *The Iliad.* Translated by Robert Fagles. Introduction and notes by Bernard Knox. New York: Penguin Books.

Ignatieff, Michael. 2000. *Virtual War: Kosovo and Beyond.* Washington, DC: Cato Institute.

Imtiaz, Saba. 2015. "What Do Pakistanis Really Think about Drones?" In Bergen and Rothenberg 2015: 89–110.

Inge, Thomas. 1987. *Truman Capote: Conversations.* Jackson: University Press of Mississippi.

Isaacson, Walter. 2007. *Einstein: His Life and Universe.* New York: Simon and Schuster.

Jackson, Richard. 2015. "The Epistemological Crisis of Terrorism." *Critical Studies on Terrorism* 8 (1): 33–54.

Jacobsen, Annie. 2011. *Area 51: An Uncensored History of America's Top Secret Military Base.* New York: Little, Brown.

Jaffer, Jameel. 2016. Introduction to *The Drone Memos: Targeted Killing, Secrecy and the Law,* edited by Jameel Jaffer, 1–55. New York: New Press.

Jameson, Fredric. 2016. *An American Utopia: Dual Power and the Universal Army.* Edited by Slavoj Žižek. London: Verso.

Johns, Larry C. 2017. *The Baneberry Disaster: A Generation of Atomic Fallout.* With Alan R. Johns. Reno: University of Nevada Press.

Johnson, Chalmers. 2007. *Nemesis: The Last Days of the American Republic.* New York: Macmillan.

Johnson, Natalie. 2014. "At Pro-Palestinian Protest, Cornel West Calls Obama a 'War Criminal.'" *Daily Signal,* August 4. https://www.dailysignal

.com/2014/08/04/pro-palestinian-protest-cornel-west-calls-obama-war-criminal/.

Johnston, David, and Eric Schmitt. 2004. "Uneven Response Seen to Terror Risk in Summer '01." *New York Times*, April 4.

Jones, Seth, Charles Vallee, Danika Newlee, Nicholas Harrington, Clayton Sharb, and Hannah Byrne. 2018. *The Evolution of the Salafi-Jihadist Threat: Current and Future Challenges from the Islamic State, Al-Qaeda, and Other Groups*. Washington, DC: Center for Strategic and International Studies. https://csis-prod.s3.amazonaws.com/s3fs-public/publication/181221_EvolvingTerroristThreat.pdf.

Josephs, Allen, and Juan Caballero. 2016. Introduction to *Bodas de sangre*, by Federico García Lorca, 1–85. Madrid: Cátedra.

Junger, Sebastian. 2016. *Tribe: On Homecoming and Belonging*. New York: Twelve.

Kaag, John, and Sara Kreps. 2014. *Drone Warfare*. Cambridge: Polity Press.

Kavanaugh, John F. 1981. *Following Christ in a Consumer Society: The Spirituality of Cultural Resistance*. Maryknoll, NY: Orbis Books.

Kelly, Kathy. 2005. *Other Lands Have Dreams: From Baghdad to Pekin Prison*. Oakland, CA: CounterPunch.

Kelly, Kathy. 2018. "The Long, Brutal War on Children in the Middle East." *Voices for Creative Non-Violence* (blog), November 29. https://countercurrents.org/2018/11/30/the-long-brutal-u-s-war-on-children-in-the-middle-east/.

Kennebeck, Sonia, dir. 2016. *National Bird*. Documentary film. Produced by Wim Wenders and Errol Morris.

Kierkegaard, Soren. 1941. *Fear and Trembling and The Sickness unto Death*. Translated with an introduction by Walter Lowrie. Princeton, NJ: Princeton University Press.

Kilcullen, David. 2009. *The Accidental Guerrilla: Fighting Small Wars in the Midst of a Big One*. New York: Oxford University Press.

Kilcullen, David, and Andrew Mcdonald Exum. 2009. "Death from Above, Outrage Down Below." *New York Times*, May 16.

Klaidman, Daniel. 2012. *Kill or Capture: The War on Terror and the Soul of the Obama Presidency*. Boston: Houghton Mifflin Harcourt.

Knox, Bernard. 1990. Introduction to *The Iliad*, translated by Robert Fagles, notes by Bernard Knox, 11–65. New York: Penguin Books.

Kurnaz, Murat. 2007. *Five Years of My Life: An Innocent Man in Guantánamo*. New York: St. Martin's Griffin.

Kurzman, Charles, and David Schanzer. 2015. "The Other Terror Threat." *New York Times*, June 16.

La Bella, Gianni, ed. 2007. *Pedro Arrupe, general de la Compañía de Jesús: Nuevas aportaciones a su biografía*. Bilbao: Mensajero.

Leach, Edmund. 1977. *Custom, Law, and Terrorist Violence*. Edinburgh: Edinburgh University Press.

Leahy, William D. 1950. *I Was There*. New York: Whittlesey House.

Lincoln, Bruce. 1989. *Discourse and the Construction of Society*. Oxford: Oxford University Press.

Linschoten, Alex Strick, and Felix Kuehn. 2012. *An Enemy We Created: The Myth of the Taliban-Al Qaeda Merger in Afghanistan*. Oxford: Oxford University Press.

Lotchin, Roger W. 1984. *The Martial Metropolis: U.S. Cities in War and Peace*. New York: Praeger.

Macdonald, Helen. 2014. *H Is for Hawk*. New York: Grove Press.

MacFarquhar, Neil. 1995. "In Bombing, a Deluge of Details." *New York Times*, March 19.

Madley, Benjamin. 2016. *An American Genocide: The United States and the California Indian Catastrophe, 1846–1873*. New Haven, CT: Yale University Press.

Maier, Klaus. 1976. *Guernica: La intervención alemana en España y el "Caso Guernica."* Madrid: Sedmay Ediciones.

Mander, Jerry. 1991. *In the Absence of the Sacred: The Failure of Technology and the Survival of the Indian Nations*. San Francisco: Sierra Club Books.

Margalit, Avishai. 1994. "The Uses of the Holocaust." *New York Review of Books*, February 17, 7–10. https://www.nybooks.com/articles/1994/02/17/the-uses-of-the-holocaust/.

Marshall, S. L. A. 1947. *Men against Fire: The Problem of Battle Command in Future War*. Washington, DC: Combat Forces Press.

Martin, Matt J. 2010. *Predator: The Remote-Control Air War over Iraq and Afghanistan: A Pilot's Story*. With Charles W. Sasser. Minneapolis, MN: Zenith Press.

Masco, Joseph. 2006. *Nuclear Borderlands: The Manhattan Project in Post-Cold War New Mexico*. Princeton, NJ: Princeton University Press.

Masco, Joseph. 2014. *The Theater of Operations: National Security Affect from the Cold War to the War on Terror*. Durham, NC: Duke University Press.

Mayer, Jane. 2009. "The Secret History." *New Yorker*, June 22. https://www.newyorker.com/magazine/2009/06/22/the-secret-history.

Mayer, Jane. 2015. "The Predator War." In Cohn 2015a: 63–76.

Mazzetti, Mark. 2007. "C.I.A. Details Errors It Made before Sept. 11." *New York Times*, August 22, A1.

Mazzetti, Mark. 2013. *The Way of the Knife: The CIA, a Secret Army, and a War at the Ends of the Earth*. New York: Penguin Press.

Mbembé, Achille. 2003. "Necropolitics." *Public Culture* 15 (1): 11–40.

McGowan, Todd. 2016. *Capitalism and Desire: The Psychic Cost of Free Markets*. New York: Columbia University Press.

McKelvey, Tara. 2015. "Defending the Drones: Harold Koh and the Evolution of US Policy." In Bergen and Rothenberg 2015: 185–205.

McMaster, H. R. 1997. *Dereliction of Duty: Lyndon Johnson, Robert McNamara, the Joint Chiefs of Staff, and the Lies That Led to Vietnam.* New York: HarperCollins.

McNamara, Robert S. 1995. *In Retrospect: The Tragedy and Lessons of Vietnam.* New York: Times Books, 1995.

Merton, Robert K. 1968. *Social Theory and Social Structure.* New York: Free Press.

Miller, John, and Michael Stone. 2002. *The Cell: Inside the 9/11 Plot and Why the FBI and the CIA Failed to Spot It.* New York: Alfred A. Knopf.

Miller, William D. 1973. *A Harsh and Dreadful Love: Dorothy Day and the Catholic Worker Movement.* New York: Liveright.

Mirer, Jeanne. 2015. "US Policy of Targeted Killing with Drones: Illegal at Any Speed." In Cohn 2015a: 135–68.

Moehring, Eugene P. 2000. *Resort City in the Sunbelt: Las Vegas, 1930–2000.* 2nd ed. Reno: University of Nevada Press.

Moehring, Eugene P., and Michael S. Green. 2005. *Las Vegas: A Centennial History.* Reno: University of Nevada Press.

Monk, Ray. 2012. *Robert Oppenheimer: A Life inside the Center.* New York: Doubleday.

Morris, Errol, dir. 2004. *The Fog of War: Eleven Lessons from the Life of Robert S. McNamara.* Documentary film.

Mothana, Ibrahim. 2012. "How Drones Help Al-Qaeda." *New York Times,* June 12.

Mueller, John. 2006. *Overblown: How Politicians and the Terrorism Industry Inflate National Security Threats, and Why We Believe Them.* New York: Free Press.

Nadelson, Theodore. 2005. *Trained to Kill: Soldiers at War.* Baltimore, MD: Johns Hopkins University Press.

Nader, Laura. 2012. "Rethinking Salvation Mentality and Counterterrorism." *Transnational Law and Contemporary Problems* 21:99–122.

National Commission on the Terrorist Attacks upon the United States. 2004. *The 9/11 Commission Report: Final Report of the National Commission on the Terrorist Attacks upon the United States.* New York: W. W. Norton.

Needham, Rodney. 1980. "Dual Sovereignty." In *Reconnaissances,* 63–105. Toronto: University of Toronto Press.

New York Times. 1995. "The Trial of Omar Abdel Rahman." Editorial. October 3.

New York Times. 2010. "Judicial Scrutiny before Death." Editorial. December 12.

New York Times. 2011. "The Truth about American Muslims." Editorial, April 1.

New York Times. 2016. "America Is Complicit in the Carnage in Yemen." Editorial, August 17.

New York Times. 2017. "511 Days. 555 Mass Shootings. Zero Action from Congress," Editorial. October 2.

Nickel, Robert V. 2005. "Dollars, Defense, and the Desert: Southern Nevada's Military Economy and the Second World War." *Psi Sigma Siren* 3 (1), Article 5. http://digitalscholarship.unlv.edu/psi_sigma_siren/vol3/iss1/5.

Obama, Barack. 1995. *Dreams from My Father: A Story of Race and Inheritance*. New York: Broadway Paperbacks.

Obama, Barack. 2006. *The Audacity of Hope: Thoughts on Reclaiming the American Dream*. New York: Crown.

Obama, Barack. 2009. "Remarks by the President at the Acceptance of the Nobel Peace Prize." December 10. https://www.whitehouse.gov/the-press-office/remarks-president-acceptance-nobel-peace-prize.

Obama, Barack. 2013. "Obama's Speech on Drone Policy." *New York Times*, May 23.

Palmerton, Patricia. 1988. "The Rhetoric of Terrorism and the Media Response to the 'Crisis of Iran.'" *Western Journal of Speech Communication* 52 (2): 105–21.

Pape, Robert A. 2005. *Dying to Win: The Strategic Logic of Suicide Terrorism*. New York: Random House.

Parker, Quentin, Paula Munier, and Susan Reynolds. 2011. *The Sordid Secrets of Las Vegas*. Avon: Adams Media.

Patton, Phil. 1998. *Dreamland: Travels inside the Secret World of Roswell and Area 51*. New York: Villard.

Pauc, Francis. 2015. *A Father at War: Reflections of a Father Whose Son Fought in Iraq*. N.p.: Self-published.

Perry, William J. 2015. *My Journey at the Nuclear Brink*. Stanford, CA: Stanford University Press.

Pew Research Center. 2015. "Public Continues to Back U.S. Drone Attacks." May 28. https://www.people-press.org/2015/05/28/public-continues-to-back-u-s-drone-attacks/.

Piehl, Mel. 1982. *Breaking Bread: The Catholic Worker and the Origin of Catholic Radicalism in America*. Philadelphia: Temple University Press.

Portela, Edurne. 2003. *El eco de los disparos*. Barcelona: Galaxia Gutenberg.

Powell, Colin. 2003. "Remarks to the United Nations Security Council." *Washington Post*, February 5.

Press, Eyal. 2018. "The Wounds of the Drone Warrior." *New York Times Magazine*, June 13. https://www.nytimes.com/2018/06/13/magazine/veterans-ptsd-drone-warrior-wounds.html.

Priest, Dana, and William M. Arkin. 2011. *Top Secret America: The Rise of the New American Security State*. New York: Little, Brown.

Pulliam, Sarah, and Ted Olsen. 2008. "Q&A: Barack Obama." *Christianity Today,* January 23. https://www.christianitytoday.com/ct/2008/januaryweb-only/104–32.0.html.

Putnam, Robert D. 2015. *Our Kids: The American Dream in Crisis.* New York: Simon and Schuster Paperbacks.

Queally, Jon. 2014. "Leaked Internal CIA Document Admits US Drone Program 'Counterproductive.'" *Common Dreams,* December 18. https://www.commondreams.org/news/2014/12/18/leaked-internal-cia-document-admits-us-drone-program-counterproductive.

Redfield, James M. 1975. *Nature and Culture in the Iliad: The Tragedy of Hector.* Chicago: Chicago University Press.

Rhodes, Ben. 2018. *The World as It Is: A Memoir of the Obama White House.* New York: Random House.

Riegle, Rosalie G. 2003. *Dorothy Day: Portraits by Those Who Knew Her.* New York: Orbis Books.

Rodman, Jami. 2016. *The Las Vegas Madam: The Escorts, the Clients, the Truth.* [US]: Maktub Press.

Rogers, James. 2017. "Drone Warfare: The Death of Precision." *Bulletin of the Atomic Scientists,* May 12. https://thebulletin.org/2017/05/drone-warfare-the-death-of-precision/.

Rosaldo, Renato. 1989. "Introduction: Grief and a Headhunter's Rage." In *Culture and Truth: The Remaking of Social Analysis,* 1–24. Boston: Beacon Press.

Samuels, David. 2016a. "The Aspiring Novelist Who Became Obama's Foreign-Policy Guru." *New York Times Magazine,* May 5. https://www.nytimes.com/2016/05/08/magazine/the-aspiring-novelist-who-became-obamas-foreign-policy-guru.html.

Samuels, David. 2016b. "Through the Looking Glass with Ben Rhodes." *New York Times Magazine,* May 13. https://www.nytimes.com/2016/05/12/magazine/through-the-looking-glass-with-ben-rhodes.html.

Sanger, David E. 2012. *Confront and Conceal: Obama's Secret Wars and Surprising Use of American Power.* New York: Crown.

Santner, Eric L. 2005. "Miracles Happen: Benjamin, Rosenzweig, Freud and the Matter of the Neighbor." In *The Neighbor: Three Inquiries in Political Theology,* by Slavoj Žižek, Eric L. Santner, and Kenneth Reinhard, 76–133. Chicago: Chicago University Press.

Sartor, Linda. 2014. *Turning Fear into Power: One Woman's Journey Confronting the War on Terror.* Mt. Shasta, CA: Psychosynthesis Press.

Savage, Charlie. 2015. *Power Wars: Inside Obama's Post-9/11 Presidency.* New York: Little, Brown.

Scahill, Jeremy. 2013. *Dirty Wars: The World Is a Battlefield.* New York: Nation Books.

Scahill, Jeremy, ed. 2016a. *The Assassination Complex: Inside the Government's Secret Drone Warfare Program.* New York: Simon and Schuster.

Scahill, Jeremy. 2016b. "The Drone Legacy." In Scahill 2016a: 1–12.

Scahill, Jeremy. 2016c. "The Heart of the Drone Maze." In Scahill 2016a: 68–82.

Scahill, Jeremy, and Glenn Greenwald. 2014. "The NSA's Secret Role in the U.S. Assassination Program." *Intercept,* February 10. https://theintercept.com/2014/02/10/the-nsas-secret-role/.

Scahill, Jeremy, and Glenn Greenwald. 2016. "Death by Metadata." In Scahill 2016a: 94–106.

Schlosser, Eric. 2013. *Command and Control: Nuclear Weapons, The Damascus Accident, and the Illusion of Safety.* New York: Penguin Press.

Schei, Tonje Hessen, dir. 2014. *Drone.* Documentary film. Produced by Tonje Hessen Schei.

Schmidt, Ann. [1986] 1994. "Nevada Desert Experience: Arrest as Sacrament." *Peace Action* (Redlands, CA, Peace Group newsletter), December. Included in John Dear, *The Sacrament of Civil Disobedience.* Baltimore, MD: Fortkamp.6Schmitt, Eric. 2018. "U.S. to Saudis and Emiratis: Pay This Bill," *New York Times,* December 14.

Schmitt, Eric, and Charlie Savage. 2019. "U.S. Airstrikes Kill Hundreds in Somalia as Shadow Conflict Ramps Up." *New York Times,* March 10.

Schwartz, David N. 2017. *The Last Man Who Knew Everything: The Life and Times of Enrico Fermi, Father of the Nuclear Age.* New York: Basic Books.

Schwartz, John. 2009. "Obama Backs Off a Reversal on Secrets." *New York Times,* February 9.

Schwartz, Mattathias. 2018. "A Spymaster Steps Out of the Shadows." *New York Times,* June 6.

Schwitzer, Yoram. 2006. *Female Suicide Bombers: Dying from Equality.* Tel Aviv: Tel Aviv University, Jaffee Center for Strategic Studies.

Shachtman, Noah. 2009. "CIA Chief: Drones 'Only Game In Town' for Stopping Al Qaeda." *Wired,* May 19.

Shah, Naureen. 2015. "A Move within the Shadows: Will JSOC Control of Drones Improve Policy?" In Bergen and Rothenberg 2015: 160–84.

Shane, Scott. 2013. "Targeted Killing Comes to Define War on Terror." *New York Times,* April 8.

Shane, Scott. 2015a. "The Lessons of Anwar al-Awlaki." *New York Times,* August 27.

Shane, Scott. 2015b. *Objective Troy: A Terrorist, a President, and the Rise of the Drone.* New York: Tim Duggan Books.

Shay, Jonathan. 1994. *Achilles in Vietnam: Combat Trauma and the Undoing of Character.* New York: Scribner.

Shay, Jonathan. 2002. *Odysseus in America: Combat Trauma and the Trials of Homecoming.* New York: Scribner.

Singer, Peter W. 2009. *Wired for War: The Robotics Revolution and Conflict in the 21st Century*. New York: Penguin Books.

Singer, Peter W. 2012. "Do Drones Undermine Democracy?" *New York Times*, January 21.

Sites, Kevin. 2013. *The Things They Cannot Say: Stories Soldiers Won't Tell You about What They've Seen, Done or Failed to Do in War*. New York: Harper.

Slahi, Mohamedou Ould. 2015. *Guantánamo Diary*. Edited by Larry Siems. New York: Little, Brown.

Sluka, Jeffrey A. 2011. "Death from Above: UAVs and Losing Hearts and Minds." *Military Review*, May-June, 70–76.

Solnit, Rebecca. 1994. *Savage Dreams: A Journey into the Landscape War of the American West*. Berkeley: University of California Press.

Solotaroff, Ivan. 2001. *The Last Face You'll Ever See: The Culture of Death Row*. New York: Perennial, 2001.

Sorley, Lewis. 2012. *Westmoreland: The General Who Lost Vietnam*. Boston: Mariner Books.

Sperber, Dan. 1975. *Rethinking Symbolism*. Cambridge: Cambridge University Press.

Stampnitzky, Lisa. 2013. *Disciplining Terror: How Experts Invented "Terrorism."* Cambridge: Cambridge University Press.

Stanford Law School and NYU School of Law. 2012. *Living under Drones: Death, Injury, and Trauma to Civilians from US Drone Practices in Pakistan*. September. Stanford, CA: Stanford Law School; New York: NYU School of Law. https://www-cdn.law.stanford.edu/wp-content/uploads/2015/07/Stanford-NYU-Living-Under-Drones.pdf.

St. Clair, Jeffrey, and Alexander Cockburn. 2005. "Afterword from the Publishers." In Kathy Kelly, *Other Lands Have Dreams: From Baghdad to Pekin Prison*, 167–68. Oakland, CA: CounterPunch.

Stewart, Mary White. 2014. *Ordinary Violence: Everyday Assaults against Women Worldwide*. 2nd ed. Santa Barbara, CA: Praeger.

Stone, Oliver, and Peter Kuznik. 2012. *The Untold History of the United States*. New York: Gallery Books.

Sullivan, Margaret. 2013. "'Targeted Killing.' 'Detainee' and 'Torture': Why Language Choice Matters." *New York Times*, April 12.

Suskind, Ron. 2006. *The One Percent Doctrine: Deep inside America's Pursuit of Its Enemies since 9/11*. New York: Simon and Schuster.

Swanson, David. 2016. *War Is a Lie*. 2nd ed. Charlottesville, VA: Just World Books.

Terrell, Brian. 2016. "My Visit to a Las Vegas Jail." *Voices for Creative Non-Violence* (blog), May 3. http://vcnv.org/2016/05/03/my-visit-to-a-las-vegas-jail-by-brian-terrell/.

Thompson, Hunter S. 1998. *Fear and Loathing in Las Vegas*. New York: Vintage Books.

Titus, A. Constandina. 1986. *Bombs in the Backyard: Atomic Testing and American Politics.* Reno: University of Nevada Press.

Tlusty, Ann. 2015. "Invincible Blades and Invulnerable Bodies: Weapons Magic in Early-Modern Germany." *European Review of History—Revue Européenne d'Histoire* 22 (4): 658–79.

Travis, Alan. 2014. "UK Counter-terrorism Bill to Include Campus Ban on Extremists." *Guardian,* November 24.

True, David. 2015. "Disciplining Drone Strikes: Just War in the Context of Counterterrorism." In Bergen and Rothenberg 2015: 285–99.

Tuchman, Barbara W. 1984. *The March of Folly: From Troy to Vietnam.* New York: Knopf.

Tutu, Desmond. 2015. Foreword to Cohn 2015a: 11–12.

Veyne, Paul. 1988. *Did the Greeks Believe in Their Myths? An Essay on the Constitutive Imagination.* Translated by Paula Wissing. Chicago: University of Chicago Press.

Vidal-Naquet, Pierre. 1991. "Atlantis and the Nations." Translated by Janet Lloyd. In *Questions of Evidence: Proof, Practice, and Persuasion across the Disciplines,* edited by James Chandler, Arnold I. Davidson, and Harry Harootunian, 325–50. Chicago: University of Chicago Press.

Vitale, Louie, OFM. 2015. *Love Is What Matters: Writings on Peace and Nonviolence.* Edited by Ken Butigan. Corvallis, OR: Pace e Bene Press.

Vitello, Paul, and Kirk Semple. 2009. "Muslims Say F.B.I. Tactics Sow Anger and Fear." *New York Times,* December 18.

Vitoria, F. Javier. 2008. *El Dios cristiano.* Bilbao: Universidad de Deusto.

Weil, Simone. 1986. *Simone Weil: An Anthology.* Edited and with an introduction by Sian Miles. New York: Grove Press.

Welsome, Eileen. 1999. *The Plutonium Files: America's Secret Medical Experiments in the Cold War.* New York: Random House.

Wemple, Erik. 2014. "Glenn Greenwald and the US 'Assassination' Program." *Washington Post,* February 10.

West, Cornel. 1993. *Race Matters.* New York: Vintage Books.

West, Nigel. 2017. *Encyclopedia of Political Assassinations.* Lanham, MD: Rowman and Littlefield.

Westmoreland, Cian. 2014. "The Day I Stopped Being Afraid: Living the Dream." *Project Red Hand* (blog), November 12. https://projectredhand.wordpress.com/2014/11/12/the-day-i-stopped-being-afraid/.

Westmoreland, Cian. 2015. "Diffused Responsibility: Focusing on Network Centric Aerial Warfare and a Call for Greater Understanding." *Project Red Hand* (blog), July 30. https://projectredhand.wordpress.com/2015/07/30/diffused-of-responsibility-focusing-on-network-centric-aerial-warfare-and-a-call-for-greater-understanding-2/.

Westmoreland, Cian. 2016. "Interview with Drone Technician Westmoreland."
     Interview by Bob Meola. *Courage to Resist*, September 21. https://couraget-
     oresist.org/westmoreland/.

Whippman, Ruth. 2016. *America the Anxious: How Our Pursuit of Happiness
     Is Creating a Nation of Nervous Wrecks*. New York: St. Martin's Press.

White, Hayden. 1978. *Tropics of Discourse: Essays in Cultural Criticism*.
     Chicago: University of Chicago Press.

Wilkerson, Lawrence. 2010. "Declaration by Lawrence Wilkerson in the Case
     of Adel Hamad." Center for the Study of Human Rights in the Americas,
     March 24, CV 05–1009 JDB. http://humanrights.ucdavis.edu/projects
     /the-guantanamo-testimonials-project/testimonies/testimonies-of-
     foreign-affairs-officials/
     declaration-by-lawrence-b-wilkerson-in-the-case-of-adel-hamad.

Williams, Terry Tempest. 1991. *Refuge: An Unnatural History of Family and
     Place*. New York: Vintage Books.

Wilson, Frances. 2016. *Guilty Thing: A Life of Thomas De Quincey*. New York:
     Farrar, Straus and Giroux.

Woods, Chris. 2015. *Sudden Justice: America's Secret Drone Wars*. Oxford:
     Oxford University Press.

Worth, Robert F. 2018. "They Break Us or We Break Them." *New York Times
     Magazine*, November 4, 69–72.

Wright, Ann. 2008. *Dissent: Voices of Conscience*. With Susan Dixon. Kihei, HI:
     Koa Books.

Young, Kevin. 2017. *Bunk: The Rise of Hoaxes, Humbug, Plagiarists, Phonies,
     Post-Facts, and Fake News*. Minneapolis, MN: Graywolf Press.

Zinn, Anthony. 1999. *A People's History of the United States: 1492–Present*. New
     York: HarperCollins.

Žižek, Slavoj. 1989. *The Sublime Object of Ideology*. London: Verso.

Žižek, Slavoj. 1997. *The Plague of Fantasies*. London: Verso.

Žižek, Slavoj. 2005. "The Empty Wheelbarrow." *Guardian*, February 19.

Žižek, Slavoj. 2007. *How to Read Lacan*. New York: W. W. Norton.

Žižek, Slavoj. 2009. "Dialectical Clarity versus the Misty Conceit of Paradox." In
     The Monstrosity of Christ: Paradox or Dialectic?, edited by Crestin Davis,
     234–306. Cambridge, MA: MIT Press.

Žižek, Slavoj. 2012. *Less Than Nothing: Hegel and the Shadow of Dialectical
     Materialism*. London: Verso.

Zuckerman, Jessica, Steven P. Bucci, and James Jay Carafano. 2013. *Sixty
     Terrorist Plots since 9/11: Continued Lessons in Domestic Counterterrorism*.
     Special Report #137 on Terrorism. Washington, DC: Heritage Foundation.
     http://thf_media.s3.amazonaws.com/2013/pdf/SR137.pdf.

Zulaika, Joseba. 1988. *Basque Violence: Metaphor and Sacrament*. Reno:
     University of Nevada Press.

Zulaika, Joseba. 1989. *Chivos y soldados: La mili como ritual de iniciación.* San Sebastián: Baroja.

Zulaika, Joseba. 1990. *Ehiztariaren erotika.* Donostia: Erein. Translated into Spanish as *Caza, símbolo, eros* (Madrid: Nerea, 1992).

Zulaika, Joseba. 1995. "The Anthropologist as Terrorist." In *Fieldwork under Fire: Contemporary Studies of Violence and Survival,* edited by Carolyn Nordstrom and Antonius C. G. Robben, 201–22. Berkeley: University of California Press.

Zulaika, Joseba. 2009. *Terrorism: The Self-Fulfilling Prophecy.* Chicago: University of Chicago Press.

Zulaika, Joseba. 2012. "Drones, Witches and Other Flying Objects: The Force of Fantasy in US Counterterrorism." *Critical Studies on Terrorism* 5 (1): 51–68.

Zulaika, Joseba. 2014. *That Old Bilbao Moon: The Passion and Resurrection of a City.* Reno: Center for Basque Studies, University of Nevada–Reno.

Zulaika, Joseba. 2018. "What Do You Want? Evidence as Fantasy in the War on Terror." In *Bodies as Evidence: Security, Knowledge, and Power,* edited by Mark Maguire, Ursula Rao, and Nils Zurawski, 201–27. Durham, NC: Duke University Press.

Zulaika, Joseba, and William A. Douglass. 1996. *Terror and Taboo: The Follies, Fables, and Faces of Terrorism.* New York: Routledge.

Zulaika, Joseba, and Imanol Murua. 2017. "How Terrorism Ends—and Does Not End: The Basque Case." *Critical Studies on Terrorism* 10 (2): 338–56.

Zupančič, Alenca. 2000. *Ethics of the Real: Kant, Lacan.* London: Verso.

Zupančič, Alenca. 2003. *The Shortest Shadow: Nietzsche's Philosophy of the Two.* Cambridge: MIT Press.

Index